D0855962

ELEMENTS OF INTERNATIONAL
POLITICAL THEORY

Elements of International Political Theory

MICHAEL DONELAN

CLARENDON PRESS · OXFORD
1990

Oxford University Press, Walton Street, Oxford OX2 6DP
Oxford New York Toronto
Delhi Bombay Calcutta Madras Karachi
Petaling Jaya Singapore Hong Kong Tokyo
Nairobi Dar es Salaam Cape Town
Melbourne Auckland
and associated companies in
Berlin Ibadan

Oxford is a trade mark of Oxford University Press

Published in the United States
by Oxford University Press, New York

© Michael Donelan, 1990

All rights reserved. No part of this publication may be reproduced,
stored in a retrieval system, or transmitted, in any form or by any means,
electronic, mechanical, photocopying, recording, or otherwise, without
the prior permission of Oxford University Press

British Library Cataloguing in Publication Data
Donelan, Michael
Elements of international political theory.
1. Foreign relations. Theories
I. Title
327.101
ISBN 0-19-827851-9

Library of Congress Cataloging-in-Publication Data
Donelan, Michael D.
Elements of international political theory / Michael Donelan.
p. cm.
Includes bibliographical references.
1. International relations—Methodology.   2. International
relations—Philosophy.   I. Title.
JX1391.D67 1990   327'.072—dc20   90-6855
ISBN 0-19-827851-9

Typeset by Hope Services (Abingdon) Ltd.
Printed and bound in Great Britain by
Courier International Ltd,
Tiptree, Essex

Acknowledgements

I SHOULD like to thank for many hours of enjoyable argument
my friends and colleagues of the one-time British Committee
on International Theory, and of the International Political
Theory Group, and of the LSE 'Theories Seminar'. In particular,
I am grateful to Mr John Charvet and Mr James Mayall, who
commented on a draft of the book. I thank with equal warmth
those at the LSE and OUP who did the work of producing it.

M.D.D.

January 1990

University Libraries
Carnegie Mellon University
Pittsburgh PA 15213-3890

Contents

Introduction   1

Part I.   Ways of Thought

  1. Natural Law   7
  2. Realism   22
  3. Fideism   38
  4. Rationalism   56
  5. Historicism: 'Nation' and 'State'   74
  6. Historicism: 'Proletariat' and 'World'   84

Part II.   Kinds of Relations

  7. Conflict   101
  8. Alliances   121
  9. Intervention   137
 10. War   157
 11. Commerce   178

Bibliography   203

Index   207

Introduction

T HIS book depicts a series of eleven meetings at The Perpetual Peace in Kaliningrad about international political theory. As the first meeting gathers, the Chairman says to you:

Now that we have found you a seat, I will point out the main people. The man in the middle of the group over there is the Historicist. He thinks that he has the strongest voice in political theory these days. He may be right. The man by the door is our first speaker, the Natural Law Man. The woman facing him is the Realist. She is second. They are waiting for our awkward member, the Fideist. He will say why he should not come in; they will say why he should; it is a ritual; he will speak at the third meeting. Then I will speak for Rationalism. The Historicist comes last. He plans to talk for twice as long as anyone else.

We shall be giving you five different views of the nature of international politics. We would have liked to do this in the form of digests of the works on international politics of the great political theorists: Locke, Rousseau, Hegel, and so on. Unfortunately, as you probably know, there are none worth talking about. The great men wrote about the nature of society or the state or about the class struggle, and only said something about international politics on the margins of their work, and thin soup it is mostly.

So we shall have to do the best we can ourselves, and we hope you will not be too hard on us. We chose the word 'Elements' in our title with care. We shall take the basic thoughts of the great men and try to widen them out to international politics. We shall be helped by the writers on relations between states: Vitoria, Grotius, Vattel, Gentz, down to the present. Also, by journalists and statesmen: Salisbury, Cavour, Wilson, Churchill, Bernadotte. We are building with other men's bricks, and are grateful to them. As to why *five* views, E. H. Carr and Hans Morgenthau managed with two: Realism and Idealism. Martin

Wight was content with three: Realism, Rationalism, and Revolutionism.[1] But we think that further analysis suggests five. Inflation, you may think. You will have to decide.

Our five views, taken together, may look like a history of thought about international politics. If they are of some use in that way, we shall be glad. But please be warned: our aim is not to describe past thought, but to use it to build theory. To describe past thought as dividing overall into five strands may be roughly right; but to assign particular past thinkers to one or other of five views would mostly be quite wrong. For example, in constructing Rationalism, I draw on the Stoics and Cicero, but so does the Natural Law Man for his stuff. I rely heavily on Kant, but I admit that he has many Historicist traits. Even apart from that, Kant would probably disagree with some of my opinions; for instance, that raising the condition of the poor is no proper task for the state.

What did you say? How does the question of the state and the poor come into a discussion of international political theory? You ask this because you take for granted the division of the world into separate states: that the Austrians are Austrians; that the British poor are Britain's poor; and Zambia's poor are Zambia's. We do not assume this. We think it needs to be explained. We do not take 'international politics' to mean 'relations between states', but 'world politics'. Statehood and citizenship are not self-evident. The question of 'the state and the poor' may not be divisible into 'domestic' and 'foreign'.

Most people recognize this vaguely nowadays. Political theorists feel it sharply. We have advertised meetings in recent years about political theory of the traditional sort, and attendance has been good, but it is still better this evening. Political theorists are more willing today to accept that Kant was right: political theory has to be international theory.[2] Times may change back again, of course. Talk of 'one world' and 'global

---

[1] Exactly, E. H. Carr, 'realism' and 'utopianism', in *The Twenty Years' Crisis* (London, 1939); Hans J. Morgenthau, 'realism' and 'the legalistic–moralistic approach', in *Politics among Nations* (New York, 1949), ch. 1. For Martin Wight's 'Three Rs', see Brian Porter, 'Patterns of Thought and Practice: Martin Wight's "International Theory" ', in Michael Donelan (ed.), *The Reason of States* (London, 1978), ch. 3.

[2] 'Idea for a Universal History', 7th proposition, in Hans Reiss (ed.), *Kant's Political Writings* (Cambridge, 1970), 47 ff.

village' may cease to be the mode. Meetings about The Separate State may become popular again. Let us make the most of the present opportunity. What a crowd tonight!

Have you noticed the Chinese couple in the middle? I admire the Chinese because they are a crowd but still each has a space around him. We have thought from time to time of holding our meetings in China. The name, The Perpetual Peace, could well have come from there. We have always rejected the idea, though. This is not because we think that the substance of our views is purely Western and not relevant to the Chinese. Only the Historicist thinks that. The rest of us think that the substance of our views is universal. On the other hand, our idiom is Western, and our examples are drawn almost exclusively from Western history, because that is what we know about, and this would be bound to reduce the interest to most Chinese of what we have to say. Universal thought needs local dress, and, alas, we could not provide it. You will hear most plainly what I mean when the Fideist speaks in two weeks' time. Fideists are not enthusiasts for faith but for a particular faith. Our Fideist is a Christian, and you will quickly realize that he is a European Christian. The four traditions of thought about the Christian in politics that he sets out are those of Christianity in Europe.

There are lots of people here besides political theorists. The woman with the fashionable red hair is an art dealer; London today, Tokyo tomorrow. What is politics, after all, but building a house for the arts? The man just sitting down is in agriculture; world-wide company, plant genetics; very shrewd. We shall hear from him at question-time. The man on his left is the local undertaker. The fellow next but one is a captain at the naval base; here to keep an eye on us, I suppose; very sensible of him. You probably recognize the landlord, talking with the Realist; hundreds of years old; very funny. I have not asked you what you are, political theorist or other, but I assume, since you are here, that you value political theory. It is part of understanding life. It is a civilized discussion that keeps us human in committees.

After each of us has stated his view of international politics in a general way, there will follow five further meetings, in which we will discuss together the main kinds of relations that countries have with each other: conflict, alliances, intervention, war, commerce. The audience question-times will not be recorded so that people can speak freely, and not because we are nervous about them, which, of course, we are.

As to which of the five views is the right one, I obviously say as a Rationalist: Rationalism. But the proper thing for me to say as Chairman is that there is some value in all of them. All are observable in the world's thought and action. It would be a mistake to neglect any of them, or to think, in so far as they are a sequence, that the later supersedes the earlier, and the more sophisticated abolish the more basic. You should use them all in reaching your own view of the truth.

I see that the Fideist has arrived; the cellarman has closed the hatch; the Natural Law Man is shuffling his notes. Goodbye. We must begin.

I

WAYS OF THOUGHT

1

Natural Law

M Y starting-point, says the Natural Law Man, is that our morality is built into us. Other theorists use the words 'nature' and 'natural law' and share with me many further terms, but there is a big difference. The Realist thinks that our morality is dictated by the facts of how the world behaves; the Fideist, that it is revealed by a prophet; the Rationalist, that we invent it by reasoning; the Historicist, that our morality is our history; but Antigone says to Creon in Sophocles' play:

I did not think your edicts strong enough to over-rule the unwritten, unalterable laws of God and heaven, you being only a man. They are not of yesterday or today but everlasting, though where they come from, none of us can tell.[1]

We take first principles for granted in our sciences, physical or moral. Morally, we look at the world and ourselves and find the categories 'good' and 'evil'. 'Good' is what is 'sought for', 'evil' is what is 'shunned'. The goods or ends, that we as a species seek, are roughly clear. Like all biological being, we strive to maintain our lives; like all mammals, we have an instinct to produce young and to care for them; and, distinctively as men, we have a drive to virtue, which is 'to know the causes of things' and to live socially. This is more than animal gregariousness and more than need to co-operate as a group with some others and so to have an expedient regard for them; it is a demand of our being to live as companions, without offence to each other.[2]

We see what this means by looking at a man we think good and noticing how he acts. We are guided in looking: we derive from the first principles some secondary principles almost as

---

[1] *Antigone*, 450–7, trans. E. F. Watting.
[2] Based on St Thomas Aquinas, *Summa Theologiae*, 1a. 2ae. 94. 2; Aristotle, *Politics*, 1253^a.

obvious as they are. As regards people's striving for life, we are not wrongfully to kill or allow to be killed or allow to die. Similarly, we must not offend against the relationship of spouses and the care of children; against people's honour and their property; and against their drive to knowledge and to living companionably. We should avoid and avert wrongs and harms not only in our simple acts but in acts that make the conditions under which we live: arrangements, rules, laws, systems, and public ideas. These conditions should be for the good of all, the common good. To use another word, acts and conditions should be just, they should give everyone his due.

What 'wrong' and 'common good', 'just' and 'unjust' mean in detail is mostly agreed among us. If this were not so, life would stop. We argue at the margin: 'what he did was right', 'you do not understand this principle', 'this law should be reformed', 'that system neglects the good of some people'. In arguing, we are seeking knowledge; if not, we are sophists, seeking victory for our opinion. We have to argue and not simply declare that we know; for even Socrates says that he does not know, notwithstanding he is spoken to by a god; so even a philosopher king needs counsellors to contradict him. In our arguing, the principles of natural law, broad as they are, act as strong limits. We do not think of saying some things; we stop ourselves when we consider saying others; what we do say faces the challenge: show how this will help people to get their food, to be a family, to have dignity and property, to live fully and companionably.

The principles of natural law are, in other words, the guidelines of reason. Within them, other philosophies such as utilitarianism, which by themselves are inane or dangerous, are helpful to us in trying to decide what to do. 'It is reason reflecting on human nature that is the guide to conduct, not reason working in pure abstraction.'[3] This is what divides a Natural Law Man from the Rationalist.

Finally, we need prudence, the virtue of knowing how to apply general reasoning to a matter in hand. Prudence differs from Realist cleverness or expediency or timidity which try to pass under its name;[4] it is bound by natural law; it works out

---

[3] F. C. Copleston, *Aquinas* (Harmondsworth, 1955), 216.
[4] Aristotle, *Nicomachean Ethics*, vi. 12.

how to follow natural law in practice. Especially, it reckons
with stupidity and ignorance in men, which are the source of
malevolence. It is strong against them because, as in the old
simile of the chariot, it is powered by the virtues of justice and
courage and self-mastery.

The area within which natural law is recognized, says the
Natural Law Man, is the whole world. This claim is not much
controverted as to its early stages. The human species everywhere
at all times strives for the same primary goods: to live, to have
young and raise them, and so on. All men agree that this
implies no murder, no slander, no thieving, and the rest, and
that conditions should be for the common good. 'Which nation
does not love courtesy, kindliness, gratitude, and remembrance
of favours bestowed? Which does not despise and hate the
arrogant, the wicked, the cruel and the ungrateful?'[5]

Controversy begins at the stage of the application of these
generalities. We see in world history great differences as to
what counts as cruelty and an immense variety of laws and
systems, which those who live by them would claim promoted
the common good. Much of this diversity can be explained as a
reasonable response to the variety of circumstances of time and
place, and as an expression of human creativity in finding
varied means to the same ends. The main objection to the idea
of a universal natural law is that men have never treated the
human species as a single moral community.[6] They have never
applied the same code to women as to men, to slaves as to free
men, to higher caste as to lower, and to other tribes, races,
nations, or countries as to their own. To pursue Aquinas's
example, the ancient Germans did not consider robberies
outside the frontiers of their settlements wrong.[7] For Plato,
Greeks and Barbarians were 'naturally enemies' whereas Greeks
among themselves were 'naturally friends'.[8]

The reply of a Natural Law Man is that Plato and Aristotle,
despite what they say about Barbarians, none the less do all
their reasoning in ethics and politics in terms of 'Man'. Moreover,
all of us everywhere acknowledge that the starting-point in

---

[5] Cicero, *Laws*, I. xi. 32.
[6] John Finnis, *Natural Law and Natural Rights* (Oxford, 1980), 97, 2nd note.
[7] Summa Theologiae, 1a. 2ae. 94. 4; Caesar, *De Bello Gallico*, vi. 23.
[8] *The Republic*, 470^c.

dealing with any other man is not to harm him unless we have a reason to do so. Constantly, other men give us a reason to harm them or we assume one. We see facing us, not a man but a subhuman, a slave, a woman, an hereditary enemy, a thieving German, a Persian aggressor, a murderous Sioux, an infidel, a fascist, a white oppressor; and so we think it not wrong to kill the man, rob or defame him, or refuse to consider him in arrangements for the common good. The basic fact is, none the less, that all these epithets are justifications; the norm is that, if we ill-treat any other man, we have to justify ourselves; the norm is not that we are indifferent or hostile to other men until they show us why we should not be. When the Europeans first came to Tasmania, they naturally treated the natives well whom later they killed in a man-hunt. In Cicero's words, 'we are biased by nature towards loving other men, and that is the foundation of law'.[9]

We can argue with all other men in today's world and in the past about what the law ought to be. An attacking Sioux or Crusader or fascist or white is not best met with arguments, but, at quieter moments, we of one culture can reason with people of another about conduct and customs and institutions. If there were no basis for mutual criticism between cultures, there would be no basis for mutual respect.[10] We influence one another. Social practices are abandoned or adopted. The prejudice that it is permissible to steal from Germans because the Germans are all thieves dies away, and the notion that Persians are natural enemies is seen to be untenable. Plato himself accepts that the best society may exist in 'some barbarian country beyond our horizons'.[11]

Time is important in various ways but it is not the essence of the matter. Some see history as a grand progress of Man in an ever-widening conception of the common good, from tribe, to nation, to world. This is not the natural law perspective; for man's instinct to treat those outside his tribe and nation for the common good cannot have started at some historical moment; it must have been present in him from the first.[12] This instinct is

---

[9] *Laws*, I. xv.
[10] Mary Midgley, *Heart and Mind* (Brighton, 1981), ch. 5.
[11] *Rep.* 499ᶜ.
[12] T. H. Green, *Prolegomena to Ethics* (Oxford, 1883), bk. 3, ch. 3.

of man's essence. It is and always has been a norm for him. There seem to be no grounds for thinking that primitive men felt its force any less or more than modern men.[13] Man's prevailing desire has always been harmony, not discord, as within himself, so within a wider body.[14] 'The law of nature, which binds us to show humanity in every way, assuredly is that we defer to each other like the parts of one body.'[15] The wider body is and always has been limitless; there is no frontier at which the bias of our being stops so that we can say, this man is a companion being but that man is not. 'The good man remembers that all rational beings are akin to himself and that to care for every man accords with the nature of man.'[16]

Men being a moral community, they are also a political community. Within the guide-lines of the moral law, they need to decide on more detailed, positive laws, and enforce them, and ensure that the other conditions of life are for the common good. The world is 'in a way, one single state'.[17] It has 'a quasi-political and moral unity'.[18] 'The community of a province includes the community of a city; and the community of the kingdom includes the community of a province; and the community of the whole world includes the community of a kingdom.'[19]

When Vitoria and Suárez wrote thus, they had in mind the making by the world of the most basic of all positive laws, the *ius gentium*, the laws common to men of all nationalities and hence applicable to dealings between them, whatever their nationality, the ancestor of international law. But the world has also to decide about another basic condition of human life, even more momentous. We have to decide whether, for the common good, we should organize the world-state as a single world-wide state or whether we should be divided into separate states.

The decision on this, taken in practice by many piecemeal decisions on how to organize affairs, is always open for argument

---

[13] Ragnar Numelin, *The Beginnings of Diplomacy* (Oxford, 1950).
[14] Plato, *Rep.*, bk. 4; Cicero, *De Officiis*, bk. 1.
[15] St Ambrose, *De Officiis Ministrorum*, bk. 3, ch. 3.
[16] Marcus Aurelius, *Meditations*, iii. 4.
[17] Francisco de Vitoria, *De Potestate Civile*, 3rd conclusion. The idea was common in the 16th cent.; see A. R. Pagden, *The Fall of Natural Man* (Cambridge, 1982), 63.
[18] Francisco Suárez, *De Legibus et Deo Legislatore*, bk. 2, ch. 19, sect. 9.
[19] St Thomas Aquinas, *Commentary on the Sentences*, bk. 4, distinction 24, Q. 3, quoted in E. B. F. Midgley, *The Natural Law Tradition and the Theory of International Relations* (London, 1975), 24.

and change. The obvious opinion is that large states or empires can work but that a world-wide state or empire cannot. The Judicial Committee of the Privy Council is too far from Canada, India, and New Zealand to be helpful in making legal judgments for the people there. The same is even more obvious as regards the other functions of a state: legislation, enforcement, the supervision of the economy, the provision of public goods, and, the supreme duty, the cult of the gods. These must be settled locally. A way of putting the point is the principle of subsidiarity. This says that the purpose of associations is to help the individual members, and that this is best done by handling any matter in the smallest possible association. Don't handle through the province what can be done by the city. Don't try to do through a world-state what can be done by Australia, Bolivia, and China. In sum, the human community needs to be divided as a matter of practicality into separate countries with separate states. Around these, naturally, a special sense of community, patriotism, grows.

The central point in natural law thought about world politics is that this division of the human community is not absolute; it is limited by the reason for which we make it, namely, the common good. A state is an institution of a country, its political aspect. The purpose of a state is to ensure the common good of the people of the country. Also its purpose is to work with the other states to ensure the common good of the people of them all.

So a state should have a certain quality in its constitution. 'Those constitutions which consider the common interest are right constitutions, judged by the standard of absolute justice. Those constitutions which consider only the personal interest of the rulers are all wrong constitutions or perversions of right forms.'[20] Such are tyrannies of one man or a section of the community or the majority. In law-making 'what is right is what is equally right and that means for the benefit of the whole state and for the common good of its citizens'.[21] Here law-making should be understood as all the acts of the state, embracing, notably, the ordinary laws, which should be for the good of all, not just some, and the regulation of the systems

[20] Aristotle, *Pol.* 1279^a; see also Aquinas, *Summa Theologiae*, 2a. 2ae. 42.2.
[21] Aristotle, *Pol.* 1283^b.

under which we live, commerce, communications, utilities, welfare, education, arts and sciences, and so on. 'The common good of all embraces the sum total of those conditions of social living whereby men are enabled to achieve their own integral perfection more fully and more easily.'[22]

The common good is not collectivist or totalitarian. Simply, it contrasts with the good that individuals pursue privately; it consists of the goods that they pursue as a community. The common good expresses the principle of solidarity but accompanied by the principle of subsidiarity. The community has a good which is prior to and superior to that of any particular individuals; but it is so because it consists of the conditions that are for the good of all the individuals.

Each person or business company and so on, in pursuing their private good, helps to make the systems under which all do this. Systems should assist all, and each should try to ensure that this is so. The purpose of the state is to supervise and regulate as necessary. It should ensure that all have the basic necessaries of life, either by correcting the relevant systems or by direct assistance, and that all are considered equally in the conduct of systems. It should see to the provision of things that are necessarily public goods.

In deciding what is for the common good, the state is not a mediator between interest groups. It should not be concerned for who has most power but for all equally; and not simply with interests but with good. For the concept of the common good (or public interest) is vacuous unless it leads to 'laws, policies, etc. which are indeed in the valid interests of some individuals and not in the valid interests of others'.[23] The loss inflicted on the latter cannot be justified only by bringing into the calculation gains to their wider interests or on other occasions. The numbers of people affected on the two sides and the amounts of gain and loss are important in coming to a decision, but a further important element is the comparative worth of the clashing interests as human goods. Argument about the hierarchy of goods is the highest argument in a community because it guides public decisions and individual decisions towards the good life.

[22] John XXIII, *Pacem in Terris*, 1963 (Catholic Truth Society, London), 25.
[23] Virginia Held, *The Public Interest and Individual Interests* (New York, 1970), 156; see also pp. 163 ff.

The conditions under which we live include the ideas of our community. The community should attend carefully to the content and conduct of education, beginning with music, and to the institutions for debate, notably political assemblies and the news media. Few expressions of opinion should be banned, perhaps only two: advocacy of outrage to the cult of the gods and of the exclusion of some category of people (those of some religion, race, class, or the like) from equal consideration in deciding the common good.

That much about states internally; next internationally. We make as individuals, as countries, and as states a climate of ideas that affects the whole community of mankind. In politics, to say nothing of religion, the arts, sciences, and technology, at one time or another, Egypt and Greece, Spain and France, Germany and Japan, the United States and the Soviet Union have had great influence on common opinion about what is good in state conduct. The character of international relations varies according to the ideas of the leading states.

States create international conditions of life in a more precise way. In their foreign policies, they are not persons as national-ists think. Poetically, this idea may be harmless, and it is perhaps a useful fiction in making law, including international law; but it is dangerous politically because it suggests that states have a good that should be pursued at the cost of their citizens, if necessary; whereas the truth is that the good of states is the fulfilment of the purpose for which they exist, namely, in foreign policy as in domestic, to ensure conditions in which individual men and women can achieve their good.

States, in their foreign policies, maintain the division of the world into separate countries: they establish the frontiers and the limits of citizenship and, while allowing foreigners to have some share in their communities, resist foreign interference in affairs of state. They make agreements under which their citizens have commerce everywhere. Many of their acts, it is true, do not create conditions for individuals in a direct sense. Customary international law and such arrangements as the organization of diplomacy, security alliances, and many other international treaties, create a structure of relations between states; within that structure, states do many things, small or vast, negotiations, propaganda, spying, economic pressure, and war, which are directed at one another as states; action aimed at individuals (for example, state trading, famine relief) are subordinate. Still, the significance of all the foreign-policy activity of states lies in the fact that it ultimately affects individuals and that its outcome is to create the conditions under which individuals must make their lives. It decides with whom they shall be a country; in what extent of territory; with what degree of independence; and so under what laws and systems; and what access they shall have to the people and resources of other countries.

In the natural law view, not only are states best understood as a matter of fact as makers of conditions under which men live but their purpose is to make conditions that are good. Every act of foreign policy of a state should aim at the good of all the states involved, with, as the ultimate aim, the achievement of conditions that are for the good of the citizens of them all.

We can distinguish three settings in which states should do this: bilaterally, as groups, and world-wide. As to the first (to take examples from everyday business) when one state complains to another about the infernal conditions in which its citizens are being made to queue for visas or about dumping of golf cars, it should consider what is fair to the people of the other state as well as of its own.[24] This is required not in mere expediency or desire for reciprocity but in recognition of why the two states exist at all; even towards a weaker state or one that does not reciprocate, it is an obligation. All this applies as much to diplomatists as to policy-makers. Some people think that diplomacy is a neuter skill, displayed in the service of a good state or a tyranny indifferently; but skills are part of men, and men are not indifferent. As the *raison d'être* of the state is the good, so is the *raison d'être* of the diplomatist. The Vienna Convention was right to discern, as the final function of diplomacy, the promotion of good relations between states.

This remains true in great affairs where the words of the diplomatist have overtones of coercion and even where his message is war. The purpose is the good of both the states in relation to each other. 'When it comes to politics most people

[24] *The Times*, 15, 16 May 1987; Robert L. Meuser, 'Dumping from "Controlled Economy" Countries: The Polish Golf Car Case', *Law and Policy in International Business*, 11 (1979), 777–803.

appear to believe that mastery is the true statesmanship; and men are not ashamed of behaving to others in ways which they would refuse to acknowledge as just, or even expedient, among themselves. For their own affairs, and among themselves, they want an authority based on justice; but when other men are in question, their interest in justice stops.' Though this is how most people seem to think, 'how can such a thing which is not even lawful be proper for a statesman or law-maker? And how can it ever be lawful to rule without regard to the right or wrong of what you are doing? Conquerors may be in the wrong.'[25]

So states and alliances should not seek aggrandizement or even the national interest but their good and that of opponent states. This means, as regards disputes over territory, that they should aim at the good of the inhabitants, bearing in mind that this is not necessarily the same as the inhabitants' opinion of their interests but takes into account all the other people affected. Similarly, as regards independence, states should do nothing by way of interference and intervention that sacrifices the good of another state and its people.

Economic policy-making should have regard as much to the prosperity of the other states as to one's own. In all policy towards other states, strategic considerations should not be paramount, as the Realist thinks, but subordinate; they are satisfied best in this way. A state must maintain its reputation for power and not tolerate small wrongs; the Romans had a maxim, *principiis obsta*, 'stamp on it at the start'; a Greek applies this with moderation. We should remember also, as the Rationalist does not, that an injustice is dishonourable and a blow not merely to the interests but also to the honour of the other side. An injustice enforced is a humiliation that may one day explode.

These questions of territory, independence, economic policy, and honour also arise among states that are a group, whether by geography, history, culture, or association for a common purpose, for example, a common market or a defence alliance. A common purpose, as the Realist stresses, restrains conflicts among associates; 'they hang together for fear of hanging separately'. A Natural Law Man goes further: the existence of a common purpose should facilitate a spirit of the common good.

---

[25] Aristotle, *Pol.* 1324[b].

An expert has written of the commissioners of the European Community: 'Their task should not be confused with that of national ministers or ambassadors. The ministers and ambassadors represent and must, if necessary, fight for their own national interest. The commissioner, by contrast, must seek to ensure that Commission proposals and compromises take fair and reasonable account of all such interests. Naturally he will be particularly concerned with those of 'the country he knows best', as the Brussels euphemism has it, but that must be within an overall European context.'[26] In the Natural Law view, politicians and diplomatists should not be contrasted with commissioners but should act exactly in the spirit here ascribed to commissioners.

The distinctive question in associations of states is distributive justice. The associates may be trying to federate their countries into one country with one state. They have not only to promote shared laws, systems, and ideas that are for the good of the people of them all but also to create an inter-state organization which will ultimately become a shared constitution, and financial arrangements which will ultimately become a shared tax system; and these powers and payments have to be allocated fairly. More usually, the associates have some less ambitious purpose such as economic development or a military alliance. Here, too, authority and other benefits and costs have to be shared out justly.

The basic principle of justice in associations is that those who contribute most should benefit most and conversely those who benefit most should contribute most. Applying this is a matter for discussion and judgement and is impossible without a general concern for the common good. For example, in NATO, the people of the United States are mostly richer than those of Turkey and in that respect have more to lose in a war and therefore benefit more from the alliance and so should bear more of the costs; on the other hand, the Turks benefit more in the sense that the danger of being attacked, from which the alliance protects them, is greater for them than for the Americans.

As to financial principles, it should be said against the Realist that what matters is the charge on the per capita wealth

---

[26] Christopher Tugendhat, *Making Sense of Europe* (London, 1986), 142.

of people, not on the collective wealth of countries; comparisons
of the gross amounts contributed by each country or of their
percentage shares of total alliance defence expenditure and
total alliance gross national product are misleading. Against
the Rationalist, it should be said that the reason why the
wealthy pay more is because they have more wealth at risk, and
not the arbitrary notion that the utility of each additional
pound declines and therefore the wealthy should pay more
pounds so that they make equal sacrifice.

In associations, as in states, each type of tax raises questions of
equity. The European Community is at present funded mainly by
a small percentage of the value added tax imposed by the member
states, and this kind of tax is usually considered to bear more on
the poor than on the rich. The rest of the funds are the charges
on imports from outside the Community, and the British, who
import most, pay most; initially, anyway, until an overriding
'financial mechanism' operates, based on the comparative
wealth of the member countries.

Authority in associations of states should be proportionate to
contribution, not population. Where an association is bent on
federation, a point may one day be reached where the people
directly elect the authorities, and then certainly the larger
member populations will have the stronger voice; but, at that
point, they are supposedly no longer truly separate member
populations but a single population under a single amalgamated
state. Until then, and in all associations with lesser purposes,
the question is how to weigh types of contribution.

In peacetime military alliances, where the abilities of the
various national commanders in war conditions are unknown,
supreme command of the alliance can only follow supreme
contribution of men and money. At the United Nations, the
World Bank, and the International Monetary Fund, and in the
European Community, inasmuch as the immediate purpose is
the administration of wealth, the rich should have most say;
inasmuch as the ultimate purpose is 'a peace-keeping operation'
or the promotion of further wealth, ability directed to the
common good should count most, and so statesmen and experts
should be heard without regard to their origin in a small or poor
or rich or large state. A gesture in the direction of this principle
is the only merit to be found in the otherwise misguided method

adopted in the United Nations charter of 'one nation, one vote'. Even weighted voting should be no more than a convenient device for bringing a discussion to an outcome; basically there should be 'consensus', meaning not that all agree but that all can accept the decision, even the outvoted, because they believe that all have discussed the matter with a desire for the common good.

The third and last setting in which states should seek the common good is world-wide. Much that they do domestically, their political upheavals, their management of their economies and so on, has effects unintentionally on all other states. Much that they do bilaterally or in associations, for example, a border conflict or a common agricultural policy, has consequences everywhere. This has always been true, long before modern systems of communications speeded and intensified and made us aware of it. The Roman Empire was broken by a chain reaction of barbarian explosions that began on the borders of the Chinese Empire, of which it had scarcely heard. Even now that we know that our actions may have ill effects far away, there is often nothing we can do about it. Countries cannot be expected to ask permission to have a rebellion. Sometimes, though, there is something they can do.

States act intentionally towards all other states by making international rules, setting up global organizations, propagating general ideas. The best idea for countries, some say, is to have a free economy; others say, a controlled economy. All want agreements between states or anyway understandings or customs and technical systems under which world commerce shall proceed. The practice of states in commerce and in all matters becomes international law; occasionally also, states assemble to make law; and they need ways of regulating this world legal process.

Inter-state law is a development of the *ius gentium*, itself a first detailing of natural law. Another necessary development of the *ius gentium* is the universal law of states, that is, the basic conditions of the common good that ought to be followed within all states; in other words, the basic political, civil, and economic rights that the citizens of a state should accord to one another.

Whenever these rights are denied by any state the world over, the other states have a duty to be concerned and to intervene to the extent that they prudently can. Similarly, whenever states are in dispute with one another and whenever one attacks another, the rest have an obligation. They should not consider only the narrow interests of their own people; on the other hand, they should not be automatically committed to spending blood and money on far-away quarrels of which they know nothing; their obligation is to do what is prudent for the common good.

To handle these world matters, states need a world authority. Some have thought that this should be an emperor, as Dante argued in his *De Monarchia*, or a supreme council, elected in either case by governments or populations. Such forms would be appropriate to a world government of a world-state. What we are talking about here is an authority to regulate relations between states. This, it seems, should be no other than the states themselves. In a world-state, as in any state, all could not come together to conduct affairs and so would have to appoint a person or a council; but states can all come together, and so there is no such necessity. The world authority is the states themselves; it is a polyarchy, an ethnarchy.[27]

Realists and Rationalists see only a world of independent states in a condition of anarchy or, in the case of the Rationalist, of society; but a Natural Law Man sees states as constituting a world authority by virtue of the fact that they exist not solely for their independent good but for the common good of the community of mankind. The practical problem is not the supersession of the states-system by a supranational organization but the dispelling of the sovereign mentality in favour of the desire for the common good.

The world authority meets in many different assemblies according to the matter in hand. One matter is common to all. Natural law is not the kind of law that tells us in detail what is right; rather it is the law of our being by which we desire what is right. It operates only to the extent that we have knowledge. Here is the world authority's greatest responsibility. The world hardly heard that there was famine in China in 1959; so it did nothing and the Chinese government did less than it would

---

[27] Luigi Taparelli D'Azeglio, *Saggio Teoretico di Diritto Naturale Appoggiato sul Fatto* (Palermo, 1841), no. 1365; see Midgley, *The Natural Law Tradition and the Theory of International Relations*, pp. 202 ff.

have done, faced with publicity; and twenty million people died. In those same years, domestic debate in the United States and the Soviet Union about world politics was paralysed by anti-communist and anti-capitalist dogma; the international debate between the two countries was propaganda; and so the desires of the people of the world were distorted, misunderstood, or altogether neglected. The world authority of states should aim before anything else at a pattern of education, news media, and assemblies, within countries and internationally, that ensures the full access of us all to knowledge.

2

Realism

IF you want to survive, even be successful, says the Realist, start by studying how people behave, not how they ought to behave. The rules Aquinas lays down for princes like Frederick II have some use no doubt, but it is secondary.[1] Begin with Frederick himself, the *stupor mundi*, begin with the behaviour of princes. Idealism muddled the Americans when they first came to world power; their later Realism and Behaviouralism were more useful to them.

As to the place to begin in studying how people behave, it is international relations. Some famous political theorists have begun with a fiction, with men in a state of nature, before politics; but real people are always under states. Other political theorists do indeed begin with states; but they leave international relations to their last chapter; and this is unreal; for the first fact about states, not the last but the very first, is that there is not one state but many. The state does not first exist and then have international relations; it exists as a thing that has international relations. So international relations is where we should start in studying people.

Suppose that, for the sake of Thomas Hobbes, we entertain for a moment the thought of a state of nature. Hobbes was an academic who would not have survived in practical politics as Duke of Devonshire, let alone as Duke Valentine; still, the drift of his thinking deserves praise. Consider, then, the state of nature. Where do we come closest to this, to seeing people dealing with one another without benefit of common authority, common laws, common culture? In international relations.

The most important characteristic of human beings, from the viewpoint of survival, is easy to see in international relations. To be sure, periods of history vary in overall spirit: the seven-

[1] St Thomas Aquinas, *De Regimine Principum*.

teenth century was terrifying as Fideist, the eighteenth was
hardly better as Rationalist, the nineteenth was tolerably peaceful
under Realists of different sorts, the canting English, the honest
Bismarck. Then again, we see that individuals vary in their
behaviour almost infinitely on the scale from cruelty to love.
Against the Natural Law Man with his human inclination to
fellowship, we might with Hobbes put in the first place 'for a
general inclination of all mankind, a perpetual and restless
desire of power after power that ceaseth only in death'.[2] This
may or may not be correct; and that is the crucial point: we are
not sure. The fact glares at us in international relations that we
cannot rely on others to be benevolent or to be ruthless. Men
are untrustworthy.

Our untrustworthiness is more obvious in international relations than in any other area of life for one basic reason. This is
not the suspicion arising from lack of common culture, nationalist
animosity, or ideological hatred; these make the characteristic
worse but it is still manifest at times and places where they are
insignificant. The reason is the senselessness for survival of
being moral when you can have no confidence that the other
will be also; when there is no common power over you all.

The study of international relations is especially instructive
about us as people in that there we are acting as association to
association (state to state) rather than person to person. Most
of our dealings with others in life (families and friends apart)
are done as representatives of associations. A bit of the day we
spend bumping into other persons on the way to work but most
of it we spend being, say, a bank clerk dealing with customers.
If we are a self-employed electrician, we represent a quasi-
association, we enact the social role considered proper for
electricians.

There is a difference between our behaviour as persons and
as associations. As persons we desire the good of others. The
Natural Law Man thinks this is ontological; the Rationalist,
that it is a matter of mutual interest. A Realist says it is a desire
to placate; for the other and I have more or less equal power as
persons to do each other harm. The desire for the good of others
passes from potential to actual and issues in a working morality
so soon as we can be sure of reciprocity.

[2] *Leviathan*, ch. 11.

As associations, we have no desire for the good of others. For we cannot assume that the others are equal to us in power; that remains to be tested; often they are not. So, states, business corporations, trade unions, interest groups of all sorts have no spontaneous concern for others; all, as de Gaulle said of states, are 'cold monsters'. As employees of Maximerge Plc, we do things to the public that we would be ashamed to do as persons; for it is not we as persons that are acting but we as an anonymous, impersonal power.

The central point in Realism is, then, this. Sometimes we as persons and, still more important, as associations, are made moral; for we have a common power over us, the state. Sometimes we are not made moral; there is no common power; and that is international relations. The frontiers of the state are the limits of morals. On the one side, we have the security of the state, on the other the bleak wastes of international relations, where the states, great associations, confront each other in cold hostility.

Let us dwell for a while on the state internally, first driving home a point made at the outset. The power of the state is not a domestic power as most political theorists assume but primarily an international-relations power. It is exerted over us and also against the foreigners. Its brute nakedness is clothed in authority to the extent that it succeeds in giving us security among ourselves and against the foreigners. The two spheres interact, but it is the latter, the external, that has the final influence. The authority of the state turns ultimately on success or failure in foreign policy. When the Chinese or the Europeans are humiliated by the world, their states lose legitimacy in their own eyes. This, and not merely the obvious insecurity of the external sphere, is why the Realist insists on 'the primacy of foreign policy' in national life. The traditional phrase should be amended, however, to 'the primacy of intenational relations' on the following thought: the power that gives the people of one state security among themselves is in the end the power of the other states pressing upon them. Leviathan is not one but many.

From the success of the state in establishing security, and thereby morals, grows society: industries, markets, the arts and sciences, religion. Realists disagree about the deep origin of these things. Perhaps the state is to be seen as a contract

between men who are equal in their personal power to do each
other harm; or perhaps such a contract is impossible because
big men would always prefer to recruit some associates and
dominate the rest. Historically, states seem to have been founded
by big men, usually with force. As to what morality is, Thrasy-
machus thinks it is what suits the powerful, Nietzsche, that it is
the way of heroes. For Spinoza, society is 'a balance between
forces of self-assertion', while, for Hobbes, 'reason suggesteth
convenient articles of peace'.[3] A Realist might even think with
the Rationalist that the source of morals is the rationality of co-
operation; with the Natural Law Man, a universal natural law;
with the Fideist, a prophet; with the Historicist, history. All this
is secondary. The prime concern of a Realist is to point out that,
whatever the origin of the state, morals, society, and all the rest
of civilization, the first step is the successful organization of
power. This is the pre-condition of all else. This is the sense in
which 'might is right'.

Every state is fundamentally a *Machtstaat*. Its basic purpose
is to monopolize the legitimate use of force. To this end it must
use force and any other means as necessary. *Raison d'état*
overrides morality and legality in order to serve them. A Realist
has his ideals; he prefers a republic to a tyranny, respect for
'human rights' to a so-called 'national security state'. But
organizing power depends on the means available. Power is not
a stuff whose ingredients can be listed; it is not even exactly an
ability of persons; it is a relationship, a situation. It is always a
situation of constraint, a manipulation of the ambitions of the
few and the fears of the crowd; but the means may be pleasant
or unpleasant, force or suasion, damage or benefit. A society
held together by power contrasts with one held together
by exchange relationships between members in their mutual
interests, as in the Rationalist vision, or by a sense of community or faith or tradition; it is, all the same, a civilized
society, not crude. Sometimes, though, what has to be done
is crude. If Augustus had not been wicked when a young
politician, he would not have survived to be the venerable
father of his country. *Debet Octavianus esse qui Augustus esse cupit.*[4]
The need for ruthless vigilance never ends. Long-established

---

[3] Stuart Hampshire, *Spinoza*, (Harmondsworth, 1951), 189; *Leviathan*, ch. 13.
[4] He has to be Octavian who wants to be Augustus.

states should not sneer at the newer, more turbulent; they had best remember that their own foundations are the same.

When considering any measure of national policy, the statesman should first assess how it will affect the power of the state, and only secondly its specialized merits. He must, above all, promote the resources for national security. This means war industries or, more widely, a rich, modern economy, so as to have war potential and peacetime influence. In the Less Developed Countries today the character of economic development is determined as much by desire for governmental and national power as by desire for prosperity. The Realist state need not own or manage industry but it must oversee and co-ordinate. Economic planning was invented by the Realist state, by states fighting two world wars and by the Stalinist state besieged, and was perpetuated as a method of peacetime development. Earlier, the open-handed, paternalist Welfare State was started by Realist rulers, wishing to retain the loyalty of the people.

The temper of politics should be undogmatic, non-ideological, dispassionate, and pragmatical. Nationalist ardour, the enthusiasm of faith, or any sort of fundamentalism are the ruin of successful policy at home and abroad. Practical Marxists are Leninists. It is an error to think that a creed is necessary in order to arouse popular support for national policies. The danger of that course is populism, demagoguery, statecraft as a ride on the back of a tiger. The people is a great beast, as Hamilton said. Democracies lack exactly the qualities needed for success in foreign policy: skill at detail, perseverance, flexibility, secrecy, patience. They are impulsive, not prudent, and abandon mature policy for the gratification of a momentary passion.[5] The statesman must accordingly take care to control public opinion, mobilizing it and mastering it, but calmly. Totalitarian methods are unnecessary and have depressing side-effects on society. So long as the government is the centre of national activity and is the main supplier of information to the news media and has charge of the agenda of national debate, it can safely allow the debate to proceed 'freely'. On a deeper level of ideas, the government should encourage the intellectuals to believe that there is a value-free science of

[5] Alexis de Tocqueville, *Democracy in America*, ed. Phillips Bradley (New York, 1945), 235.

society. This belief castrates them as controversialists; it cuts off their facts from their values, so that their values become mere opinions, which, after some turbulence, settle down in favour of power. Sociology is not, as it sometimes appears superficially, the enemy of Realism but its ally, and should be given large government subsidies.

The more a state succeeds in these various aspects of the organization of power and the more a society rises upon this foundation, the more it differs from the conditions prevailing outside its frontiers in international relations. To the extent that a state fails, the more it knows conflict, lawlessness, bribery, oppression, diffused force, and, at the worst, collapse or civil war, the more it is comparable with international relations.

Strictly speaking, the Realist continues, I mean inter-state relations. Between persons of different nations there is, of course, much friendliness; between associations, for example, business companies, world-wide co-operation. For, in their dealings across frontiers, they are under the power of one state or another. It is between the states, the princes, the nations as states, that there is no common power and so no peace. Between them, there can be no morality. They are powers, engaged in power politics. The Melians argued that Athens should show restraint towards them because it might itself need to be shown restraint one day. But, as the Athenians replied, dealings between states are not like that: how one state treats another today has no effect on how other states will treat it tomorrow. Simply, 'the strong do what they can and the weak do what they must'.[6] Inter-state relations are a vicious circle of competition; in area after area, each separately may wish to do nothing but dare not for fear that the other will not. Spain and Portugal discover America, and the Soviet Union and the United States are in Space because they are rivals. A security dilemma torments states. What one does for its defence might, so far as its neighbours can know, be for attack. Nothing can be taken on trust.

In this situation, the statesman must first of all be an expert in military force. But not as the so-called experts are expert; his

[6] Thucydides, *The Peloponnesian War*, bk. 7.

grasp of strategy must be realistic. The experts have a self-confidence in peacetime that bears no relation to the muddle of war. They overawe the impressionable statesman with apparent Realism when in fact they are Rationalists. Note, as regards contemporary strategy, that nuclear deterrence is a rational relationship between adversaries, based on hypothetical warfare, not directed towards real nuclear war.[7]

As the statesman must be a real general, so, a real quartermaster. The British spent millions on being a world military power after 1945, and could not properly equip a brigade for Korea in 1950; further millions, and they had no force ready in 1956 that they could use to strike Egypt. The statesman needs his Realist wits most of all in dealing with the arms businessmen. These people and their friends among officials are seduced by technical possibilities, excellent in every way except that they are irrelevant to the realities of combat. They sold fleets of battleships to the great powers in 1900 that did nothing when The Day came in 1914; and nowadays they sell to every kind of power Goliath weapons systems that David strikes down.

The statesman must above all be a politician. Military force is only an instrument, and can only be as successful as the political skill that wields it. If war comes, it is 'a continuation of politics by other means'.[8] Political considerations must remain paramount.

The first step in political skill is understanding that inter-state relations are an anarchy. The statesman cannot create the current of events; he keeps afloat, he steers.[9] The second step is understanding that inter-state relations, though an anarchy, are not a chaos; on the contrary, they have a deep, continuous movement towards order. Policies that do not conform to this fact, that are excessive, extreme, arrogant, which is to say, chaotic, will fail.

The reason for this bias towards order lies in the nature of power. The matter has many aspects. First, defence is more powerful than offence. Of course, not every defender wins. States decay and are taken over by neighbours. Where there is a

[7] Paul J. Bracken, *The Command and Control of Nuclear Forces* (New Haven, Conn., 1983).
[8] Karl von Clausewitz, *On War*, bk. 1, ch. 1; bk. 8, ch. 6.
[9] A. J. P. Taylor, *Bismarck* (London, 1955), ch. 4.

power vacuum in a state or region, external power moves in. Some states are strong in their way but others are strong in a superior way; so the great empires of history were formed, and Europe took over most of the world. Sometimes states of comparable power attack and destroy each other. Six empires collided in the First World War, and, at the end, four were dead.

On the whole, though, throughout history, more states deter or defend successfully more of the time than conquer successfully. Militarily, defence has an inherent advantage over attack, and this is equally true politically and socially. A mere heap of bananas has an in-built resistance; the force to push it over takes more organizing. The nature of states is to expand, through ambition or fear and the fact that there is no reason why their frontiers should lie here rather than there;[10] but to say this is not to say that they are usually successful. Sometimes they are. Usually, the impetus slows in alien surroundings and dies away.

We come, with this, to the second cause of order in inter-state relations: balance of power. The struggle of states never ends in final victory. They seek hegemony but they frustrate each other, balance each other. Their efforts result in a stalemate in which they survive.

This is the Germanic way of looking at balance of power. It is a gloomy way, influenced by Historicism; balance of power is to be understood as an outcome. In Fichte's words, 'Nature strives after and maintains an equilibrium through the very struggles of men for superiority'.[11] The Italians are more cheerful: they are interested in the possibilities of making balances against rivals or as *tertius gaudens* between rivals. Lorenzo constructs his complicated alliance against Venice. Venice manipulates the hostility of Florence and Milan.

[10] Jean-Jacques Rousseau, 'The State of War' in M. G. Forsyth, H. M. A. Keens-Soper, and P. Savigear (eds.), *The Theory of International Relations, Selected Texts from Gentili to Treitschke* (London, 1970), 170.

[11] Johann Fichte, 'The Characteristics of the Present Age' in Moorhead Wright (ed.), *Theory and Practice of the Balance of Power 1486–1914, Selected European Writings* (London, 1975), 90; also, Carsten Holbraad, *The Concert of Europe* (London, 1970), 152; Kenneth N. Waltz, *Theory of International Politics* (Reading, Mass., 1979), 116–23; Coral Bell, *The Diplomacy of Détente* (New York, 1977), ch. 2.

The English way is purposive, like the Italian: the balance of power is not something automatic; it needs close attention.[12] But the English think their way nobler: the Florentines and Venetians were crafty primitives; the perfection of the idea of balance of power came with the understanding in the eighteenth century that it is a general field of forces, a states-system, an international order, higher than mere state egotism.[13] The powers must be ever vigilant against attempts at hegemony by any of their number, Spain, France, Germany, Russia, and immediately coalesce to fight and defeat such ambitions. This English picture of 'a society of states', gathering to defend its freedom, must not, of course, be taken at face-value. The reality was that the English organized a balance on the mainland of Europe which left them free to build their empire everywhere else. They were *tertius gudens* in a stalemate of the rest.[14] Still, though the English view was as egotistical as the others, it had, like them, some effect of order among states.

The principle of balance of power prevents incessant war but does not by itself create a peaceful order. By itself, it is tense and unstable. For each state would prefer to find its security in a balance of power in the sense of a margin of power over its rivals. A competition ensues. Coalitions form. There is uncertainty about whether there is a balance. One side, fearful or ambitious, attacks. After a war, a victorious power, having a clear margin of power over the others, may establish a *pax britannica* or a *pax americana*. But soon its ascendancy is challenged, and the cycle begins again.

All proceeds at a higher tension when the rival powers fear not only the strength of the others but weakness in themselves, caused by domestic political and social turmoil, as was the case in Europe in the years before 1914. The highest tension is reached when the powers are struggling with one another on the politico-social front as much as the military front in a total 'correlation of forces', as they claimed to be in the mid-twentieth century, first in Europe and later world-wide.[15]

---

[12] Hedley Bull, *The Anarchical Society* (London, 1977), 112.

[13] Herbert Butterfield, 'The Balance of Power', in Herbert Butterfield and Martin Wight (eds.), *Diplomatic Investigations* (London, 1966), ch. 6.

[14] Gerhard Ritter, *The Corrupting Influence of Power* (Hadleigh, Essex, 1952).

[15] Antonio Gramsci, *The Modern Prince* (London, 1957), 168 ff.; Julian Lider, *Correlation of Forces* (Aldershot, 1986).

· The process of rivalry for security and supremacy among the great powers, the central balance, is replicated in miniature among the lesser powers in the various regions of the world. On all levels, balance of power is not a structure that will keep the peace, but a dynamic, always dangerous. Sometimes statesmen try to halt the process, make a structure. Castlereagh and Metternich were so tempted at Vienna. Bismarck, in his later years, made a system out of his achievements but it came to nothing. The nuclear balance of terror nowadays is delicate.[16] To rely for peace simply on constructing an equilibrium of armaments is unrealistic.

Not mechanical balances but only the will of the powers can keep the peace. The third cause of order in inter-state relations is the will of the powers to order.

Such a will is possible. There is nothing about the states-system that makes war inevitable. Whatever the case with Hobbes's fictitious individuals in a state of nature, there is no reason why what he calls 'the condition of war' among princes must lead to actual war.[17] States do not trust each other, and fundamentally they never can; there is always the spiral of competition and the security dilemma; there is therefore always the potential for explosion; but the explosion is not inevitable. Inter-state relations are a realm of necessity in that certain kinds of policies are demanded, and any state that omits them is utopian and may not survive; and some of the policies are repugnant, such as armaments and willingness to fight; the necessities of inter-state relations are harsh. But inter-state relations are not a realm of necessity in the sense that they must lead to war. Even the most determinist of Realists, the Marxist-Leninists, finally accepted that. In Nikita Khrushchev's historic phrase, 'war is not fatalistically inevitable'.[18]

This is not the same as to say that there will come a time when there will be no more wars in the world. On the contrary, a Realist predicts that there will always be wars or organized violence of some sort so long as men are men. But this is because he thinks

[16] Albert J. Wohlstetter, 'The Delicate Balance of Terror', *Foreign Affairs*, 37 (Jan. 1959), pp. 211–34.
[17] *Leviathan*, ch. 13.
[18] 'Report of the Central Committee to the 20th Party Congress, February 1956', in L. Gruliow (ed.), *Current Soviet Policies, II* (London, 1957).

it likely that sometimes a state will choose to attack another, calculating correctly or incorrectly that it will profit; and that sometimes states will stumble into war through incompetence. It is not because any of this is ever inevitable. Miscalculation and incompetence are not inevitable.

Inter-state relations are a realm of necessity but also of virtue. Virtue is not the ideal, Natural Law virtue; it is magnificence, the drive to superiority that promotes human civilization. Virtue is also awareness of limits. The fault of the Athenians, Thucydides believed, was excess. Ulm, Austerlitz, Jena, Eylau, Friedland must stop at Tilsit or they will end at Leipzig and Waterloo. Ordinary men want to follow magnificence; in battle, they do not 'give all their fame for a pot of ale and safety'; in the end, though, they do. Napoléon learns that France is not worthy of him; Hitler, Germany; that is Realism.

The Realist statesmen of today understand that the age-old pursuit of power has reached a limit. The continuum between politics and force has been broken in one respect, namely, that no longer can states use the greatest force of which they are capable as an instrument. Each must possess ultimate force, actually or potentially, because the others might, but none can sanely use it. Disarmament among states is a Rationalist fantasy; it would require trust; but arms-control is possible. Arms-control is an expression by states of the will to order, consisting of the clarification to each other that they are indeed doing what it would be sane for them to do whether the others did it or not. Thus, they can make agreements with appropriate solemnities to abandon or avoid weapons systems that they do not really want because the systems do not add to their security. They can make shared arrangements for improved communication and verification so as to confirm to each other that they are observing those limits of policy which it would be unrealistic for them to overstep.

States cannot abolish the ultimate destructive power that they have invented, but they can seek to push it into the background of world affairs and thus abate the fears and tensions that surround it. The way to do this is for them to concentrate equal effort on building an array of political and economic agreements between them. These will not, of course, consist of Rationalist discoveries of mutual interests but will be agreements to do with mutual consent and, if possible, in co-operation, things in the political and economic spheres that they will do separately anyway. It is a gross breach of Realism, of a kind that marred English policy towards Germany in the earlier part of the twentieth century and stultified United States policy towards the Soviet Union in the middle part, to resent and to try to deny to another state, for motives of nationalism, prestige, or ideology, that position at home and in the world to which its power or potential entitle it and which it will one way or another at length achieve.

The great powers should, in addition, seek agreement in one crucial area: consent or co-operation in keeping order among the lesser powers. The search for such agreement is Realist in that disorder among the lesser powers can lead to unwanted and perhaps limitless collision among the great powers. The latter traditionally dress up this task of keeping world order in some such grand phrase as 'the exercise of responsibility in the international community'. The reality is, of course, that a 'responsible' power is merely a one-time trouble-maker that is now satisfied. The English, having plundered the world for some generations, called a halt at the beginning of the twentieth century just when Germany, Italy, and Japan thought they might have their turn.[19] For states, as for the Emperor Augustus, virtue is a matter of dates. Still, if declaring the game of power politics over is hypocrisy, if the highest art of diplomacy is knowing where to resist a rising power and where to let it have its head, the most basic is controlling lesser powers and limiting great-power rivalry about them. 'Great Powers are no more restrained and responsible than small powers, as they like to assert; they simply aim at monopolising the right to create international conflict.'[20] Realistically so.

The lesser powers resent great-power 'concert' and 'pentarchy' and 'responsibility'. Their worst nightmare, in Kissinger's phrase, next to collision between the great powers, is collusion. However, the facts of power have to be faced: the great powers should seek a degree of condominium in world affairs and the lesser powers must accept it. The feelings of the more important among them, the medium powers, can be somewhat appeased.

[19] Harold Nicholson, *Lord Carnock: A Study in the Old Diplomacy* (London, 1930), Introduction.   [20] Martin Wight, *Power Politics* (London, 1946), 22.

These need, for their own security, to perform in their region the same order-keeping role as do the great powers in the world. Great and medium powers have here a basis for a degree of toleration, even collaboration.

These remarks amount to saying that the fourth source of order in inter-state relations is the inequality of states. There is a hierarchy of power among them. The authority of great states does not end at their frontiers, as legalists think, but extends to a sphere of influence around them. As Realists, the small states in the spheres should conform the conduct of their politics to this fact, and the great powers should reach understandings about which small states are in whose sphere and to what degree. The Churchill–Stalin agreement of 1944 on the Balkans is a model. When conflicts occur further afield between small powers or between small and great, the great powers should temper their rivalry with understanding that one or other of them has primary 'responsibility', though with due respect for the other's prestige.

A major aspect of order-keeping is the struggle to control world opinion. Propaganda will have no degree of success if it consists of unqualified hostility to rival states; it will simply anger the rivals and be disbelieved by everyone else. The basic rule of Realist propaganda is that it is not fantasy but the persuasive presentation of fact. World opinion is shocked by crude displays of power; it is frightened; but it is alienated completely by lies about power. States must be concerned to maintain their reputation for power, their prestige; but this is not the same as to pursue a policy of prestige, which is an error, often fatal.[21]

In economic affairs, the maintenance of order requires acceptance that the basic policy of states is mercantilism. States support national industries against the foreigners to the extent needed for state power and national prosperity. From time to time, the propaganda prevailing in the world advocates free trade. Free trade is an academic theory with some usable insights; in practice, it is on the whole simply the mercantilism

---

[21] This follows Bismarck's usage of the phrase 'a policy of prestige'; see William L. Langer, *European Alliances and Alignments 1871–1890* (New York, 1931), 453. Hans Morgenthau adopted a different usage but to the same effect: *Politics among Nations*, 3rd edn. (New York, 1960), ch. 6.

of the strongest. The English preached it in the mid-nineteenth century; they would benefit most from a general reduction of trade barriers; the Americans similarly in the mid-twentieth. Of course, all states were to some extent impressed by the theory and still more by the English and American propaganda, and anyway had to conform to it somewhat because it was the policy of the dominant power. Surreptitiously, though, all maintained their basic mercantilism: as fast as they cut their tariffs after 1945, they replaced them with non-tariff barriers; the Common Market created by the Western Europeans among themselves was simply a larger unit for protectionism against the rest of the world; the Japanese felt thereby approved in their trade warfare ways. In sum, the great powers must impose an economic order but one that is realistic about themselves and states generally. The small states, resenting the economic order of the great, must coalesce to make propaganda for a new order, while accepting that on the whole they must make the best of what is imposed on them.

In all aspects of world affairs, the Realist is a bilateralist. To form other states into a group may suit him from time to time: a United Nations, so long as he can dominate it; a military alliance; the countless technical bodies. But a Realist fears that by promoting groups he will encourage coalitions against him, as the Northern states did among the small states by telling them that they were 'the Less Developed Countries'. Above all, he fears the paralysing effect of multilateralism on diplomacy. Not all so-called multilateral organizations really proceed so; GATT procedure is the multilateralization of bilaterally negotiated deals; but to the extent that an organization really does act multilaterally, it inevitably substitutes speech-making for the efficient dispatch of business. The worst in this respect are those organizations that do 'open diplomacy'; useless even for effective propaganda, their only value is that they may help statesmen of small countries to cut a world figure in the eyes of their own people; but open or closed, the tendency of all group diplomacy is towards striking attitudes. The law of human contact is that two is best; realism diminishes in the presence of more.

A more profound danger to diplomacy is naïvety about international law. The battle about this is not so noisy at present as it was at the beginning of this century; the Americans have ceased to be legalists and have become strategists instead. None the less, there is a deep human disposition to think that in the end security internationally has the same source as it does domestically, namely, the observance of law. Just as citizens should obey the law at home, so should states conform to it in their diplomacy abroad. The fact is, of course, that domestic and international law are clean different things: the one has a common power behind it, making it and enforcing it more or less impartially; the other is merely a record of the methods and results of power politics. Respect for international law is expedient because it is respect for the power of other states. Also, it is important not to antagonize the believers in international justice and morality. When a state breaks or sets out to alter international law on some matter, it should do so with the greatest diplomatic and propaganda finesse, and avoid such blunders as calling treaties 'scraps of paper', even though that is in fact what they are.[22]

First and last, the true source of security in international relations is national power and military force, handled with true diplomacy. Diplomacy is the recognition and communication of the facts of power. It is the peaceful enactment of otherwise violent conflict. It is *le tact des choses possibles*. Power is never absolute, always relative to particular adversaries. When a state has a margin of power it should use it; when it has not, it must concede. The correct calculation of what can and cannot be done is difficult; but, because it deals in realities, it is not outright impossible as are the moral, utilitarian, and historical calculations of other breeds of statesman. Power should be exercised in a manner that is firm but never brutal or arrogant. Because the forces at work in international life are complex and uncontrollable, the outcome of a policy is unpredictable, and therefore the style in which things are done is as important as what is done.[23] The last, worst enemy of diplomacy is Fideism, that disastrous combination of inexperience of the world and zealotry. 'Surtout, messieurs, point de zèle.'[24]

[22] Bernhard von Bülow, *Denkwürdigkeiten* (Berlin, 1930), ii. 109.
[23] Gwendolin Cecil, *Life of Robert, Marquis of Salisbury* (London, 1921), ii. 136.
[24] Attributed to Talleyrand. In the same vein, Duff Cooper, *Talleyrand* (London, 1932), 330.

Beside Necessity and Virtue, there is another power:

> Mortal prudence, handmaid of divine providence,
> Hath inscrutable reckoning with fate and fortune.[25]

What statesman can trust himself to be a Realist, leave alone trust all the others to be so who manage the world with him? And, even if all were, failure could still come by chance. Realism is rightly called a pessimistic, even tragic view. This is not its last word, however. It is empirical. The fact is that fortune favours the brave.[26]

[25] Robert Bridges, *The Testament of Beauty*, bk. 1.
[26] Niccolò Machiavelli, *The Prince*, ch. 25.

3

Fideism

BROTHERS and sisters in the Faith, we are full of a truth revealed by a power beyond ourselves: men without God are lost. The glories of their civilization end in the graves of Auschwitz and Hiroshima. They wander in the vast void of space. 'La silence éternelle de ces espaces infinies m'effraie.'[1] Within them, their hearts are empty. They hear nothing but the beat of time passing until their lives stop.

Men set up idols to worship in the desert. They bow down to reason. They build a reasonable society; they view the structure with complacency. Then the storm comes; they are tested; and all breaks. Reason succeeds when men are reasonable, but cannot withstand evil. 'If someone approves, as a goal, the extirpation of the human race from the earth,' wrote Einstein, 'one cannot refute such a viewpoint on rational grounds.'[2]

Morality, based on reason, is selfishness. It says: 'I must behave well or I will be in trouble.' If not selfish, it is purposeless. It says: 'The point of my existence is to serve others.' But what is the point of their existence? The final inanity is the categorical imperative: duty is duty.[3]

Morality, based on reason, cannot control men. The pagans will object: 'We have had great sages who lived by reason.' But must they not admit that, for the mass of men, reason is too cold an authority? Even their sages are answered out of their own mouths by the tale in Plato of the ring of Gyges: no man, however rational, could resist the temptation to do wrong if he could be sure that he would not be discovered.[4] As to doing good, let the Rationalist answer this: how many men over the

---

[1] Blaise Pascal, *Pensées*, iii. 206.
[2] Quoted in Arnold Brecht, *Political Theory* (Princeton, NJ, 1959), 9.
[3] Emil Brunner, *The Divine Imperative* (London, 1937), 67 ff.; N. H. G. Robinson, *The Groundwork of Christian Ethics* (London, 1971), 17–21, 47, 100.
[4] *The Republic*, bk. 2.

centuries who have dedicated their lives to others have been atheists?

Because reason is not enough, men worship a pantheon of idols, called natural religion. Sometimes they crouch and mumble before effigies of sticks, straw, and mud; sometimes they believe in the gods of Olympus and the heroes of Valhalla; or they live in an age of competing world religions or secular faiths; or these fade and they fall back on the oldest superstition, belief in the stars. These are all human fictions to repel fear. Man's life is unbearable without a power beyond himself that will help bear it. The historian shows us the variety of these fictions over the ages, and, since they come and go, the vanity of them all. History itself is just another fable. Only a truth that comes into history from beyond it can fill the emptiness, a star like no other. Only this can cast out fear.

The ugliest idol is this: men, refusing to worship even the natural gods, leave alone the true God, worship Man. Some idolize their own person; they inflate themselves into Leaders. Most bow down to the Group. Kierkegaard prophesied this: men that turn from God turn to collectivism. Jung wrote: 'Once we have lost the capacity to orient ourselves by religious truth, there is absolutely nothing that can deliver man from his original biological bondage to the family, as he will simply transfer his infantile principles, uncorrected, to the world at large, and will find there a father who, so far from guiding him, will lead him to perdition.'[5]

The idol state is, at worst, a glittering, conjuring tyranny: its subjects gasp, spellbound. At best, it is liberal and rational; it deceives more subtly; for in truth, even the best of godless states is, as the Realist says, only an organization of power so that its citizens shall have law and order, and a Welfare State so that they shall be comfortable. The best community of godless men has no higher reason for existence than Man. Man is his own reason. He is his own God.

Even the greatest empire ends in disillusion. Men lose heart. 'I have come to hate life because what is done under the sun is grievous to me, for all is vanity and a striving after wind.'[6] In the emptiness of the great desert, men finally despair before

---

[5] *The Collected Works of C. G. Jung*, xvii (London, 1954), 85.
[6] Ecclesiastes 2: 17.

suffering and death. 'And I thought the dead who are already dead more fortunate than the living who are still alive; but better than both is he who has not yet been, and has not seen the evil deeds that are done under the sun.'[7]

Unknown to infidels, death, the last enemy, is God. It is the wrath and judgement of God upon men for their disobedience. Because they have chosen Satan, they are delivered into his power. God is terrible. 'Woe to you who desire the day of the Lord! Why would you have the day of the Lord? It is darkness and not light.'[8]

Yet, in the desert, there is also mercy. 'Hate evil and love good, and establish justice in the gate; it may be that the Lord, the God of hosts, will be gracious to the remnant of Joseph.'[9] And this has indeed come to pass; there is in truth 'a remnant chosen by grace'.[10] It is a people that believes what God has revealed and that worships and obeys him.

This Community of the Faithful, our Community, is attacked on its journey through the desert by many enemies. The most dangerous are those who pretend to belong to the Faith but who distort it, false teachers, false communities.

Some of them are tainted with paganism. They rejoice in the Faith but they refuse to believe that infidels are lost. For, they say, human nature is diseased by disobedience to God but not totally; men can still please him in that they can still follow the Natural Law, though not in its original perfection. They quote St Paul: 'When the Gentiles who have not the Law do by nature what the Law requires, they are a law to themselves, even though they do not know the Law.'[11] This means, they think, that the moral law does not require divine revelation; the unbelievers follow it already; the same moral law binds the Faithful; there is no 'religious ethics'.

What then, in their opinion, is the Revelation? They say it is not law but love. It shows us Man's obedience in its original perfection; 'grace does not replace nature but perfects it'.[12] It is a new spirit in the law; 'Love is the soul of the virtues.'[13] The

---

[7] Ecclesiastes 4: 2–3.   [8] Amos 5: 18.   [9] Ibid. 5: 65.
[10] Romans 11: 5.   [11] Ibid. 2: 14.
[12] '. . . gratia non tollat naturam sed perficiat . . .', St Thomas Aquinas, *Summa Theologiae*, 1. 1. 8, *ad* 2; see also St Benedict, *Rule*, Prologue ('et quod minus habet . . .').
[13] 'Caritas anima virtutum.' I should be grateful to anyone who can tell me the origin of this phrase.

unbelievers do not know the joy of this, but they need not fear the saying 'There is no salvation outside the Church.'[14] It means that there is no source of salvation except the Church, that, without it, the world is heartless. Because of the Church, the good pagan will live in Paradise.

The climax of their errors is their doctrine that, even as a man who does not accept the Faith can still be pleasing to God, so a state that is not founded on the Faith can still be a good state. They quote St Paul again: 'The powers that be are ordained of God.'[15] and these in his day were pagan. Man, they say, has two kinds of good: natural and supernatural. The purpose of the state is to administer the fulfilment of the first of these. Among the Faithful, the Church dispenses the supernatural good.

Against these distortions by fleshly reasoning, let us now declare the true Faith. 'We believe, teach and confess that Original Sin is no trivial corruption but is so profound a corruption of human nature as to leave nothing sound, nothing uncorrupt in body or soul of man, or his mind or bodily powers.'[16] Depraved humanity has a dim 'light of nature' to guide it, and there are men of virtue in every age; but this is so by a special act of God, lest wickedness destroy the earth;[17] men, of themselves, can do nothing pleasing to God; they are 'a mass of perdition'.[18] Only those to whom God grants faith, the faith to believe what he has revealed of himself and of his Law, and who worship and obey, will live in Paradise.

The states that the infidels form are in the same condition as they are. Man's depraved will has a certain ability to do civil justice and to choose rightly in matters of reason, but it has no power to do the justice of God, spiritual justice.[19] Godless states, like men, are in the power of Satan. 'The powers that be' are demonic; they are 'of God' merely in that God tolerates Satan, uses him, permits infidel states, provisionally.[20] If a state

[14] St Augustine, *De Baptismo contra Donatistas*, bk. 4, ch. 17.
[15] Romans 13: 1.
[16] 'Formula Concordiae' (1577), in Philip Schaff, *The History of the Creeds* (London, 1877), iii. 100.
[17] John Calvin, *Institutes of the Christian Religion*, bk. 2, ch. 3, sects. 3–4.
[18] St Augustine, *De Diversis Quaestionibus ad Simplicianum*, bk. 1, Q. 2, sect. 16; *Enchiridion ad Laurentium*, ch. 27.
[19] 'Confession of Augsburg' (1530), in B. J. Kidd, *Documents Illustrative of the Continental Reformation* (Oxford, 1911), 266; see also Schaff, *The History of the Creeds*, iii. 18.
[20] Revelation 13.

is not just, what is it but a great gang of thieves? And how can a state be just that takes a man from God and subjects him to demons? The only state pleasing to God is one that worships and obeys him.[21]

This is a state that is a Church. There is no difference between state and Church, natural good and supernatural. The error of dividing them springs from pagan thought and Romano-Christian history. As the medieval Christians found, torn between pope and king, such ideas turn the Community of the Faithful into a monstrosity, one body with two heads or, yet more monstrous, two bodies with one head. The truth is that the Community of the Faithful is one and has one sole good which is, in every act and instant of life, the service of God.

There is another set of false teachers of a quite different colour: those who think that the Faithful should run away from the godless state back to a little Garden of Eden of their own making, secluded from the world. These are the pacifists. They abhor the states and all the other power structures of the world, the oppression and the killing; and in this they are right. They see that the difference between legal killing by the states of this world and illegal killing by criminals is not fundamental; all of it is human self-serving, rotten with pride and greed; all of it is evil. In this too they are right; but totally wrong is their response; they refuse to fight against the wickedness of the world; they take the command to be meek, to 'turn the other cheek', to mean that they should renounce power and force; they fail to see that godless power and force are wrong, not godly.

Many men who seem to be pacifists are not truly so. The violence that they repudiate is that of 'the powers that be', not their own. Their doctrine is not 'that nobody has the right to take up the sword, but that no worldly person has the right to take up the sword'.[22] Such people can be strong soldiers for the godly state or, by millenniarism and antinomianism, like the Anabaptists of old, very dangerous to it. But, as for the peaceful pacifists, they are shepherds without rod or staff in a world of wolves. The true godly, praise be, raise against the Midianites 'a sword for the Lord and Gideon'.[23]

---

[21] St Augustine, *De Civitate Dei*, bk. 4, ch. 4; bk. 19, ch. 21.
[22] Ronald Knox, *Enthusiasm* (Oxford, 1950), 148.   [23] Judges 7: 20.

Very different again is a tradition of teachers who obey the Faith with their hearts but the world with their heads. They say that the Faithful live under two kingdoms or disciplines, both ordained by God, but contrasting in quality. The first is spiritual, the Church. If the Faithful were truly spiritual, there would be no need of any other discipline. But the Faithful are only partly so; they still adhere partly to the depraved, corrupt, fallen world. In addition, there are the infidels to be controlled. So God ordains a second discipline, the state, to keep men in hand with bridle, bit, and lash.[24]

The contradictions and dangers of this theory are manifest. It exalts the state; the state exists by 'divine right'; but the state is at the same time still a creature of the corrupt world; it is unredeemed. The more a man is spiritual and belongs to the Faith, the less he truly belongs to the state; and the more he belongs to the state, the less he truly belongs to the Faith. The state is a sinful thing for sinful men. Therefore, in this tradition of teaching, all political action is sinful. ' . . . if I take what I believe to be a Protestant Christian view, I do not *expect* to find a politically practical course of action which is without a degree of sinfulness.'[25] Such are the terms in which these people attack the pacifists. Reinhold Niebuhr said to a pacifist once: 'Your difficulty is that you want to live in history without sinning.'[26] A later member of the Union Theological Seminary defended United States possession of nuclear weapons with these words: 'It is more important to prevent nuclear war than to preserve my sinlessness.'[27] These people face manfully what they take to be the insoluble and tragic dilemma of politics: 'There never was a state but was committed to acts and maxims which it is its crime to maintain and its ruin to abandon.'[28] The best that these people can say of the state is: 'Utimur et nos pace Babylonis': 'We too use the peace of Babylon.'[29]

---

[24] Martin Luther, 'Temporal Authority: To What Extent Should it be Obeyed?' in *Works* (St Louis, Mo., 1962), xlv.

[25] Lawrence Martin, 'The Reith Lectures', 2, BBC, Nov. 1981, pub. as *The Two-Edged Sword* (London, 1982), 27.

[26] C. W. Kegley and R. W. Bretall (eds.), *Reinhold Niebuhr: His Religious, Social and Political Thought* (New York, 1956), 69.

[27] Roger Shinn, 'Everyman', BBC TV, 6 Dec. 1981.

[28] Terence Kenny, *The Political Thought of John Henry Newman* (London, 1957), 73.

[29] St Augustine, *De Civitate Dei*, bk. 19, ch. 26.

The danger for those influenced by this doctrine is surrender to evil. Many are strong, valiant for truth; but many ordinary spirits are misled. They succumb to pietism. They despair of political action as a means to overcome the sufferings of men; the state can do no good; it can at most prevent wickedness. And suppose the state turns tyrannical? What else do you expect of states? It is God's will; resistance would be wrong. As Weber put it: 'Protestantism legitimated the authoritarian state.'[30] The international system of states is power politics; it is repugnant but ordained; accept this, teach it, but play no part in the violence.[31]

An alternative form of surrender is alliance with Realism. Just as Machiavelli divided politics from religion, so the Faithful are to engage robustly in politics but are to keep this activity quite separate from the ideals of their Faith. The convergence of the two doctrines can be seen in Meinecke, who wrote the history of Machiavellism and, in it, that the state necessarily lapses back into 'the kingdom of evil'.[32] Responsible for Britain's world policies at the height of its power was Lord Salisbury, a devout Christian who at the same time declared repeatedly that foreign policy cannot be conducted according to the Sermon on the Mount.[33]

Such thoughts can lead to compromise with wickedness. Salisbury had the code of honour of an English gentleman to protect him. Weber saw alongside 'the ethic of ultimate ends', 'the ethic of responsibility'. Some such shield is needed, for, in this peril, Faith will not protect a man. He has left Faith behind as he enters politics, except as a tragic emotion. All is sinful. He must sin bravely. He must calculate the lesser evil, and do it.

It is time to cast light amid this wandering in the dark. The fundamental truth is this: God's grace regenerates nature in those whom he has chosen.[34] The Faithful are a people created anew, born again. Accordingly, the state that they establish is regenerate. The godless state is not God's kingdom; it is God's

[30] Max Weber, 'Politics as a Vocation', in H. H. Gerth and C. W. Mills (eds.), *From Max Weber* (London, 1948), 124.
[31] Brian Porter, 'Patterns of Thought and Practice: Martin Wight's "International Theory" ', in Michael Donelan (ed.), *The Reason of States* (London, 1978), 68.
[32] Friedrich Meinecke, *Machiavellism*, ed. W. Stark, trans. D. Scott (London, 1957), 12.
[33] Gwendolin Cecil, *The Life of Robert, Marquis of Salisbury* (London, 1921), i. 121.
[34] Calvin, *Institutes of the Christian Religion*, bk. 2, ch. 3.

relinquishment of men to their chosen master, Satan. The state made by the Faithful is a 'dominion founded in grace'.[35] Its politics and its policies to the world are godly.

Those whose doctrine is the sinfulness of every state, their own in common with the rest, say that their doctrine makes for humility and restraint in relations between states. They accuse us of a dangerous self-righteousness. Niebuhr attacks Dulles: 'Self-righteousness is the inevitable fruit of simple moral judgments placed in the service of complacency.'[36] We might answer that it is better to be righteous than to be worldly. And must we not believe that God will guide those who trust not in themselves but in him and are no mad fanatics but use every skill of statecraft that he has given them, and that he will lead them, yes, into danger and tribulation but through it to victory? If we do not believe this, what is our Faith but a bed to cry on?

The state made by the Faithful is truly natural, truly realist, truly rational. In it, the feeble light of civil righteousness is electrified by the revelation of the Law. The state is no longer a mere structure of power and force; these are now sanctified by being put to the service of God. The state is no selfish contract among men but a covenant with God, obedience for salvation. It is a theocracy.

So far, I have been casting down the idols of the infidel and exposing the distortions of false teachers of the Faith. Hear next the principle of the Community of the Faithful, the true state. It is, above all, unity: God is one, the Faith is one, the people is one. In government, there should be no division into 'temporal' and 'spiritual' authority. 'Unam sanctam . . . ecclesiam credere cogimur,' declared Boniface VIII; 'The material sword and the spiritual, both are in the power of the Church.'[37] Even such language is imperfect, still in tension between 'Church' and 'State' and 'clergy' and 'laity'. There should be a single set of rulers of the Community with undivided oversight of every aspect of its life. Athens should not be the capital city over Jerusalem nor Jerusalem over Athens. No one is less fitted to

[35] R. L. Poole, *Illustrations of the History of Mediaeval Thought* (London, 1884), ch. 10, 'Wycliffe's Doctrine of Lordship', p. 295; see below, p. 61.
[36] Townsend Hoopes, *The Devil and John Foster Dulles* (Boston, Mass., 1973), 37.
[37] 'Unam Sanctam', Nov. 1302, in Brian Tierney, *The Crisis of Church and State, 1050–1300* (Englewood Cliffs, NJ, 1964), 188–9.

have charge of the well-being of men than politicians who do
not study God's Law; unless it is clerics, ignorant of God's
world. The rulers of the Faithful are to be those who are at once
the best in the observance of the Law of worship and conduct
and in the skills of state.

'Best' is utterly different from popular and ambitious. Government should be in the hands of a Small Council, chosen by a
Council of Two Hundred, itself chosen by it from the citizenry.[38]
Open discussion is godly at all levels of the Community except
at this highest level, where discussion should be secret and
decisions not subject to question. For the unity of the people,
which requires at first pluralism, publicity, and the effort to
harmonize opinions, requires finally self-sacrifice and obedience.

The supreme task of the rulers is to ensure the teaching of the
true Faith and only the true Faith. Teachers of rival religions
will arise as a test of fidelity imposed by God; they must be
suppressed.[39] Heretics must be purged. The medieval papacy
overrode as regards heretics the principles of law which it
otherwise laboriously promoted.[40] Correctly. Heretics are not
fighting for religious freedom; they believe in the unity of the
Faith; they wish to impose their view of what the Faith is. They
are like forgers; like them, they should be destroyed.[41]

We know about God only that he is One, Terrible, and
Merciful. He is, for the rest, beyond human reason. So there
should be no theology, least of all schools and factions of
theology. Better for the medieval Christans if they had followed
their St Bernard, not their clever Abelard. The Faith is not a
continual personal torment about salvation; it is obedience to
the Law; in this lies a man's assurance and his hope. The Faith
is not about creating heaven on earth. Men can be godly but
they cannot on earth be spirits, ruled by spirits. Puritanism is an
error; imprudence is another; antinomianism is an abomination.
Savonarola's Florence, John of Leyden's Münster, America's
Great Awakening are in their different degrees all madness.
The Community of the Faithful fights every day here on earth

---

[38] Borrowed from Calvin's Geneva.   [39] Deuteronomy 13: 3–5.
[40] H. C. Lea, *The Inquisition in the Middle Ages*, Introduction by Walter Ullmann
(London, 1963), 31 ff.
[41] Aquinas, *Summa Theologiae*, 2a. 2ae. 11. 3.

the battle against Satan, the apocalyptic battle, but it is not yet the glorious community of the end of days. It struggles in the desert, and its very life is obedience to the Law.[42]

The second duty of the rulers is practising the Law and teaching and administering it and clarifying it for new contingencies in its two great branches, worship and private and social conduct. The latter includes all covered by the codes of law of pagan states but with a great difference throughout: there are no injuries to persons, only to God, no wrong, only sin. For persons in themselves, being part of the corrupt world, have no value; only as purified and made obedient have they value; and so injuries are done not to them but to their Master. The Community of the Faithful proclaims, as do infidel states, a code of human rights but with this proviso: the rights are not natural rights; they are subject to the Law of God, which is to say, granted by it. The practical effect of this spirit of the laws is the reinforcement of unity. The parties to a conflict approach it not as wilful, self-assertive individuals but as servants in a community of servants. The work of a law court is not decision between the parties but reconciliation; not prevarication and legal nicety but the diagnosis of an ill and the prescription of a remedy; at the broadest, the subordination of legalism to the political good. The Law is severe but its severity is accepted because all are under obedience.

The Law grants a degree of tolerance to unbelievers, living in the Community of the Faithful, as a matter of prudence. They should not be forced to profess the true Faith, and yet they should be put under pressure. Those of them that acknowledge the unity of God may be permitted for a time to continue their mistaken ways of worship and upbringing of children, but polytheists, never. Their beliefs are blasphemy, and, besides, they suffer a double blindness, not seeing 'that even this world's prizes are not in the gift of demons but in the power of the true God'.[43]

The Law, having been revealed once and for ever, is a fixed and certain guide. Not for the Faithful the motto of the godless:

---

[42] Luther, 'Temporal Authority: To What Extent Should it be Obeyed?', p. 91 ff.; Calvin, *Institutes of the Christian Religion*, bk. 4, ch. 20.

[43] St Augustine, *De Civitate Dei*, bk. 5, ch. 26; see also Deuteronomy 20: 17–18.

Plurimi pertransibunt et multiplex erit scientia.[44] But the Faithful must not become fixed. They are not a settlement but journeying. In interpreting the Law, they must not stop. They must not look backward to their first centuries or forward to the mirage of modernity, but upward. They must dispute about what the Law requires in face of new problems, always, though, restrained by obedience. Each remembers that he is nothing. The motto of the Faithful is: *Dominus illuminatio mea.* [45]

So it shall be in every aspect of the life of the Community: politics, economics, the arts, and the sciences. The Faithful must not fear change, and must avoid archaism equally with beguiling novelty. The common Faith will restrain extremism in controversy and encourage self-sacrifice. It will, above all, give fire and purpose to the Community and so advancement. For the heart of the Faith is obedience; and men demonstrate that they are obedient to God by work and the achievement of prosperity.[46]

No darkness is deeper among the pagans than their mis-understanding of prosperity. They dispute as to how it should be distributed among some or many or all, but they agree that it is theirs. But prosperity is God's. Did men make the world? God made it; we are his; he gave us our talents. To question why he did so and to fail to use our talents is disobedience; we must fill sea, earth, and sky with our achievements. To use our talents for ourselves is disobedience. For what have I achieved, heavy with gold rings, grey-haired? Or what even if I share my wealth with a spiteful beggar? Our achievements must be not for ourselves or for other men but offerings to God.

The Faithful must seek for each of their number a living that is decent, not luxurious, the weak aided by the strong, the strong required to show by their work that they are indeed of the Faith, and all despising greed in the income that they accept and the prices and interest that they charge. 'To a foreigner, you may lend upon interest but to your brother you shall not lend upon interest.'[47] They must seek beyond this the utmost

---

[44] Inscription in the Bodleian Library, Oxford; St Jerome's Latin translation of Daniel 12: 4. A modern English translation (the Jerusalem Bible) is: 'Many will wander this way and that and wickedness will go on increasing.'

[45] Psalms 27: 1. The motto of Oxford University.

[46] R. H. Tawney, *Religion and the Rise of Capitalism* (London, 1922).

[47] Deuteronomy 23: 20.

that their skills can attain in raising up men and nature, in design and manufacture, in concept, form, colour, and music. This is their godly joy. Should it wither in disaster, they are consoled by remembering that all is God's.

In everything, in economics, politics, philosophy, the sciences, the arts, and even in the Law itself, the God-given skills of the Faithful are kept sharp by controversy. Yet there must be continual watchfulness lest diversity of opinion and the rivalry of bodies of opinion result in infidelity. Any hint of relativism and scepticism must be suppressed. Ideologies, such as liberalism, fascism, communism, must not be permitted. The duty of vigilance, as much over oneself as over others, lies with all the Faithful, but especially with the news media, and, finally, with the rulers who must be ready to censure any deviant developments. In any uncertainty, the question is whether this or that opinion makes for the fervour of the people in the Faith and for their unity.

This unity should be world-wide. The whole of the earth, all its peoples, should acknowledge one God and obey one Law. The highest duty of the Faithful is to struggle for that consummation. Until it is achieved, the fundamental feature of international politics is that the world is divided into two, the Camp of the Faithful and the Camp of the Infidels. The Camp of the Faithful is the abode of those peoples who live in obedience to God; the Camp of the Infidels consists of the peoples still under the dominion of Satan, the empire of evil.

In the Camp of the Faithful, there must above all else be unity so that it is truly an abode of peace and so that it is strong for the struggle against the infidels. It is not divided as they are into sovereign states. The only sovereign is God and all the Faithful are one community. The so-called states of the Faithful should better be called 'statelets'. They are a practical necessity of great importance but still of restricted scope. They have at most 'a limited sovereignty'. They are like the divisions of one single, great army.

Accordingly, set over the whole Camp of the Faithful, there should be a Central Authority, drawn from the states, deliberating in secret, and pronouncing upon the principles of the Law regarding worship and conduct and also upon the principles of the constitution of states and their governance and of relations between them. Within these limits, the states of the Camp rule themselves in their own way, deciding what the Law requires and what is best to be done in public affairs. They organize co-operation with other states in the same region of the Camp and methods of settling disagreements.

They remember throughout how different they are in spirit from infidel states. They are not obsessed with rule over territory; they are primarily jurisdictions over people. Their frontiers are mere administrative lines, not great symbols of a barrier between brothers and aliens. Their economies are not theirs but God's and fundamentally one single economy in his service. They avoid, above all, the poison of nationalism. Though the migration of the Faithful between states must be controlled, this is an act of prudence, not done in the spirit of exclusion; for all are brothers in the Faith. A state may be peopled by the Faithful but it is still not a true state of the Faithful so long as it is not open to all of them without regard to nationality or race. A state may experience an explosion of enthusiasm for the Faith, of revolutionary ardour, of valiant defiance of 'the great Satan' that has oppressed it; but all this may represent not true fervour for the Faith but the use of the Faith as a symbol of national identity, and as the banner, not of God, but of a profane ideology, and thus be blasphemous and doomed to transience and failure.

Any state in the Camp that deviates from the path of the Law and political principle or becomes contaminated with false enthusiasm must be corrected by the others in its region at the command of the Centre. Take a parallel from the profane world. Throughout the negotiations for the Helsinki Accords of 1975, the Communist Russians argued, in the end unsuccessfully, that the principles of sovereignty, non-interference, and territorial integrity applied absolutely only among states with different social systems, not among those that belonged to the camp of socialism. So it is in the Camp of the Faithful. To be sure, there must be proper respect for brethren in inter-state relations as in all matters. Limitless interference would be as offensive and impractical as limitless sovereignty. But there will be all the time a fraternal voice across frontiers in the affairs of fellow states, and, if the unthinkable happens and deviation begins and the state concerned will not listen to friendly admonition, its rulers must be changed. Let 'the servant of wickedness' be anathema and deposed, declared Pius V, a one-time Central Authority, against Elizabeth of England.[48] Invasion is destructive, humiliating, and costly, and the best method may well be assassination (understood as execution of the Law) backed by the threat of heavier sanctions. Heretics and infidels often ask whether such interventions between the states of the Faithful are motivated by religion or politics, and how we can expect to impose ideas with the sword. This is shallow talk. Oxenstjerna put the matter correctly: Gustavus Adolphus did not invade Germany for religion, which is spiritual, but for the *status publicus*, ecclesiastical and political, in which religion is comprehended.[49]

The Central Authority also has the happier duty of promoting great common enterprises that require the resources of all the states of the Camp in industry, technology, arts, and sciences, and organizing rites and festivals, and celebrating the Faith and the unity of the Camp. Its final responsibility is coordination and leadership in relations with the Camp of the Infidels.

These relations are eternally hostile. Where the guilt of this lies is plain. The infidels refuse obedience to God; they are in rebellion against him. They form the army of Satan in the war that he declared of old. The manner in which the infidel states attack the Camp of the Faithful varies. Sometimes they encircle it with force, sometimes they practice appeasement, sometimes they declare the struggle obsolete. At all times, they do not understand what they are doing; they cherish their own superficial interpretations of world politics; Satan misleads them. For always, whether assaulting with force or corrupting with scepticism and atheism, they are attacking the Faith. All hostility that the Faithful meet in world politics is religious hostility, springing in one way or another from disobedience to God. Thus, for example, 'Soviet Communism starts with an atheistic, Godless premise. Everything else flows from that premise.'[50]

The duty of the Faithful is to wage continual crusade by one means or another against the infidel states. This is not

[48] 'Regnans in Excelsis', Feb. 1570, in Thomas Fuller, *The Church History of Britain*, ed. J. S. Brewer (Oxford, 1845), iv. 361.
[49] Michael Roberts, *Gustavus Adolphus* (London, 1958), ii. 419.
[50] John Foster Dulles, *War or Peace* (New York, 1950), 8.

'aggression'; crusade is an act of recovery.[51] Just as the communists used to say that, since the Revolution is the law of history, promoting it is simply defending it, so the Faithful are not imposing the Faith, but restoring it.

The institutions of the infidels, being godless and illegitimate, have no right to respect. Their states are not entitled to independent existence. When the Spaniards conquered the New World, they did so with the conviction that the Aztecs and Incas and the rest had only provisional dominion, and that this should be overridden in order to spread the Faith. The infidels claim that there is a states-system or a society of states or a world community, and that this, the widest institution of man, has foundations in reason and history that all must acknowledge. They have also at one time their empires, at other times their hegemonies or their concerts of powers. Their deepest justification for all this is peace: *pax romana, pax americana*. But they are 'saying peace where there is no peace'![52] This is no *dar al-Islam*. 'They make a desert and they call it peace.'[53] What is a peace worth that is a mere structure of external quiet among men who are spiritually fevered and despairing? It is the peace of Babylon.

The equality of states is the foundation of Rationalist international law; but there can in truth be no equality between Faithful and infidel states. Therefore, any so-called international law, any treaties that it may suit the Faithful to make with their opponents, are, on a profound understanding, not truly multilateral or bilateral agreements but edicts of the Faithful. The inequality of states is the foundation of Realist diplomacy, which consists of communicating the facts of power; but diplomacy in the Camp of the Faithful consists of discussion and decision among brothers, and between the Camps, diplomacy is a continuation of war by other means. Natural Law attitudes, according to which the true diplomatist always seeks to build community, are false, as is the belief that diplomacy must always be honest. There is no obligation to keep faith with infidels. Least of all can the Faithful admit any validity in the conception of an 'international community' or any legitimacy in the pronouncements of world organizations. When, in August

[51] Jonathan Riley-Smith, *What Were the Crusades?* (London, 1977), 17–27; Eric Christiansen, *The Northern Crusade* (London, 1980), 56.
[52] Jeremiah 6: 14.   [53] Tacitus, *Agricola*, 30.

1980, the United Nations Security Council passed a resolution presuming to condemn Israel for incorporating Jerusalem into itself, Israel replied: 'The people of Israel does not need the Security Council's recognition to know that Jerusalem is the eternal capital of Israel.'[54]

Thus much as to our fundamental attitude to the infidel. Always remember, though, that this is strategy; tactics are a different matter. Overt force is sometimes the correct approach but usually peaceful or semi-peaceful methods will be more productive. The merest prudence dictates this, and equally obviously we bear in mind that there are degrees of turpitude among the infidels. Some of them are nations that profess to acknowledge God; truly they do not; they are neither cold nor hot, they are fit to be spewed out, a horror, a thing to be hissed at; and yet often use can be made of them.[55] Others are states that are genuinely progressing in the direction of the Faith, and these should be encouraged with acts of friendship. Besides, we cannot advance against the enemy Camp on all fronts at once. We need co-operation here in order to attack there, we need stability in some respects among the infidels so that we can undermine them more profoundly.

Thus, the economic prosperity of the infidel Camp can greatly assist our cause. To be sure there will be times when collapse and distress there will create opportunities for us: discontent will breed disunity, and disunity, weakness. But to suppose that this is the general rule of human life would be to succumb to the materialist thought of the infidels themselves. On the contrary, our knowledge of men tells us, and history confirms, that the rich are easier to conquer than the poor. No doubt also we must be cautious in our use of infidel prosperity. We must not allow the strength of our economy to become dependent on theirs; our policy must be autarky; and, above all, we must guard against the infection of our people with the spirit of luxury. None the less, with due vigilance, the infidels can be made to work for us, inventors, financiers, industrialists.

So much for tactics, often involving co-operation with our enemies. The great problem for our leaders is how to maintain among our people the strategic spirit of crusade. The Historicist

---

[54] Government of Israel Press statement, 24 Aug. 1980.
[55] Jeremiah 19: 8; Revelation 3: 15–16.

will say that this is impossible; countless faiths have arisen but always at length their fervour has died away; he refuses to accept that there is one Faith that is different, the true one. Co-operation, periodic truce, prolonged coexistence must not be allowed to confuse and enervate our people. No task is more vital for our teachers than to define the limits of goodwill between the Faith and Infidelity, and to expound it to our people in ever fresh terms with all possible animation. Our fundamental principle is plain: we pity the infidels in their slavery and do not tolerate it. How long the great struggle will last, only God knows; it may be very long, but each one of the Faithful must constantly be reminded that his life is short and that the task of making his contribution to the long struggle is therefore urgent; and that there must be no weariness, only a great ardour that bursts out in the same battle-cry whether in military crusade or in the years of civilian struggle: 'Make them come in.'[56] Byzantium became degenerate, learned to coexist with the Arabs, and was therefore rightly despised by the real Crusaders from the West, and in the end justly destroyed by the Ottomans from the East. Our acceptance of the Camp of the Infidels is always only provisional. We make use of the peace of Babylon. In the end, Babylon falls to Cyrus.

Between the Camp of the Faithful and the Camp of the Infidels, there is no fixed frontier. A Camp is not a place but a movement; around it there is a no man's land; mingling in it are a multitude of witting and unwitting followers of the enemy. In the Camp of the Faithful, besides the infidel groups, heretics, ideologists, the luxurious, the disobedient, and the disunifiers of all sorts, there are also lurking agents of the enemy, termites and moles, gnawing and burrowing, Guy Fawkeses, sapping and mining, working to destroy us. They must be sought out and dealt with. In the Camp of the Infidels, we for our part, besides the millions whose actions unconsciously serve us, have our mission-aries and, because of them and our ceaseless propaganda, countless fellow believers in the true Faith. In this way, the whole of world society is one great battlefield. We have to assess not just the balance of power between the Camps as groups of

---

[56] Luke 14: 23; a slogan of the Crusaders; e.g. B. Scott James, *The Letters of St. Bernard of Clairvaux* (London, 1953), no. 394.

states, but the total 'correlation of forces', political, economic, and social, in the struggle for the obedience of mankind.[57]

Missionaries will usually best concentrate their efforts on the conversion of the leading classes. These will then exert pressure of some kind on the rest of the people. When St Augustine had converted Ethelbert of Kent, the king so far encouraged the conversion of the people 'as that he compelled none to embrace Christianity, but only showed more affection to the believers, as to his fellow-citizens in the heavenly kingdom'.[58] Until the rulers of a pagan kingdom have been converted, the Faithful who live there have grave tactical problems. They must organize as communities so as to be strong, and yet, by submissiveness and even collaboration, they must avoid seeming to pose a threat to the state until the right time comes. They will not succeed in this in periods of crisis in the great struggle, and they will suffer fearful persecution.

They will endure it, and their martyrdom will inspire the rest of us, because they have faith in final victory. Nothing at all moves in human life without faith. Even the pagans bear distorted witness to this. In their political movements, rebellions, and wars, their men struggle and die, not for interests or reason or justice or history, but because these are a faith. Afrikaner or Zionist, nationalist, imperialist, and communist draw on religion or transform their cause into a religion. In all peaceful pursuits also, in the arts and sciences and industry, it is only by faith that a man can move a mountain. If this is how even the profane world works, how much more can be achieved in the Camp of the Faithful by the true Faith? And how much more yet will be achieved in the whole world when in the last times with the coming of the Prince of Peace the final battle, of which all our work and warfare are a foreshadowing, that Armageddon that will end in triumph over Satan, has been fought, and the glorious community of a thousand thousand years lifts up every moment of life as a joyful offering of obedience to God!

[57] See above, ch. 2 n. 15.
[58] St Bede, *The Ecclesiastical History of the English Nation* trans. John Stevens, bk. 1, ch. 26.

4

Rationalism

THE Great Khan Möngke ordered that a conference be held at his capital, Karakorum, on 30 May 1254. His empire was the widest that the historian had ever seen, stretching from the China Sea across the steppes of Asia to the little kingdoms of the West. Thirteen years earlier, after the Battle of Liegnitz on the borders of Germany, the Mongols had 'filled nine sacks with the right ears of the slain'.[1] The Khan wanted to know which was the best religion. The Moslems, Buddhists, and Roman and Nestorian Christians debated. None convinced the others. The Khan's successors inclined towards Buddhism.

This piece of history, says the Rationalist, is a simple way of showing that the First Cause of things cannot be known. Moslems, Buddhists, and Christians have their 'revelations', but these are conflicting. Wars of religion cannot settle the matter; a medieval Mongol could see that, even if Christians could not. Reason cannot decide the matter either. Our beliefs about God are private, their status uncertain.

Let us move from the dark origins of the world into the world itself. Consider physical and human nature. The essences of these, things in themselves, the Good, Ends, and Laws of Nature are not accessible to us and cannot be discovered by reasoning. For between us and the world there is an intermediary, our senses; the world for us is not as it is but as it seems. Yet this seeming is not arbitrary. We bring intellect to our perception, that is, first, concepts: space and time; quantity, quality, substance, cause, mode; I, World, First Cause. All men share these concepts. With these concepts, we construct the world.[2]

In constructing the social world, the first idea that reason uses is 'I'. We are aware of thought, and we interpret this as 'I' thinking. We pick up a bit of wood, and it becomes different

---

[1] Edward Gibbon, *The Decline and Fall of the Roman Empire*, ch. 64.
[2] Based on Immanuel Kant, *Critique of Pure Reason*.

from the others lying about: 'my' bit of wood. Moreover, it is mine as opposed to anyone else's. By appropriating the world we create our identity and by mapping frontiers ('mine', 'yours', 'hers', 'his') we make the world a place we can live in.

Reason uses, next, the idea of 'freedom'. We are aware of a multitude of men and of a moral law among them. Neither God nor Nature imposes this moral law on us; for, as I have said, we do not know God or Nature. The moral law is the free creation of our reason; we are autonomous. Again, neither God nor Nature has appointed anyone to rule others. Parents rule children because adults know more than infants. All of us enforce the moral law on those who break it. But men who keep the law are free.

We also perceive men as being 'equal'. In basic faculties, as Cicero wrote, 'Nothing is so one to one similar, so equivalent, as all of us are to each other.'[3] In basic power, we are the same; to put this point in a crude way, men have the same ability to kill one another until in the course of social interaction they divide into stronger and weaker.[4] Men, lastly, are the same in that each has interests. 'The poorest he that is in England has a life to lead as the greatest he.'[5]

Freedom and equality are the foundation of society and the moral law among men. From our sameness of faculties, 'we understand that the whole human race are associates', wrote Cicero.[6] Reason 'teaches all mankind who will but consult it, that being equal and independent', wrote Locke, 'no one ought to harm another in his life, health, liberty or possessions'.[7] It is because we are free and equal that, in reason, we ought to act to others as we think they should act to us, and not treat others merely as means to our ends, but as having ends of their own.[8] 'Everybody to count for one and nobody for more than one', as Bentham put it.[9]

The Natural Law Man, the Realist, and the Fideist will object that such reasoning is too arithmetical and disembodied

---

[3] *Laws*, I. x. 29.   [4] Thomas Hobbes, *Leviathan*, ch. 13.

[5] Colonel Thomas Rainborow, Army Debates, Putney, 29 Oct. 1647, in C. H. Firth (ed.), *The Clarke Papers* (London, Camden Society, II, 49, 1891), i. 301.

[6] *Laws*, I. xi. 32.   [7] John Locke, *Second Treatise of Government*, ch. 2.

[8] Kant, *Groundwork of the Metaphysic of Morals*, in H. J. Paton, *The Moral Law* (Hutchinson, 1983), 55, 84, 91.

[9] Quoted in John Stuart Mill, *Utilitarianism*, ch. 5.

to move men to act morally. Very well, let us add for their sake more passionate reasoning: men, to pursue their interests successfully, must respect the interests of others. No doubt, men often come into conflict, and sometimes, admittedly, they gain more by enforcing their interests on others than by respect; but these cases are the exception; on the whole, men gain most by making a convention called 'justice', and by taking it as their rule. Of this convention, the three laws are, as Hume says, stability of possession, transfer by consent, and the performance of promises.[10]

That respect is best is obvious wherever men are co-operating with some others in a common purpose. That among men generally respect is best is almost as clear. There is a fundamental 'harmony of interests' among men.[11] Whenever one progresses in the pursuit of his interests, opportunities for progress are created for others. If I impede someone by injuring him, this is more often than not a mistake; for even if his progress does not directly benefit mine, it benefits someone else's, and that in turn benefits mine. Conflict among men, however prevalent, is basically unreasonable because it impoverishes them. Each prospers as others prosper.

The dynamic throughout is 'I', the 'self', 'self-interest'. Neither freedom and equality nor utilitarian respect nor harmony of interests require that I subordinate my interests to anyone else's. Agreed, I must not injure others. Agreed, also, that something more positive is entailed by equality. In Locke's words, 'Everyone, as he is bound to preserve himself, and not to quit his station wilfully, so by the like reason, when his own preservation comes not in competition, ought he as much as he can to preserve the rest of mankind.'[12] In Kant's terms, 'Humanity could no doubt subsist if everybody contributed nothing to the happiness of others but, at the same time, refrained from deliberately impairing their happiness. This is, however, merely to agree negatively and not positively with humanity as an end in itself, unless everyone endeavours also, as far as in him lies, to further the ends of others. For the ends of a subject who is an end

[10] David Hume, *A Treatise of Human Nature*, bk. 3, pt. 2, sect. 6.

[11] A common 18th-cent. idea; see Thomas Spragens, *The Irony of Liberal Reason* (Chicago, 1981), 86–9.

[12] *Second Treatise of Government*, ch. 2.

in himself must, if this conception is to have its *full* effect in me, be also, as far as possible, my ends.'[13] Still, these considerations do not amount to a duty to promote the prosperity of others, such as we have to avoid harming them. In the more passionate terms of Hume, we feel 'a sentiment of humanity', and it, in fact, moves us to help others; still, this is not a demand made upon us by 'justice'. Men have no positive obligations to others (apart from family and friends, no doubt) except those that they take upon themselves by agreements made in the course of pursuing their interests.

These facts of reason that I have so far been trying to make clear, says the Rationalist, are facts for all men, the whole world over. They make of the human species 'a great and natural community'.[14] I need no Realist or Historicist to tell me that all men do not at all times and everywhere observe these facts. Because this is so, reason does not rest with constructing a single great and natural community, but constructs separate civil societies under government. Even if there were no irrationality and aggression, men would still need government as the means of preventing accidental collisions among them.

Reason does not prescribe a single world-wide government. That would be impractical, and, besides, reason proceeds by diversity, by having many different experiments in the constitution of liberty. Moreover, legions of men, here and there on the globe, are irrational and aggressive, and could seize a central government and corrupt or oppress all. Separate societies are needed in the world to prevent this and to provide refuge and defence.[15]

The making of separate societies does not, of course, obliterate the wider society of all mankind; on the contrary, as we shall see, it should reinforce that society; that society should flourish the more strongly. But, first, let us discuss the separate civil society and its government.

We should begin with a clear grasp of what kind of association civil society is. It consists of a multitude of people engaged in the harmonious pursuit of separate purposes. It is not the kind

---

[13] *Groundwork of the Metaphysic of Morals*, p. 92.

[14] Locke, *Second Treatise of Government*, ch. 9.

[15] Gibbon, *The Decline and Fall of the Roman Empire*, ch. 3; Kant, 'Theory and Practice', in Hans Reiss (ed.), *Kant's Political Writings* (Cambridge, 1970), 90.

of association where men come together to co-operate in a single common purpose, as, for example, in a business company. The more mercantile type of Realist habitually talks as though his country were one great trading corporation, competing with the rest of the world, but this is a false picture. Still less does civil society have the common purpose of joint striving for "the good". The Natural Law Man is forever on the brink of this notion with his 'common good' and hierarchy of goods; the Fideist is engulfed in it, and so are nationalists who serve the nation and Marxists who serve history; but they also are wrong.[16]

Only in one respect does civil society have a common purpose, namely, as government.[17] Here, all join together, as citizens, legislature, executive, judiciary, police, armed forces, and so on, to make and enforce laws. The language that reason uses at this point should be noticed. Reason, that begins with 'I', property, freedom, equality, and harmony of interests, necessarily speaks as if these things existed before government, and as if men came together to set up government with the purpose of protecting them. Men of reason, like Bentham and Hume, who call such language nonsense, and say no more of the origin of government than that it is a rational convention, speciously diminish reason and enfeeble it against its enemies.[18] Reason must use the concept of 'a great and natural community' in 'a state of nature', under 'a law of nature or reason' which embodies the 'natural, human rights' of life, property, freedom, and equality, prior to government; and of a 'social contract' whereby men consent to come together and to put themselves under government for the purpose of protecting their rights.

John Stuart Mill wrote: 'The sole end for which mankind are warranted, individually or collectively, in interfering with the liberty of action of any of their number is self-protection.'[19] This and nothing more being the right of individuals and the purpose of governments, reason requires them to be vigilant against any aggrandisement. As 'society', they should take care not to oppress each other with the weight of common opinion, and to be

---

[16] F. A. Hayek, *Law, Legislation and Liberty* (London, 1973), vol. i, ch. 2; Michael Oakeshott, *On Human Conduct* (Oxford, 1975).

[17] Kant, 'Theory and Practice', p. 73.

[18] Jeremy Bentham, *Anarchical Fallacies*, art. 2; Hume, *A Treatise of Human Nature*, bk. 3, pt. 2, sects. 1–2.   [19] John Stuart Mill, *On Liberty*, Introductory.

agreeable to non-conformity and creativity. As government or, to use the word that the Realists have made customary, as a state, they must ensure that they, as voters, and their representatives, officials, and judges do not undermine the privacy of the individual and the diversity of society, which it is their function to protect. State and society should not be conflated; the one is a subordinate activity of the other. Society is not created by the power of the state, as the Realist thinks. The state is no ideal reason such that it can presume to civilize society, as the Hegelians think and as do all totalitarians before and after them. Government does not exist for the satisfaction of rulers, but for the benefit of the governed. As to what this is, it is not the 'general will', Rousseau's dangerous fiction, but the will of each and all. Any government that neglects these principles, and itself becomes oppressive, breaks the social contract, and rightly meets resistance and, at the extreme, rebellion.

The 'checks and balances' between the parts of government, designed to prevent oppression by any of them, that characterize a good political constitution, extend to the voting part. The legislators, office-holders, officials, and judges are not mere puppets of the voters, but should think for themselves about how the interests of all are to be protected equally. The first principle is that every law should apply to all generally, and not be directed for or against any individuals or groups particularly. There should be no privilege, no prejudice, no persecution. This is the old principle that there should be rule not by men but by laws.

On this much, the Natural Law Man and the Fideist agree with me, says the Rationalist; but only verbally; how we differ in substance! For, according to the Fideist, what ensures the making of good laws and obedience to them, is common belief in God; according to the Natural Law Man, it is a sense of community and of good that is beyond perception, metaphysical. I say, on the contrary, that the First Amendment needed to all constitutions is the separation of God from politics, Church from State. Every religion should be tolerated except any that are intolerant and believe that government should be founded on grace.[20] Similarly, good is for debate in society and for

---

[20] Locke, *A Letter on Toleration*, ed. R. Klibansky and J. W. Gough (Oxford, 1968), 85.

decision by the individual. The concern of government is not good but right, not ends but means; it is with making laws that enable each of us to pursue his idea of the good life, without infringing the equal liberty of others. These laws are obeyed precisely because they say nothing of God or the good, and because (this is the second great principle) they are made according to agreed procedures.

The laws differ in kind according to the different aspects of the prevention of injury: criminal laws; company, traffic, health, and environment laws; laws concerned with the carrying-out of the common purpose, for example, taxation and military service. In all aspects, making laws and decisions under them involves such problems as: What counts as an injury? what is an equal burden, say, in taxation? When does property infringe equal liberty? What is to be done when one public good conflicts with another? Various models can be given of the political process, but none should disguise that men argue from their personal and group self-interest and should do so. There are no known absolutes. When a motorway clashes with a national park, there is no taking refuge in some such Aristotelian nonsense as that Rest is more perfect than Motion. In this, as in greater matters, there is only one recourse: the procedural. If the procedures for law and decision-making, from the constitution downwards, are based on the principle that all are equal in having interests and in the right to voice them, if all do in fact have their full say, and if they are reminded in the course of this how each benefits from the progress of others, then the impulse to short-sighted individual and factional and majority selfishness will be curbed, and self-interest will be enlightened, and the best possible law or decision on a given matter will be made, and 'the greatest happiness of the greatest number' will have been achieved.[21]

I have implied throughout, the Rationalist continues, and now stress that the purpose of government is negative, that is, to defend the people by laws at home and by diplomacy and armed force abroad in their pursuit of their prosperity; not to engineer their prosperity itself. The latter deplorable notion is sometimes called 'Rationalism in politics' but I say that it is a perversion of

---

[21] Francis Hutcheson, *An Inquiry into the Original of Our Ideas of Beauty and Virtue*, 5th edn. (London, 1753), 185; see also Ross Harrison, *Bentham* (London, 1983), 115.

Rationalism. This perversion occurs whenever liberals ally with so-called 'benevolent despots' or ideologues such as jacobins and socialists, or are seduced by victory in war, as in 1945, into believing that they can use the same power to do good to the people in peace. Such liberals become indistinguishable from Realists in their *dirigisme*.[22]

For government to move beyond making a structure of laws around a society, to confuse politics with economics, and to give directions to the people in the pursuit of their interests is not only tyrannical; it is presumptuous and foolish. Since the economy consists of a myriad individual purposes, neither politicians nor bureaucrats nor anyone else can comprehend it. That it should consist of a myriad individual purposes and should not be centrally directed is required not only for freedom but for maximum wealth as well. For when each pursues his own prosperity in his own way, the maximum incentive is given to hard work and efficiency; and the maximum number of ideas are tried out about what prosperity is and about new processes and products. Each, while intent only on his own self-interest, and in competition with others, progresses by creating the goods and services that others most want for their own progress. Each, in a free market, in increasing his own wealth, as it were by 'an invisible hand', increases to the greatest possible extent the wealth of all.[23]

Part of maintaining the necessary separation of politics and economics is to have nothing to do with such ideas as 'economic rights', 'economic freedom', and 'economic equality'. Every man, to be sure, has, among his rights, the right not to be injured in his economic affairs, for example, not to be robbed or put to forced labour or driven off his land or excluded from a given trade; but he has no 'economic right' to a share in prosperity other than what he can earn for himself. Similarly, the only freedom is freedom to live your own life, including your economic life, within laws that you have helped to make. People who speak of 'economic freedom' mean that they would like to be richer, so as to be able to do more things; and that they would be richer, were it not that the economic system is oppressive

---

[22] Oakeshott, *Rationalism in Politics* (London, 1962); Hayek, *Law, Legislation, and Liberty*, vol. i, ch. 1.
[23] Adam Smith, *The Wealth of Nations*, bk. 1, ch. 2; bk. 4, chs. 2 and 9.

and cheats them of their due. How a market system does this
and what system would be fairer, they are never able to say
exactly. As to equality, it consists of equal freedom within equal
laws, and this includes, for example, equality of opportunity,
that is, 'the career open to the talents'.[24] Schemes for economic
equality in any other sense are simply robbery.

Government has a few proper tasks in the economy, flowing
from its appointed purpose, for example, taxation and monitoring
defence industries. Also the government may be the only
possible provider of some public goods. The organization of a
Welfare State (education, insurance, and so on) is not among
its proper tasks. The socialist advocates this for ideological
reasons, and the Realist does so in keeping with her maternalist
philosophy, but I answer: first, a citizen has no obligation to
assist the prosperity of his fellows. He has, of course, an interest
in their progress, as they have in his; but they and he will
usually do everything possible towards this on their own account;
and he has no interest in helping anyone who does not. He will
simply assist the unfortunate through his sentiment of humanity
to the extent that he chooses. Second, government is a far less
efficient organizer of people's welfare than they are of their
own; it is wasteful, labyrinthine, and slow to adapt to changing
needs.

There remains the hardest problem of civil society and
government. Whereas the Natural Law Man sees politics as
natural to man and part of the good life, a Rationalist sees it as a
second-rate activity. Private life is the important thing; public
life is merely for the creation of the necessary space. Washington
groans at leaving his estates for the capital. Ordinary people do
not want to be bothered with politics most of the time. But how,
then, can they ensure that they have the rationality and the
institutions that they need for clear self-expression on the
occasions when they do wish to have their say? How, in other
words, can they avoid falling, overtly or covertly, under the
control of manipulators of opinion: politicians, bureaucrats,
churches, big business, demagogues, and popular heroes of all
sorts? The answer is that there is one kind of political activity
that they must engage in all the time: the maintenance, through

[24] Barry R. Gross, 'Real Equality of Opportunity', in E. F. Paul, F. D. Miller, Jr.,
J. Paul, and J. Ahrens (eds.), *Equal Opportunity* (Oxford, 1987).

the public purse, of independent media of news and ideas. Those that staff the media should reflect that there is one aspect of politics that is first-rate and worthy of a man of genius: the prevention of slavery of the mind. 'Ecrasez l'infâme!'[25]

I return now, the Rationalist continues, to the subject of 'the common society of the human race'.[26] It is in every way the great society, in value as in extent. For even those of us who desire no more than a small private sphere, confined to a chosen part of one country, draw upon resources from everywhere, and their spirit is enlarged by knowing that they have the freedom of a whole world. The laws of this great society are the laws of nature or reason, and these are, or ought to be, upheld and detailed by the laws of the separate states. We deal with foreigners, for the most part, under either our laws or theirs. However, there are gaps between these laws, which need to be filled by inter-state action; worse, many states have bad laws, amounting in some cases to tyranny. Worst of all, such states are aggressive, and start wars with others, and in this way, states are the great disturbers of the peace of cosmopolis.

First, as to the quality of states, their historical origin (which often, no doubt, lay in great crimes) has no practical importance; what matters is their present and future reasonableness, internally and externally. States are, or should be, in a certain sense, nation-states. Men who have joined together freely in civil society under government may be called a nation, a political nation. They need not be an ethnic or cultural nation. They may be mostly of the same stock and the same language, customs, religion, and so on, but also they may not be. The belief that a state should be an ethnic or cultural nation, and that an ethnic or cultural nation should be a state is, with religious bigotry, the worst error of human history so far, oppressive, indeed murderous, to individuals and minorities at home, and aggressive abroad. A reasonable state will certainly reflect the historical character of its citizens as well as their personal opinions, and so arises its distinctive 'spirit of the laws'. It is national; but it is not nationalist.

From this thought follows the proper judgement on imperial states, on the empires of the Great Khan and the Empress

---

[25] Voltaire's slogan.
[26] Grotius, *De Jure Belli ac Pacis*, bk. 2, ch. 20, sect. 44.

Victoria and the like mighty structures that may be built in the future. Past imperial aggression has no practical importance; future aggression must be resisted; but, at any given moment, if an empire rules people of many cultures but does not treat them unequally as regards the constitution or the laws, for example, the Roman Empire, it is no different in reason, merely in history, from any other state, and should be applauded or condemned on exactly the same criteria: freedom, equality, and the rest. An empire that subjugates, discriminates, and humiliates is much like any other irrational state; its officials give themselves larger airs, but their insolence is the same.

I come to the reasonable relationship of states to one another: they are a society. Just as reason constructs the great society of mankind and civil society, so it constructs 'the society of states'. The elements of this society are as follows.

Each state is free. That is to say, its people, being free men and women, having a right of freedom, or, more exactly, no one having any discoverable grounding for a right to give them orders, are free in relation to the people of the other states. They are understood as having made a contract among themselves to institute government; the people of other states have their own contract; they have no part in this one, and so no right to give orders. Each state has the right to settle its affairs for itself.

Many attack this freedom in the name of an alternative notion of what freedom is. Some say that men are only truly free when they adhere to the true religion; perhaps; but who can claim a right to decide which this is? Others say, similarly, that men and states are not free so long as they do not accept the correct social philosophy; they must be liberated; but many versions of the correct social philosophy turn out to be possible, and which is really correct? The foundation-stone of the society of states was laid in 1648 in Westphalia between Münster and Osnabrück when Europe after long wars agreed lastingly: *cuius regio, eius religio*, 'whose the state, his the religion'. This was the first step towards privacy in individual belief. The event happened in Europe; the reason is world-wide.

The people of a state, having a common purpose (namely, to legislate for and defend their civil society), may be understood, like any association that has a common purpose, to be a person, that is, a corporate or group person. Like ordinary persons, group persons are equal; states are equal; they have the same basic rights and obligations. They differ, of course, vastly in size and success; accordingly, they differ endlessly in the extent of things to which they have particular rights and in the number of other states to which they have undertaken particular obligations. None the less, simply as states, they are the same.

'Strength or weakness in this case counts for nothing. A dwarf is as much a man as a giant is; a small republic is no less a sovereign State than the most powerful kingdom. From this equality, it necessarily follows that what is lawful or unlawful for one Nation is equally lawful or unlawful for every other Nation.'[27] The contribution of this thought to ridiculing pretension to religious or natural or prescriptive superiority by some states over others, and to restraining power politics and to constructing the society of states is inestimable. The first and widest contribution it makes is this: states being equal, none ought to harm another in its life, health, liberty, or possessions. A state should not be murdered (Poland is the example best remembered within Europe; the European empires were often murderers outside it, on the pretext that they were dealing with 'barbarians')[28] or subverted or made a puppet state by others. A state may be understood as having possessions; most fundamentally, it has territory; and it should not be robbed by other states.

Also, because states are equal, they must use reason in their dealings with one another and keep the agreements that they make. A treaty or lesser agreement is not a covert edict by a superior to an inferior as, for example, Fideist and ideological states think, but a transaction between equals, and therefore to break it is irrational. Though this rule holds for the great majority of cases, sometimes an agreement may itself be an offence against the equality of states, for example, some so-called 'unequal treaties' and some treaties signed 'under duress'. Then again, sometimes keeping a treaty may turn out to be seriously injurious to one of the parties.[29]

I have now completed the list of the main precepts of the law of nature or reason governing the society of states. They may be

---

[27] Emmerich de Vattel, *Le Droit des gens*, Préliminaires, sect. 18.

[28] Rosalyn Higgins, *Conflict of Interests: International Law in a Divided World* (London, 1965); Gerrit W. Gong, *The Standard of 'Civilisation' in International Society* (Oxford, 1984).

[29] Vattel, *Le Droit des gens*, bk. 2, ch. 12.

described as negative, and summed up in a rule of non-injury. They are underpinned by a further great consideration. The three laws of justice (stability of possession, transfer by consent, and the performance of promises) are as valid among states as among ordinary persons, because they serve the interests of states on the whole.[30] There is a fundamental harmony of interests between states as between persons, if only they will see it.

On these foundations, states erect the large edifice of positive international law, that is, customs and treaties. The first level is the diplomatic system. From the equality of states, their duty to use reason, and their mutual interest, follow the sanctity of envoys and the whole organization of bilateral and multilateral diplomacy. The latter is a valuable practice, including the 'open diplomacy' and the public international debate which help form the climate of world opinion and the assumptions on which inter-state dealings proceed. The Realist, instead of condemning this aspect of diplomacy because it encourages windy rhetoric, should acknowledge the deep cause of that evil, namely, the disease of propaganda in world politics which she connives at with her power-political theory. A Rationalist combats propaganda, and seeks communication and not the persuasive but the lucid presentation of the facts, not manipulation but reason in human dealings.

I turn next to the substance of relations between states. Inasmuch as states have an obligation not to injure each other in the respects mentioned (freedom, equality, possessions, and agreements) and correspondingly a right to insist on this in their diplomacy, and, at the extreme, to do so by armed force, the most momentous form, in every way, that relations between them can take is war. But we shall be better equipped to consider the solution to the problem of war if we first look at happier matters.

States can, and at the present time, of course, very extensively do, co-operate with one another for the suppression of the many lesser ills that afflict cosmopolis. They find that national action in various respects is not enough; action by the others is also desirable. Notice that such co-operation is not obligatory, as

[30] Hume, *A Treatise of Human Nature*, bk. 3, pt. 2, sect. 11.

non-injury is, and may not be demanded by one state of another
as a matter of right. Co-operation is a reasonable extension of
the purpose of a state to protect its citizens by domestic law,
diplomacy, and armed defence, but still it lies within a state's
free choice.

Thus, if a state allows its territory to be used as a base by
criminals, pirates, terrorists, and the like, this is an injury; but if it
refuses to take part in inter-state action against such malefactors,
this is not an injury, though it may well be unreasonable.

As the Realist pointed out, we spend much of our lives as
members of group persons, corporations; once particularly
important were churches; nowadays, professional groups, trade
unions, and business corporations. Both the Realist and the
Rationalist, while welcoming these as wealth-creating, have
ambivalent attitudes to them. The Modern Prince dislikes
them if they are an independent and even divisive and disruptive
force in society, but likes them if they are an instrument of
control, as in a 'corporate state'. The Rationalist likes them as
independent, as a 'check and balance' to the state, but at the
same time fears their conscienceless power.

Sometimes states discipline business corporations. 'I con-
cluded [in *Modern Capitalism* in 1965] that, in spite of differences
in the ideologies and political assumptions of individual countries,
there was a clear tendency in all of them to subordinate the
traditional independent rights of private business to institutions
designed to express the public interest.'[31] In the following years,
what rescued private business from this trend was the freedom
of cosmopolis, that is, the great growth of international markets
and of international business corporations. A corporation that is
subject to many states is less subject to any one of them. This
renewed liberty raised in its turn fears of an opposite kind, of the
capacity of international business corporations to do harm as well
as good in world society. There is continual need for inter-state
co-operation here, of a balanced sort, neither permissive nor
oppressive.

The harms that ordinary persons and corporations do in
world society range from mass migration for work and residence
and the blight of mass tourism to the depletion or pollution

---

[31] Andrew Shonfield, 'Can Capitalism Survive till 1999?', *Encounter*, Jan. 1977.

of earth, sea, and sky. States themselves abet these harms
by indulging the exploits of their national corporations and
especially liberal states, by indiscriminate encouragement of
most forms of international traffic, regardless of the nuisance
caused. Barriers to movement are the traditional enemy of
world society, but excessive movement is a new enemy, and
equally requires co-operation between states.

Barriers to world trade arising from Realist protectionism
are lamentable because trade is the great engine of world peace
and prosperity; but precisely because trade is so important and
sensitive a matter, stress should be laid on the fact that no
person or country is obliged to engage in it. Whereas the
Natural Law Man holds that access to the resources and
manufacturers of the world is a right of the community of
mankind, which, if perversely denied, may be enforced by war,
the Rationalist holds that trade may only be requested, and
that the only force to be used is that of reason. As in all relations
between states, the case is altered if a treaty is breached, and
possibly also if a refusal of dealings is intended as a hostile act.
The most famous refusals of trade historically, in the Indies,
and by China and Japan, arose from fears that were well
justified, and Western enforcement actions, as the Natural Law
Man agrees, were worthy of barbarians.[32]

The scrutiny of barriers to commerce and their diminution
where obnoxious is the great everyday task of diplomacy
between states. It should include continuous tactful and respect-
ful effort to dissuade states from the attempt at state control of
their economies; for micro-economic control, planning, is by its
nature incompatible with international commerce, and, in this
and in other ways, hinders the progress of the society which it
purports to advance, and so indirectly diminishes the progress
of every other society; and macro-economic control, economic
management, similarly, while requiring a degree of national
isolation and thus impeding international trade, works only to
the detriment of the economy controlled, or, rather, meddled
with, and of economies interdependent with it. An especially
deplorable aspect of state economic management is that the

---

[32] Francisco de Vitoria, *De Indis*, pt. 3, 1st title, 2nd proposition; Vattel, *Le Droit des
gens*, bk. 2, ch. 2; Kant, 'Perpetual Peace', in Reiss (ed.), *Kant's Political Writings*, 106–
7; Hsin-pao Chang, *Commissioner Lin and the Opium War* (Cambridge, Mass., 1970).

value of the national currency domestically and on the foreign exchanges comes to depend, not on the shifts of the market, but on the pretensions of politicians to improve on the market; and this has grave world-wide consequences when the currency is that of a leading state or group of states and is used by the whole world in its commerce. The principal aim of the foreign economic policies of states should be to reduce the activity of states in the world economy; to expel the age-old Realist spirit from economic affairs, ever new in its plausible disguises; to be rid, that is, of state management, state trading, trade as national rivalry, diplomacy as national trade promotion, trade as an instrument of foreign policy; and, having thus cleared the space in which trade can flourish in the hands of the proper agents, the merchants, producers, investors, and consumers, to surround it with the necessary structure of laws.

Some kinds of action are sometimes thought to be obligatory for states which are not so and are at their discretion. States have no obligation to assist the economic progress of poor countries; or to intervene in any other way in their economic and political troubles; or to help defend them against aggression. States may do these things through a sentiment of humanity or more likely (since that sentiment tends to decline with the distances of international relations) through interest; but, in any case, they are not a duty.

The most momentous form of interested co-operation is the making of alliances against aggression. Alliances are a wretched expedient, necessary in the society of states as it is at present. The ideal society of states would be a civil society, that is, a state of states. The present society is not a state; it has no common purpose of government. The member states are under the law of nature or reason, it is true, whereby they are obliged not to injure each other; but they have not made a social contract to renounce self-help in conflicts. International law is, or should be, a structure of reasonable customs and binding agreements, but it does not amount to a social contract; indeed, it contains provision for war. It is some comfort, and yet, as Kant says, miserable comfort![33]

The ideal is a federation of states which are republics (that is,

---

[33] 'Perpetual Peace', p. 103.

based on the right principles, whatever their form of government) and which agree: there shall be no war among us; we shall have a true law and adjudication.[34] Such a federation would be a kind of state, but in one crucial respect it would differ from the ordinary states that govern people in their civil societies: it would contain no provision for enforcement. The reason for this can be expressed in the somewhat Realist language that Hamilton used when the United States constitution was being made,[35] but Rationalist terms are deeper and more precise. Any state has ideally no need for enforcement and is concerned solely with preventing accidental collisions among the citizens. Still, the ordinary, separate state can without contradiction contain provision for enforcement because it enforces against individuals, whether persons or group persons, who are not necessarily rational; men, business corporations, and so on may be rational or they may not. But the separate state itself (when it is a republic) is necessarily rational; it is a construct of reason, a contract of rationality. Thus, provision for enforcement by the federal state would be contradictory: rational entities would be providing for the possibility that they were irrational. If the member states of the federation were to use force against any of their number, this would not be enforcement but war; the federation of states would have ended and the state of nature would have returned.

How is a world-wide federation of states, based on the renunciation of war, to be constructed? For the Historicist, this means: how might it come about over the coming generations? He sees the sad experience of the League of Nations and the United Nations with their provision for enforcement. He sees also that in the past two centuries a group of republican states has emerged among which war is unthinkable.[36] He can envisage that this unwritten quasi-federation might grow by slow accre-

[34] Kant, 'Theory and Practice', pp. 87 ff.; 'Idea for a Universal History', 7th proposition, in Reiss (ed.), *Kant's Political Writings*, pp. 47 ff; 'The Theory of Public Right', Conclusion, in *The Metaphysics of Morals*, in Reiss (ed.), *Kant's Political Writings*, pp. 171–5.
[35] *The Federalist*, Paper XVI.
[36] Michael W. Doyle, 'Kant, Liberal Legacies and Foreign Affairs', *Philosophy and Public Affairs*, 12(3) (Summer 1983), 205–35; 12(4) (Fall 1983), 323–53; R.J. Rummel, 'Libertarianism and International Violence', *Journal of Conflict Resolution*, 27(1) (Mar. 1983), 27–72.

tion, at peace within itself and defending itself against aggressors, until in time it embraces all the states of the world.

Equally, as the Historicist insists, this might not come about; perpetual peace may never be attained; we cannot know. What matters, says a Rationalist, is that states should act as if this were the direction or *telos* of history, as if progress, despite many fearful reverses, were certain. They should act, that is, continuously in inter-state relations according to the norms that would bring this about: namely, the norms that I have expounded, and that are derived from reason, whether abstract reason or utilitarian. These two kinds of reason, in some respects in tension, come together on this matter. The norms that reason might teach men in abstract, it does teach them through experience of the misery of injury and war and of the prosperity of peace.

Not men as states but men pursuing their personal interests in national and world society are taught by experience the futility of war. The state, if uncontrolled by society, drifts towards Realism; for the state is organized power; its purpose being defence, it must provide for war; it must be suspicious of other states, even adversarial; in the abstract idea of the state, there is little impulse to co-operation, none to federation. People in society make the state a contract of rationality, and so too the pressure against war comes from people in peaceful touch with one another in their homes, in their art, science, trade, sport, fun, and all the pursuits of happiness. The freedom of cosmopolis widens this contact to the whole world. The commerce of men binds the nations in mutual interest and hence in mutual respect. The goal of all politics is the least encounter between states and the widest between people.[37] From people as cosmopolis there flows into people as states a great impulse towards peace. The utilitarian passion drives men to reason.[38]

[37] Richard Cobden, 'Russia', in *The Political Writings of Richard Cobden* (London, 1867), i. 282.
[38] Kant, 'Perpetual Peace', pp. 112–14; Mill, *Principles of Political Economy*, bk. 3, ch. 17, sect. 5.

5

Historicism: 'Nation' and 'State'

Now the Historicist has his turn, and he says: the reader will have noticed that this book follows the order of history. First came Natural Law thought, whose classics belong to Greece and Rome. Then followed Realism and Fideism with their climax at the Renaissance and Reformation. Next came Rationalism, rooted in the eighteenth century. Now, last, comes Historicism, which exploded like a bomb in the intellectual life of nineteenth-century Europe, and irradiates all its thought to the present day.[1]

I entirely approve of this way of arranging the book, the Historicist continues; indeed, I am responsible for it. I deplore the refusal of the previous four speakers to admit that the historical sequence is all-important and that their theories belong to a particular time and place. They claim to have gone beyond the transient and the local to permanent, universal truth; the presentation and application of their theories will vary widely in detail, they say, but essentially they follow the special genius of Western thought, which is to see through the mists of changing phenomena to a world *sub specie aeternitatis*. Consequently, they are not content to be consulted by modern man simply as one voice in a long tradition; they each want to be his main guide.

These ambitious theorists should ask themselves why it is that philosophers have come and gone for millennia, and none has ever agreed with another, and none has ever been accepted by the world as conclusive. It is because each thinks in response to a predecessor, and is only intelligible so. Kant is answering Hume; Christianity and Islam arise out of Judaism. The life of the human race is a long drama in which no one's speech is

---

[1] 'Historicism' means here, as traditionally, the understanding of life as history, and not belief in laws of history, as in Sir Karl Popper's *The Poverty of Historicism*.

comprehensible alone, and in which each speaks to all but none can be decisive.

The significance of time and place is so obvious to modern man that we can hardly imagine the old mentality before the Historicist explosion. That started when Lessing said that poetry tells the truth, not by philosophizing, but by telling a story. Herder showed that differences of culture are profound. Scott rescued the people of the past from the museum of edifying examples, and brought them to life as people like ourselves at a different time. The idea of history now erupted everywhere, and henceforth all areas of life were to be understood *sub specie temporis*: language, literature, religion, philosophy, the arts, law, ethics, politics, society and every aspect of it.

Last, the idea reached the supreme natural sciences: geology with Lyell, zoology with Darwin, cosmology with Einstein. The deepest change, the work of Vico and Hegel, was that, as the world is historical, so is the human mind that knows it. At the level of biology, mind changes slowly; at the level of society, comparatively fast; but, from the lowest to the highest in Man's being, there is no constant human nature. Men have no essence, only an ever-changing existence.

The Historicist revolution disclosed a new dimension of human freedom. A man was no longer a mere example of timeless and placeless generalizations, as in the earlier philosophies and faiths. His actions were not conformity with or defiance of eternal norms, for these were now exploded; his actions were an expression of a unique self. Each man was now free to imagine his own life, and all were now free to make, rather than suffer, human history. The creative energy released was incalculable.

The explosion also destroyed. In Dilthey's words:

An apparently irreconcilable contradiction arises when the historical consciousness is followed through to its final consequences. The last word of the historical view of the world is the finiteness of every historical phenomenon, whether a religion, an ideal or a philosophical system, and hence the relativity of every kind of human conception of the connections of things, all flowing in process, nothing stable. Against this, rises up the need of thought and the struggle of philosophy towards generally valid cognition. The historical view of the world is the liberatrix of the human mind from the last chains that the natural sciences and philosophy have not yet destroyed—but where are the resources to overcome the anarchy of beliefs that threatens to break in?[2]

The new freedom enlarged Man's horizons until they were the desert of the Fideist, a place of mirage and nightmare. The Romantic personality 'spun from abyss to abyss with the ruins of God and the world'.[3] It went mad with Nietzsche at the transvaluation of all values. It could no longer follow the traditional wisdom 'know thyself' because, in Freud's metaphor, 'beneath the mountains of civilization, heaved the Titans, the unconscious, revealed in dreams'.[4] People turned in fear to illusionists, men of images and shadows, parading as scientific theorists: nationalists, racists, totalitarians.

These frenzies passed. A sober Historicism is the prevailing contemporary way of thought, and is where we nowadays work. Dilthey ended his speech on his seventieth birthday thus: 'I have worked all my life long on the problems that are linked in a long series with this one. I see the goal; if I remain by the road, I hope my young companions, my pupils will reach it.' Some landmarks are clear; they are definitive of the historical world-view: theories imposed on life are not reason; reason is in life; reason is continuity with history.

Truth is revealed to us, not from outside history, as the Fideist believes, but in the unfolding of history. Nature and human society and politics are not like a machine, as the Realist thinks, but like a story. Mind does not construct the world, as in Rationalism, because it is not separate from the world; mind is the world conscious of itself, and therefore the categories and concepts of mind are those of the world in itself. The old Natural Law Men understood this naïvely and were innocent of epistemology, the alienation of Man and world; but they thought that Man and world were in essence static, and did not grasp that they are essentially historical.

We understand the natural world because we are part of it; only superficially are we outside observers. The theories of the natural sciences are not imposed on nature but spring from it. Similarly, we understand the human world because we are

---

[2] 'Rede zum 70 Geburtstag', in *Gesammelte Schriften* (Leipzig, 1924), vol. 5, p. 9.
[3] François-René de Chateaubriand, *Atala*, 'Le Drame'.
[4] *The Interpretation of Dreams*, ch. 7 (c), trans. James Strachey (London, 1954), 553.

within it; we do this by studying the history of the institutions and practices of which it consists; we grasp their rationality by seeing how they developed. Our method is to take the traditional understanding and reflect on it, enquire further, argue, and amend. So we arrive at our understanding of 'how it really was', in Ranke's phrase.[5] Our understanding is never final; it is living; it will be contradicted; for the Austrian, Klopp, Ranke is 'the most dangerous of all these Prussian liars';[6] our understanding is itself within history. Yet it is not arbitrary. What is arbitrary and what fails as a procedure for understanding a given area of life is the transfer of methods from another area, for example, from the natural sciences into the human sciences. What is catastrophic is the enforcement on an area of life of theories that come from nowhere but the will of a person or the fantasies of a crowd, for example, the pronouncements of a tyrant about genetics or the ravings of another about race.

'There is no understanding of the present without knowledge of the past.'[7] This is the essence of Historicism. Certainly, this knowledge is not enough for creativity; heroism is needed; but, without knowledge of the tradition, the clever man will fail and the great man will make ruins. Our method as men of affairs is the same as our method as scholars of the humanities. When in some area of life in which we act (as in a humane discipline, so in a business company or a branch of law or a sector of politics), when there we find a contradiction, a conflict, a tension between what has been and might be, we study the tradition of our predecessors, bringing it to life in our consciousness, and reflect on it, enquire, argue, amend, and so continue it into the future. What perverts action, as it distorts scholarship, is theory brought in from outside the tradition. 'Theory' began modestly as Greek 'onlooking'; it hardened into censorship, and ascended the throne as Roman dogma; cast down, it reingratiated itself as Intellectualism. Statesmen and citizens, unless they are vigilant, dance to the latest theory, and

[5] Leopold von Ranke, *Geschichten der romanischen und germanishcen Völker*, preface to the 1st edn., *Sämmtliche Werke* (Leipzig, 1874), vol. xxxiii, p. vii.
[6] Wiard von Klopp, *Onno Klopp* (Munich, 1950), 148.
[7] Ranke, 'Über die Verwandschaft und den Unterschied der Historie und der Politik', in *Sämmtliche Werke*, xxiv. 289.

social change, which should be traditional, steady, and slow, becomes arbitrary, convulsive, and frightening. Modern men seek stability, and can only find it in respect for the past. The last contribution of history to human sanity is philosophy of history. From the beginning, Niebuhr and Hegel in Berlin, there has always been tension between the historian and the philosopher of history, the one for uniqueness, the other for pattern. Still, they remain partners, for what the historian is doing when he tells the story of a person, an episode, an institution, or a practice is to show how this fitted with that and this led to the other, which is to say, to display the rationality; not the rationality of Rationalist theory or any other, but historical rationality; and this is what the philosopher of history does with history as a whole. He shows that past and present are not a meaningless succession of lives and deaths but a play in which all can listen to and speak to all across time and place because they voice a single spirit; and in which we are freed from unbearable subjectivity because what we say is a response to what that spirit said through others elsewhere and before.

I turn now from Historicism in general to our particular subject, politics. Here the historian finds that, in modern times, the action has proceeded in terms of three words above all: 'nation', 'state', 'proletariat'.

The nation-state, once usually a monarchy, became, in the course of the nineteenth and twentieth centuries, usually a democracy, whether liberal, dictatorial, or totalitarian. The people were recognized, in one way or another, as sovereign. This development was in part evolutionary but in part revolutionary; and for the latter I hold Rationalism heavily responsible.

For, let the Rationalist protest as he may, his theories were behind the French Revolution and continued thereafter to encourage 'ideologues such as jacobins and socialists'.[8] Rationalism says that men construct society; those who believe this understandably take a fancy to reconstruct it. The Rationalist teaches impatience of tradition. He does not see that the state is 'a partnership not only between those who are living, but between those who are living, those who are dead and those who are to

_____
[8] Above p. 63.

be born'.[9] His 'liberty' and 'equality' inspired the declarations of 1789 and the countless manifestos and *pronunciamientos* and programmes of reform that then followed for generations.

Historicism, on the other hand, countered the anarchy of the ideologues, and gave the people continuity, stability, and unity. The historians, whose writings, from the most scholarly to the most popular, poured into the culture of the times, focused on the nation; they were inspired by the struggles of the nation; *sanctus amor patriae dat animum* was Stein's motto for the *Monumenta Germaniae Historica*. By telling the story of the nation, they reinforced it as a community in the minds of the people. National consciousness was heightened by the spectacle of the national past. The nation became a person with a character and a soul. Its age and splendour gave it a majesty equivalent to the old kingship. Men lived and died, but the nation was eternal, and through it, as Fichte said, each man had a share of eternity.[10]

Though old, the nation was continually new. Mazzini appealed with the glories of the past to Young Italy. Renan's famous definition of a nation was: 'To have common glories in the past, a common will in the present; to have done great things together; to wish to do greater; these are the essential conditions that make up a people.'[11] Ortega y Gasset in his *Revolt of the Masses* denied that 'nation' signified a common past; that would make it one with its oppressors; it was the conviction of a common future.[12] But, up to his time and ours, evidently the nation is both past and future; the past is the foundation laid by the historians and philosophers and by statesmen who use their work; the future is built upon it. The nation, we may say, is about time and transition. It is a refuge in the emotional stress of revolutionary upheaval, the passing of traditional society, the strains of change. Immortal and sacred, it is worthy of reverence, obedience, and loyalty. It inspires a spirit of community, self-sacrifice, self-immolation.

Alongside the unity thus created among the people went the

[9] Edmund Burke, *Reflections on the Revolution in France*, Everyman edn. (London, 1964), 93.

[10] Johann Gottlieb Fichte, *Addresses to the German Nation*, viii.

[11] Ernest Renan, 'Qu'est ce qu'une nation?', in *Discours et Conférences* (Paris, 1938), 306.

[12] (London, 1932), ch. 14.

spiritual devastation which I described earlier; the nation was
at once strong and cohesive and yet fevered; but I assert that
Historicism was not responsible for the terrible beliefs that the
nation took to at its times of frenzy: nationalism, racism,
totalitarianism. To show to the nation the varied riches of its
past and to all nations a philosophy of history is not the same as
to fabricate theories of 'nation', 'race', and 'society'. I shall
discuss this point as regards nationalism when we turn to
international relations. For the moment, we should notice that
as Historicism offers to the nation history not theory as a way to
self-consciousness, so it offers history not theory as a way to
success in the conduct of national policy.

'In a progressive country change is constant,' said Disraeli;
'and the great question is, not whether you should resist change
which is inevitable, but whether that change should be carried
out in deference to the manners, the customs, the laws and the
traditions of a people, or whether it should be carried out in
deference to abstract principles, and arbitrary and general
doctrines. The one is a national system, the other . . . a
philosophic system.'[13] The culture of the people decides the
character of the nation-state and how its politics work; therefore
the history of that culture should be the statesman's study.
Sometimes, it is true, the state is not traditional but is imposed
by aliens or theorists, for example, imperialists or revolutionaries; but their work does not endure as they intended, only as
absorbed into the traditions of the culture. In modern politics,
practitioners and academics are fascinated by the natural
sciences and technology; but these are nothing without experimental method; and how is that possible (without barbarism)
in politics? It is possible by the study of history, down to
yesterday; history is 'experimental politics'.[14] In the natural
sciences, the aim is to grasp laws; in politics, the aim of the
statesman is to grasp the spirit of the people who face him, the
country as a whole, an institution, or the men across the table,
by knowing where they come from, what they have been
through, what they have done.

   [13] Edinburgh, 29 Oct. 1867, in T. E. Kebbel (ed.), *Selected Speeches of the late Rt. Hon.
the Earl of Beaconsfield* (London, 1882), ii. 487.
   [14] Joseph de Maistre, 'Study on Sovereignty', in *Works*, ed. Jack Lively (London,
1965), 114.

Since the particular people of a nation-state settle its character,
there is no such thing as 'the state'; there is only the Austrian
state, the Bolivian, the Chinese, and so on. Hence, there can be
no 'theory of the state', no political theory; Frenchmen and
Americans should read Tocqueville, not Locke and Rousseau.
Philosophically, as Hegel said, every state is an expression of
the spirit that moves us all in human history, and of the idea of
the state; but that idea unfolds in our action and is only
understood when action is over, and does not constrain it in
advance.

The founding fathers of economics and their modern followers
were inclined to think that their science is valid at all times and
places. After a while, List showed that what holds for a country
at one stage of its economic growth does not hold at another;
but he still wrote as though his five stages applied across
countries;[15] whereas the truth is that the economy of every
country is unique because it cannot be understood in abstraction
from the whole life of the country, and that life is unique. To
understand the economy of a country, you must study its whole
history. What makes your study specifically 'economic history'
is the question you ask of the history of a country: how does it
get its living? Avoidance of economic theory in favour of
economic history is especially important for the statesman
concerned with understanding and forwarding the economic
development of his country and managing its economic progress
smoothly. The countries least influenced by economic theorists
in policy-making have done best economically. Economic science,
as one of its founders, Nassau Senior, remarked, 'depends more
on reasoning than observation'.[16] That is the trouble with it. As
a present-day economist has written, our maxim in the current
rethinking of economics should be: 'Economics is the study of
Economies.'[17]

That law-making on social questions requires experience of
how the law has so far worked, not a head dizzy with social
theories, is obvious to common sense; but let me reinforce this

[15] Friedrich List, *The National System of Political Economy*, trans. Sampson S. Lodge
(London, 1885), ch. 15.
[16] *An Outline of the Science of Political Economy* (London, 1836), Introduction.
[17] Dudley Seers, 'The Limitations of the Special Case', in Kurt Martin and John
Knapp (eds.), *The Teaching of Development Economics* (London, 1967), 27.

with a reminder of what law is. A Historicist is not a positivist like the Realist; law is not simply the will of the lawmaker, and not a constraining structure, separate from society and imposed upon it and regulating it. Rather, law is the slowly accumulating expression of the life of the nation; more exactly, it is to be seen as a succession of decisions taken in managing social change; and the basis is not will but reason. This reason is not abstract reason; law is not normative because it has foundations beyond time and place. Law is normative in a society because the members of the society take it as normative, in much the same way as they take the rules of how to speak their language. Law is the historical reason of a particular nation.

Legal traditions are inseparable from ethical, and these are the deepest matter for the statesman's study. At first sight, modern man is in ethical chaos. In a sense, 'the logical conclusion of this historical approach must be some form of ethical relativism, or perhaps the dissolution of ethics in sociology'.[18] Historicism, at first encounter, as I said, leads to boundless subjectivism, criterionless existentialism, and to worse than this in revulsion. But in a deeper sense, Historicism clears the ground for the uncovering of the true foundations of morals. It destroys the idea of moral philosophy as system-building. For the fact is, it shows that in our moral judgements 'we use a variety of different ethical considerations which are genuinely different from one another, and this is what one would expect to find, if only because we are heirs to a long and complex ethical tradition, with many different religious and other social strands'.[19] Historicism substitutes for single system-building the idea of moral philosophy as the articulation of the moral tradition of a nation and the continuance of it. Morals for the citizen and statesman consist of knowing what has usually been done, rejecting the onus of proving that it is right, and going on doing it until those who disagree can show why not.

In all aspects of national life, change should proceed by free discussion; for coercion means that change is imposed upon the nation and does not come from within it. The organization of assemblies, news media, and so on should be traditional. At the

---

[18] W. H. Walsh, 'Hegelian Ethics', in W. D. Hudson (ed.), *New Studies in Ethics* (London, 1974), i. 391.
[19] Bernard Williams, *Ethics and the Limits of Philosophy* (London, 1985), 16.

present time, in most countries, the media are controlled by governments with the backing of Realist theories; opponents of this call for reform in accordance with Rationalist theories; but the right course is for each different country to know, respect, and extend its own way of debate.

In the national discussion of change, ideas from all times and places can be considered, but nothing should be given a privileged status; there should be 'no bowing to ideologies, dogmas, and magical incantations, for example, 'human rights', 'equality', 'the master race', 'modernity'; for the only source of truth is the mind, formed by tradition, judging freely. This freedom is not uncontrolled. 'It is not chance and not arbitrary who we ourselves are and what we can hear from the past.'[20]

The part of us that is not tradition, the unique in us, the personal, the heroic, is none the less still guided by tradition. Of course, we can be merely wilful; we are free, whether as small men or as great, not to make our lives but to dictate them; but a life that lasts, that changes the tradition, and, when remembered, is imitated, is one that measures itself against the standards of the past. As for each of us, so for all, the nation: statesmen decide in moments of national crisis by how they think their actions will seem in 'the eyes of history', and that is how they rally the rest of us. 'Let us therefore brace ourselves to our duty and so bear ourselves that, if the British Commonwealth and Empire lasts for a thousand years, men will still say, "This was their finest hour".'[21] Statesmen seem to mean by 'the eyes of history', future generations; but if you reflect for a moment, you will see that they mean the heroes of the past.

[20] Georgia Warnke, *Gadamer* (Cambridge, 1987), 81.
[21] Winston Churchill, House of Commons, 18 June 1940, in *UK Parliamentary Debates*, 5th series, vol. 362, col. 60.

6

Historicism: 'Proletariat' and 'World'

I HOPE, the Historicist resumes, that I have said enough about 'nation' and 'state' until we come to international relations. I will now discuss 'proletariat'. Though the people became sovereign in 1789, not the whole of it truly did so. There was a class which, whatever the theories of the nationalists, was in fact excluded from the nation, that is, from power in the state and from prosperity and dignity. Historians saw their struggle and began to write their history. By raising the struggle to a vision of history, they gave the proletariat the same strengths that they gave the nation.

The most influential of these writers were the Marxists. They, above all others, gave the proletariat identity. They showed that the successive outbursts of the oppressed across the centuries were one struggle, the grievances not occasional and superficial but structural. The oppressed had always formed groups for the righting of this or that wrong, most recently, trade unions and socialist parties, but their membership of the proletariat was deeper. What the bourgeois writers taught the nation, the Marxists taught the proletariat: it was no mere passing interest group, like a commercial partnership, to be formed and dissolved at will, but a continuous relationship across time and place.

This is to say, the Marxists gave the proletariat class consciousness. The proletariat only comes truly into existence, they taught, when its members become aware of themselves as the proletariat. This consciousness is created, like national consciousness, in the heat of action, in conflict; but equally, like national consciousness, true proletarian consciousness is historical consciousness. The proletariat escapes from false consciousness and ceases to be a mere object of history by achieving understanding of history.

Marxism showed proletarians that the proletariat and its struggle was the highest value in their lives. Their fight with their boss was not just their fight, not selfishness, but the fight of a group; and this group was also not transient and selfish; it was enduring. Understanding this gave meaning to life: I live and die but the proletariat and its struggle goes on. I will give my life for it.

So the Marxists encouraged the proletariat and those from other classes who supported its cause; but also, they killed many millions of people; for fundamentally they were not historians but theorists. They paralleled, not the historians of the nation, but the nationalists. Though they gave the proletariat a sense of history, and some, beginning with Marx himself, were gifted historians, they subordinated history to theory. They realized that history is not a simple record of objective facts; but they did not see that it is, none the less, a discussion conducted in obedience to evidence; and so they turned history into a myth which they were sure was true, whether the evidence supported it or not. They were Rationalists in disguise; they embraced classical political and economic theory, and clothed it in time and change and called that history.

The true historian has much to offer about the 'proletariat'. He can show the nation-state that it has always been 'two nations'; there has always been an excluded class; but not permanent across time and place; changing rather, today's neglected and oppressed often becoming tomorrow's oppressors. Also the historian can show that the excluded class is not wholly so; it makes its contribution to the life of the nation-state. The Marxists understood none of this.

When Marxists spoke of 'the proletariat', they had in mind the proletariat that they conceived in theory, not the proletariat of the streets. The proletariat of the streets, while inspired by the history of its struggle and of its heroes, did not like theory and did not conform to it. Marxists, accordingly, did not follow the proletariat but led it; they were Leninist, not democratic but dictatorial. The Communist Party or some other kind of Marxist leader had the historical role of directing the proletariat according to the theoretical proletarian consciousness that it had not yet developed.

Supposedly, the leadership's grasp of theory enabled it to hold courageously to the true needs of the people whatever the temporary clamour of the people themselves. A grasp of history would have served better at this; the effect of theory was to sacrifice real people to a fiction. When the Bolsheviks discovered with amazement in the winter of 1920–1 that it was possible for workers and Party to conflict, they crushed the workers.[1] It was theory that led the German Communist Party to its disastrous refusal to ally with other political parties against the Nazis. The Red Army shot down workers on the streets of Budapest in 1956, confident that these could not really be workers but must be agents of reactionary capitalism. Theory legitimized the mass killings done by Stalin, Mao Tse-tung, and Pol Pot.

Not just theory but, far more, the particular content of Marxist theory was responsible for these crimes. Marxists rightly saw that men never meet one another as persons, as Rationalists think, but always in historically formed social roles. But Marxists imposed on this, in defiance of the evidence of history, the theory of dialectical materialism: our class roles of proletarian or oppressor are determined by the forces of production; these class roles determine all our other roles; everything in life beyond the forces and corresponding relations of production is merely ideological, superstructural, and, so far as the proletariat is concerned, oppressive; and, it follows from this, proletarians and their oppressors, the bourgeoisie, have nothing in common.

To the Marxists, the proletarians were nothing but 'toiling masses'. Their national pride was merely indoctrinated into them by the bourgeoisie. Though their struggles had influenced the development of the institutions of the nation, essentially these were merely the tools of their oppressors. Accordingly, the proletariat could not advance its cause through the use of these institutions, through the state, the law, and the economic organizations. The proletariat must overthrow what history had given, and build everything afresh in line with the blueprints of its leaders.

The theory, started by Marx himself, that the state was a bourgeois idea, alien to the proletariat, left the state exposed to the bloody and futile revolutionism of Lenin and Mao Tse-tung. The denial of value to the traditions of the nation unleashed the new rulers from all constraints, and encouraged,

[1] Isaac Deutscher, *The Prophet Armed: Trotsky 1879–1921* (Oxford, 1954), 506.

in fact, required, if there was not to be chaos, totalitarianism. In their supreme area, the economic, they dismissed economic history, and preferred economic theory like Rationalists, and economic planning like Realists, with failure as the doubly obvious result. In this area, as in all, they shattered law and ethics, not seeing that these were proletarian, in a way, as much as bourgeois, and at length alienating the majority of the proletariat for whom, in Léon Blum's phrase, socialism was a morality as much as a doctrine, so that it could not be advanced by lying, betrayal, torture, and murder. As to still higher matters, Marxists supposed that past art was not proletarian; it must be replaced. Religion must be destroyed, as not the people's possession but their opium.

Because in Marxist theory men were material, they were to be moulded and, if resistant, to be thrown away. Marxists held this the more boldly because they believed that they were scientists. Whereas Niebuhr and Hegel sought the reason of the past and thought the future free, the Marxists believed that the future as well as the past was determined. Many thinkers have been influenced by some version or other of the idea of 'progress'; every modern politician says that his proposals are better than right, they are inevitable. What distinguished the Marxists was faith that history was subject to scientific laws and that they knew them. Materialists were here claiming the same kind of authority as the Fideists. Any crime that they committed was right because it was ordained.[2]

The criticisms I have made of Marxism are derived from modern Marxists or would be accepted by many of them. They say nowadays that the notion that Marxism is a science was an aberration of late nineteenth-century German Communists and twentieth-century Russians. They declare that the growth of representative democracy was a genuine advance for the proletariat. The proletariat are not merely the 'toiling masses', and culture is no mere superstructure. The state is not simply an outgrowth of the economy. Concepts not based on the philosophical study of real men must be abandoned. There are even a few attempts to release the writing of history from the prison of theory. So Marxism today is changing; but then, like

[2] Leszek Kolakowski, *Marxism and Beyond: On Historical Understanding and Individual Responsibility* (London, 1969).

everything else, it always has done since it began; and very likely it will continue to do so until eventually it dies, leaving men free to use their minds, and, instead of Marxism, we have Marx and those who think in his tradition.

I come finally, the Historicist says, to international relations. I wish, as usual, to dispel the theories that have been fabricated, without historical evidence, of how international relations are and ought to be.

Take 'nationalism'. This is, in the first place, the name we give to the recent form of the age-old rivalry between states. With the development of popular sovereignty after 1789, competition between Habsburg and Hohenzollern gradually gave way to competition between the people of Austria and the people of Prussia; dynastic conflict became popular conflict or, as we call it, 'national' conflict.

The new rivalry was more destructive than the old because of the enrolment of greater numbers of people and modern techniques of warfare. It was heated to a still greater degree of violence by a theory: cultural nationalism, the idea of the cultural nation. I described earlier how the solidarity of each nation-state was reinforced by the historians, recounting the achievements of its people in politics, war, religion, the arts, and so on, in short, the glories of its culture. Modern peoples, like dynasties, had their *Aeneid*. Theory was a quite different thing, concocted by Fichte and his sort, and seized upon by politicians and social groups that it suited. Theory did not extol the actual culture of the nation-states; it extolled the idea of a cultural nation, and demanded that the nation-states conform to it. The state must be a cultural nation; the cultural nation must be a state; and only those in the state who belonged to the cultural nation were fit to rule, not the people of cultural minorities or, in empires, of majorities. In British India, even a Kashmiri Brahmin like Nehru was not considered good enough to be Viceroy until too late.

Of course, no one could say exactly what they meant by a cultural nation, could define or delimit it; for nation is, in reality, a historical, not an abstract thing. Politicians, in practice, made use of old frontiers; thus, Sukarno and his comrades decided after much debate that what they meant by 'Indonesians' was the subjects of the Dutch in the East Indies. At other times, politicians denounced old frontiers for outrageously separating brothers of the same language and folk-ways. Within the nation, groups considered inferior were persecuted. Nationalism swelled to racism. Because no one knew what they were talking about, incomprehension increased anger and, in the bewilderment, the worst sort sometimes took power.

Though the theory of the cultural nation was abstract, it was not, at first, a general theory. That is to say, the nationalist was passionate for the independence, the unification, and the purity of his nation, not of anyone else's, not of 'nations'. The blindness of nationalists towards others did much to spread the theory around the world; 'British' behaviour helped create 'Indians'; 'Dutch', 'Indonesians'; the nation of theory, like the historical nation-state of fact, can only be understood in terms of international relations.

Rationalist liberals were the ones who turned the theory into a general theory. They entered, with misgivings, into an alliance with nationalism; they attempted to look, not as Armenians only to Armenia, or as Zimbabweans only to Zimbabwe, but impartially at all nations; they declared 'national self-determination' a general principle of world order. The result ranged from the unfortunate everywhere to the catastrophic, for example, in Central Europe; the cosmopolitans abetted the chauvinists in making chaos. When their time of disillusion came in the late twentieth century, they spent much effort proving that the general idea of national self-determination was untenable, unaware that only they, not nationalists proper, had ever held it.

The destruction of the European empires by nationalism, as much of the rulers as of the subjects, was followed by another victory for theory in the shape of the idea of 'the state'. Rulers hesitantly, subjects vehemently supposed that the successor states in Asia and Africa should follow the Westminster or Fifth Republic model. This did not last long. The successor states, being very different nations, were likely to be very different states, and so they indeed rapidly became.

The new nation-states were much alike in one respect, it is true: in their internal and external affairs, they continued to be affected by nationalism, to which they added the idea of 'modernity', the whole amounting to a programme called 'nation-building'. The new great powers, the Soviet Union and the United States, were in a similar plight. Russian policy was distorted by their theory of communism, and American, by their theory of communism. To their cost, the statesmen on both sides knew all about 'world politics' but not much about the politics of other countries in particular. Always, no doubt, in great powers, generalists must decide high policy on countries and subjects, not country or subject specialists. But a general ideology makes this problem worse. The only sure guide for the statesman in foreign policy, as in domestic, is historical understanding of his countrymen and of the countries with which he is dealing.

In stressing the uniqueness of states, I do not mean to say that they owe nothing to each other. On the contrary, they owe to each other, in a sense, their very existence; a state is one of a number; a world state, without others, would not be a state, as we know it. A state learns its identity in its encounters with others. It does so in the dialogue about peace, about the constitution, the economy, the laws, ethics, and the arts and sciences, and in the experience that shows it to itself most clearly and shapes or destroys it: war.[3]

I do mean to say that states do not constitute a 'states-system', anyway in the sense that the theorists of international relations suppose. We have no evidence for thinking with the Natural Law Man that states are a 'community'; so far in their history, at any rate, they have never thought of themselves as parts of a whole or subordinated their good to a common good. The more modest Rationalist idea that there is a latent harmony of interests between states and that they thus form a 'society' has sometimes been true among some states and sometimes not; to assume it as a basic norm is utopian. The Realist theory is little better; to say that there is a states-system in that all the vastly diverse interaction is fundamentally about power is a simplification, only to be excused because it recurs in a Machiavelli or a Hobbes or a Morgenthau in reaction to the periodic recrudescence of the even worse simplicities of the Natural Law Men, the Fideists, and the Rationalists. The most that can be said is this: the actions of states are all human and therefore intelligible; accordingly, there is a states-system in the sense of a continuous, intelligible interaction.

[3] Based on G. W. F. Hegel, *Philosophy of Right*, sect. 321–31.

I acknowledge that sometimes, of some states, there is more to be said; they have something further in common. For example, the European states had for many centuries a certain unity as heirs of Rome. One consequence of their ancestry was that, in Ranke's words, 'the European order of things differs from others that have appeared in the course of world history by virtue of its legal, even juridical, nature';[4] another consequence was that they were linked by concern for glory and honour in each other's eyes. Then, too, they were for a long time all Christian. In sum, they felt themselves to be a group by history, and were indeed so. If the phrase 'the European states-system' means only that, means an order of things that occurred historically, well and good; it can mean no more.

In the world as a whole, there is no 'system' beyond mere interaction. The world has, strictly speaking, no 'world politics'; it is not a polity; it has only diplomacy. Diplomacy has a history; it is, at any given time, a prevailing set of methods; in no other sense is there 'a diplomatic system'. When Europeans write of 'the nature of diplomacy', of timeless, rational principles for the conduct of relations between sovereigns, they are simply describing their practices in the days of their pre-eminence. Their first principle is the inviolability of envoys; but, in other cultures, varying degrees of insult to envoys is a means of communication. In the late twentieth century, a diplomatic institution accepted as self-evident is the standing multilateral organization. Men had scarcely heard of it a hundred years ago. Perhaps the historians will have to remind them of it a hundred years hence.

We delude ourselves when we talk of an 'international economy' as though it really had *nomoi*, rules. In the economic debate between states, I see a continual tendency for some ideas to become dominating, and, with still greater dismay, how frequently writers elevate these ideas yet further into a general theory of how international economic relations ought to be conducted. 'Mercantilism' is followed by '*laisser-faire*', which is followed by 'autarky', which is followed by 'the principles of the GATT'; and so they go on. They are so certain of the truth of the current theory that they can hardly credit how certain their

[4] Leopold von Ranke, 'Die grossen Mächte', in *Sämmtliche Werke* (Leipzig, 1874), xxiv. 10.

predecessors were of the last or imagine how certain their successors will be of the next. Each state should think for itself in dialogue with the others. Today, for example, a state should not be led by a general theory of 'free trade' or 'protection' but should think for itself about what degree of openness in what branches of industry to what other economies it should best have. General conventions of conduct for international businessmen, continually developing, are to be distinguished from general rules for the management of national economies and the conduct of relations between them; these reflect the assumption that all economies are in principle the same, and are progressing towards actually being so and towards one homogeneous world economy. This may turn out to be true, but equally it may not. In the going, therefore, statesmen should best pay prudent lip-service to the dominant theories, but follow their own historically formed opinion.

Why, I ask you, are there great histories of English law but no equivalent histories of international law? It is because England exists, and international society is as yet only an idea. The historian can find a coherence or pattern, in short, a story in the one kind of law which he cannot as yet find in the other. The most that he can do for international law is to recount how in this or that area of affairs the practice of states was once thus and seems now to be changing to so, and the circumstances which apparently explain this. What, then, is international law? It is not a series of authoritative decisions, as is national law. It is a set of concepts that states use to communicate their conflict and co-operation. To call it a language would be to say too much, since it has neither the deep structural coherence nor the unquestioned status of a language.

International law is thin because there are no international ethics. Each nation-state has its own beliefs about what is just, right, dishonourable, cruel, and so on in international politics, and it can do nothing else but follow these in its dealings with other nation-states. It can do so in one of two ways. It can accept that this is the situation, recognizing that, as it has its moral beliefs, so others have theirs, and there is no one to decide between them. In my opinion, as a Historicist, when this is a nation's attitude to others, much frustration, anger, and conflict is avoided. Alternatively, a nation may believe that its values are universal and that it should set about developing the power to impose them. The philosopher of history accepts that much of world history has moved in this manner, one moral system crushing another. He also sees the suffering involved.[5]

A nation that acts in the belief that its values are universal is in the grip of a theory. It is no longer content with its historical nationhood but sees itself as the servant of a higher ideal. The highest form of nationalism is universalism. It is the worst form because it is the most extensive and is disguised as benevolence. It is a delusion because the values are really the nation's own.

The communist rulers of Russia, China, and some other countries suffered from the same delusion as the nationalists. They differed, of course, in that the higher ideal which they claimed to serve, 'proletarian internationalism', was not an inflation of their national values but the invention of theorists. The similarity lay in their belief that, in serving this ideal, it was possible for them to be more than national, and that the proletarians of other countries could be more than national. The similarity lay also in the ideal as disguise. All modern revolutionaries, like the imperialists, claim to be internationalists; for this, they suppose, justifies their crime against their country's history and their violence to their countrymen.

The source of the communists' delusion, I need scarcely point out, was their belief in theory rather than history. From Marx himself onwards, they were blind to the fact that the proletariat is different from nation to nation over time. They made light of 'nation' in world affairs altogether. A mere bourgeois concept, it was being superseded by bourgeois internationalism, which would be matched by proletarian internationalism. The workers of the world would unite. A revolution would happen all over the world at the same time. The communists made light equally of 'state' and inter-state relations. Since the state was alien to the proletariat and destined to wither away, the age-old inter-state problem was of no great concern to them. It would simply lapse.

When the proletariat proved not to be international, when The Revolution happened in one country but not in others, when in consequence foreign policy proved to be a continuing

[5] Hegel, *Philosophy of Right*, sect. 345.

necessity, communists slowly and painfully rediscovered that they were men of nation-states after all. Stalin subordinated 'proletarian internationalism' to 'socialism in one country'. After his death, communists agreed that there were 'different roads to socialism'. As to 'state', Lenin's announcement of the need for a temporary 'dictatorship of the proletariat' was followed by Stalin's decision to postpone any withering away until the conflict with the capitalist states had been won.

With Stalin gone, communists could see more and more clearly that, even if all states were socialist, the inter-state problem would not be over. For not only were socialist states, albeit united by socialism, separated by nationhood, and often by nationalism; but also they faced the dilemma that their socialism simultaneously enjoined co-operation and discouraged it; for the socialist planned and managed economy could only work in insulation from other economies. This was merely a new form of the old question 'socialism, national or international?', and the latest explanation of that paradoxical figure, influential from England to the Urals, the socialist chauvinist.[6] The socialist states had no talent for solving their dilemmas or for contributing to the control of the inter-state problem world-wide. They had for too long buried their national traditions of thought about international relations, never admittedly very strong, under a mound of theoretical internationalism. Their military and economic organizations in Eastern Europe were imitated from the West, and, in the development of international organization generally, an outstanding feature of world affairs in the mid-twentieth century, they played little creative part.

Against such strictures as these, some have protested that the writings of Lenin on imperialism, and those of a long line of Marxists and para-Marxist successors, have made a great contribution to the theory of international relations. I say, once again, that this is not the same as a contribution to the under-standing of international relations. Lenin did not begin by studying the history of what the European nations had lately been doing in Asia, Africa, and Latin America. He presupposed that capitalism was the explanation and aimed to elucidate the connections between capitalism and imperialism that he was sure in advance must exist. A historian often cannot see much connection between the condition of European economies, even as pictured by Marxists, and the activities of explorers, businessmen, missionaries, soldiers, and imperial bureaucrats; no matter to the Marxist; theory assured him that there must be a connection 'ultimately'. Theory extended yet further. Lenin's idea went beyond the title of his famous book *Imperialism: The Highest Stage of Capitalism*; rather, the highest stage of capitalism was imperialism; anything that the capitalists had lately been doing abroad was for him imperialism, especially French loans to his country, Russia.

The supremacy of theory over history continued in Lenin's successors as writers on imperialism, 'dependency', 'centre–periphery', and the like changing titles. The same trait appeared with more serious effects in Marxist thought about relations between 'capitalist' and 'socialist' states. The two kinds of state were necessarily hostile, Marxists held; beneath the tactical necessity for 'coexistence', there could never be goodwill; the capitalists must always 'encircle', seeking to prevent the progress of history; socialists must always probe and, where they found weakness, thrust; the end would be fearful collisions from which socialism would emerge triumphant. The great mitigation of these harmful dogmas was that, since the victory of socialism was inevitable, there need be no haste or recklessness in the campaign to bring it about. Gradually, the shadow of nuclear weapons over socialist and capitalist alike, the success of the Soviet Union in achieving military balance with the United States, and its failures in other areas of life, led to a change of mind. Events eroded theory.

I move, says the Historicist, to my conclusion. I have discussed 'nation', 'state', and 'proletariat', not for the sake of the past but for the sake of the future. Over many years now, a further concept has developed real force among practical men: 'world'. I hope that they will have learned to treat this concept as a possibility and not as a theory.

Doing this, using 'world' wisely in practical discussions of 'world politics', 'the world economy', 'our company's world markets', 'world athletics', and so on, demands first knowing the history. Even as we seek to understand some national matter, for example, the German or the Japanese 'economic miracle' of the mid-twentieth century, through history and not through theory, so we should do with all matters of 'world'. That people who substitute 'world' as theory for 'world' as history are in error is, I hope, by now broadly clear. No sane businessman allows his world-wide strategies to be determined by theories of the transnational corporation. A statesman, at this or that juncture of world affairs, invokes the 'world community'; but it should be as something that seems to be emerging, that is perhaps being created in action as juncture follows juncture, not as something whose norms, rules, and organization can be known theoretically in advance and treated as imperatives.

The whole world sets some value on 'Man', but we only agree what this value is nation by nation, or, at most, in groups of nations. Long ago, Burke warned the believers in 'the rights of man' of this, and the liberal nationalists warned the cosmopolitans. Mazzini declared that the first duty of man was towards humanity, that we are to be 'apostles of the brotherhood of nations, of the unity of the human race'; but he also declared that the only way we could know of doing that duty was by contributing to the life of our nation, and by each nation contributing what it had to offer to the life of the world.[7] Nowadays, we recognize that a good patriot makes the best international civil servant. We get to where we shall be from where we are, not from where we should like to be.

Though so much is, no doubt, broadly clear, notice that, ours being a Historicist age, the substitution for history of theory often takes the disguised form of the transformation of history into theory. We saw the Marxists doing this as regards 'proletariat', and it is done too with 'world'. The long experience of a businessman of some area or other of world commerce fossilizes into a covert theory. Statesmen invoke the 'lessons of history' in support of their programmes for the world, as did the enthusiasts for the League of Nations and the United Nations and a United Europe. The so-called lessons of Munich and Yalta led to the catastrophes of Suez and Vietnam. Summarized experience is the only 'theory' worth having, and even that is a dangerous guide.

Acton said: 'If the Past has been an obstacle and a burden,

[7] Giuseppe Mazzini, *The Duties of Man*, ch. 5.

knowledge of the Past is the safest and the surest emancipation.'[8] That is true at every level from the most practical to the most philosophical. It is by never accepting our tradition or our experience or the history of our times as fixed and settled, and by continually scrutinizing them anew and discussing and revising them that we achieve a mind that is historically formed and yet free, and so fit to take the decisions of the future. Philosophy of history reconciles us with history, its dark and light, suffering and creativity. But understanding of history does not mean that we can anticipate history's judgements and impose them on ourselves and others. Acceptance of the past does not imply endorsement of anything done there for the future. The past is unchangeable and the evidence of the past must be respected; but, within those limits, the history of the past and of the future is free.

[8] John Acton, *The Study of History* (London, 1896), 10.

II

KINDS OF RELATIONS

7

Conflict

IN this part of the book, the five spokesmen discuss in more detail the main kinds of relations that countries have with one another. They begin with conflict.

Before the rest of you start, says the Fideist, with your rationalizing sophistries, I say that fundamentally men conflict because they want to. I am not speaking of an unconscious desire. Experts used to tell us that the cause of conflict was vice or superstition or barbarism; later, the trouble lay in Man's psyche or his animal instincts or his genes. I believe these theories to be false in their own terms, but, in any case, they are useless. Man cannot reform Man's vices or enlighten his darkness or cultivate away his barbarism; such notions are as foolish as the supposition that he might improve his genes. The only valuable ideas about human conflict concern conscious, controllable desires. All five of us here agree on that. Where we differ is that you four think that men desire things about which they conflict, whereas I say that they desire conflict.

Among the multitude of desirable things in life, men are never sure for long what they want. All their thinking about how to live fails for lack of a starting-point of which they are certain. They lead lives of 'quiet desperation', as Thoreau put it. What gives them some relief is commitment to a cause. They find some certainty in a personal feud, in loyalty to a group against another group, in dedication to their country against other countries. Without this desire, the material for conflict between states, the particular things desired, would still exist; conflicts would still abound; but they would do little damage. It is the craving for self-sacrifice that makes conflicts dangerous, and leads in the end to violence and death.

This desire is a distortion of something true. There is, in reality, a fixed starting-point in life, which can give order to men's desires, a commitment and a cause worthy of loyalty

and self-sacrifice. There is a remedy for Man's conflict. But
I described it at length earlier, and I say no more.

My diagnosis, says the Realist, is sometimes conflated with
that of the Fideist but in fact he is too gloomy for me. Also, his
remedy amounts to converting all human conflict into religious
conflict, and that really would kill us.

You may be surprised to hear a Realist point out that in most
of world affairs, there is no conflict. Most states usually accept
the existing order. Moreover, most of the conflict that does
occur is harmless and inseparable from life: states, in pursuing
their interests and honour in competition with one another,
confront interest with interest, and bargain, negotiate, persuade,
and press. Sometimes, amid this ordinary conflict, a special
kind arises: dispute. Here there are formulated claims and
counter-claims, maybe over a small matter like fishing rights,
or a big one, like a rich piece of territory. Usually these disputes
are handled peacefully, but they may lead to the use of force,
especially if honour is involved, which is to say, 'the arguments
and signs of power', alias, prestige.[1] States acquire prestige in
the course of the pursuit of their interests, and value it for its
own sake and because it is useful. It may be challenged in a
dispute, and has to be defended.

Let us agree to call what I have just described 'ordinary
conflict' and 'ordinary dispute'. Beyond this, in international
life, there is a higher level of conflict, much more dangerous.
Here, states of similar power, regionally or world-wide, are not
merely competing with one another in the usual way; they have a
special fear of one another; they feel themselves under continuous
pressure from the illwill of the other as regards their territory,
or independence, or prestige, or religion, or ideology, or economy.
This kind of conflict (let us call it a 'tension') comes to a head in
disputes. These are either 'expressive of it' (as the Kashmir
dispute was an expression of the tension between India and
Pakistan; the Suez Canal Crisis of the tension between Britain,
France, and Egypt; the Cuba Missiles Crisis of the tension
between the United States and the Soviet Union) or 'symbolic
of it' (as are many a trifling border dispute; for example, on the
Ussuri River between the Soviet Union and China).[2]

---

[1] Thomas Hobbes, *Leviathan*, ch. 10.
[2] Hans J. Morgenthau, *Politics among Nations*, 3rd edn. (New York, 1960), ch. 25.

Great tensions, which may lead through disputes to war, are at the same time a great source of peace. I pointed out a moment ago that most states refrain from conflict with one another, that most conflict is harmless, and that ordinary disputes are mostly handled peacefully. This is because each state is restrained by the power of the others and, above all, because it needs the power of others to help it survive in the great tensions that it has or which larger powers have and in which it may be crushed. States take care not to antagonize one another because of their greater antagonisms.

Not only are many disputes averted by the power of others but many are solved by it. France and Germany, which quarrelled for centuries over their borderlands, quickly stopped when both were overshadowed by the power of the United States and the Soviet Union. A new tension transforms an old one.

As to methods of handling tensions and disputes, I have already talked about diplomacy, propaganda, balance of power, and war, and I intend to say much about alliances later. I will only add here a half-welcome to one new method, 'crisis management', and no welcome at all to another, 'economic sanctions'.

I do not doubt that economic sanctions work continually in international relations as a deterrent to conflict; but, as with nuclear deterrence, once the threat has been defied, to implement it is merely fanatical. The opponent has probably calculated that you will lose at least as much as he will, and he is probably the better judge. Usually, you will not do much damage to him, only to your good relations with other states that you try to make join in. In any case, it is a Rationalist fallacy to think that economic damage by itself brings political surrender; as a step towards force and as an adjunct to force, it helps, but it is no substitute.

Most thinking about crisis management is done from the viewpoint of states that wish to control and end crises, and little from the viewpoint of those that wish to provoke and use them; also, most of it concerns inter-state crises, but these often spring from the internal conflicts of states, and shrewdness in handling them deserves more study; still, the whole approach is in the right spirit. If I had to single out just one piece of advice about the conduct of international relations, it would be avoidance of excess; 'compromise when you are winning'. Salvation in international conflict lies in astute statesmanship by the powers to keep it within bounds, and not, as I have no doubt the Rationalist is about to tell us, in getting the powers to co-operate in the delusion that international conflict can be abolished.

At this point, the Natural Law Man intervenes, saying: I think the topic will be made clearer if I speak next. Let me say, before anything else, this much in support of the Fideist: if men do not honour the gods, they have no virtue, only arrogance, and conflicts multiply. The Fideist is also right to demand obedience to the laws of the gods; but the laws of the gods are the natural law; to forget the natural law in the name of Faith is an error with terrible consequences. Above all, the great conflict in the world is not between the Camp of the Faithful and the Camp of the Infidels but is within ourselves between our nature and our ignorance and stupidity about our nature.

What the Realist says is an improvement, but, for all her belief in facing the facts, there are some facts she refuses to face. First, everyone will contradict her when she says we refrain most of the time from harming the independence, territory, and honour of other countries simply through fear of their power or possible need of their power in other conflicts. We refrain because to attack others is against our nature. Often 'man is wolf to man' but he is not basically so.

Honour has more aspects than the Realist thinks. It is not simply reputation for power. States, like men, get honour for other kinds of eminence; for example, economic success was the way the Germans and the Japanese returned to international respect after the Second Word War; states get honour, even weak states, for working for the common good, for example, The Netherlands in the European Community. Moreover, honour goes deeper than reputation into the sense of right. Even if the people of a nation have little reputation for power or for anything else, their national honour can still be insulted. This often happens in disputes inasmuch as disputes are about injuries, and injuries are often also insults.

The Realist's distinction of three kinds of conflict, ordinary conflict, tension, and dispute, is valuable, but she is vague about the dividing line between them. The fact is that we distinguish them sharply, and we do so in terms of justice.

In ordinary conflict, which I prefer to call ordinary dealings, we want something from another state; in dispute, we want something that we believe to be 'ours'. In the first case, we expect to have to negotiate for the best that we can get; in the second, we are making a demand. In the first case, we accept that the other state is entitled to refuse to satisfy us, if it wants to; in the second, we do not accept this. In both cases, we are pursuing our interests and honour; but in disputes, we are pursuing interests and honour conceived as right.[3]

The distinction does not lie (the Realist recognizes this) in the scale of the interests involved. In ordinary dealings, the interests may be very large, as in General de Gaulle's veto in 1963 of Britain's first application to join the European Community. In disputes also, they may be very large, vital interests indeed, concerning the entire security of the country; they may, on the other hand, be small; Britain's interests in its Cod War of the same period with Iceland did not run far beyond Hull and Grimsby. The crucial difference was that the Cod War involved right, and, because of that, could and did lead to force.

We think things are 'ours' in international relations, in the first place, when we are in existing control of them. A state that challenges the existing position, saying that a thing is 'theirs', gives a justification; its opponent then justifies the continuance of the present position. In recent times, states have done this superficially in historical, geographical, ethnic, and legal terms. However, on further scrutiny, no one thinks that a thing is 'ours' simply because we have always had it or once had it; 'ours', simply because we are closest to it geographically; 'ours' because all the people of our culture ought to be in our state; 'ours' because the existing international law is that national fisheries are three miles wide and not twelve. The underlying grounds for demand and refusal are of the following sort: the thing was seized without justification in the past, and, unlike most of history's wrongs, is still a visible insult (for example, West Irian or Gibraltar); the thing is ours because we made it (consider Goa, which we turned from a village into The Lady of All the Orient, or the 'I took Panama' Canal); the existing dividing lines favour some people over others (the British over

[3] F. S. Northedge and M. D. Donelan, *International Disputes: The Political Aspects* (London, 1971), ch. 2.

the Icelanders) or harm some people (the Somalis in Kenya, the Hungarians in Romania).

The Realist rightly distinguished from ordinary disputes those that arise from a deeper source, from a tension between the states concerned; but what is a tension? It is a situation of fear, to be sure, but of fear, not that we shall be surpassed in the competition for the things states want, but that we may be attacked in what is ours. We say that our opponent is bent on aggrandizement or mastery; our meaning is that it is not content with greatness within its borders and influence beyond, but might at any time and in any place attack our territory, possessions, independence, and honour. An ideological tension is more than a difference of political ideas; it is a conviction that the opponent's system is unjust to its subjects and would be to others and eventually to ourselves, were it to spread. Something similar can be said of religious tensions, though here the argument is about truth rather than about justice.

As to the disputes that express a tension, Indians and Pakistanis are convinced that Kashmir is 'ours'. They are convinced of this on much the sort of grounds that I mentioned a moment ago in the case of ordinary disputes; and so are the British, French, and Egyptians as regards the Suez Canal. The difference is that now they take the opponent's actions to be conclusive proof of a general desire to injure them and theirs in every respect. The Soviet Union's covert installation of missiles on Cuba alarmed the Americans strategically but alarmed them still more as an expression of hostility, which must be checked if they were to maintain their reputation for power to defend what was theirs. In symbolic disputes, this kind of concern is even more central. If two states fight over some worthless bit of borderland, they justify this to themselves and to the world by saying that they are defending what is theirs, meaning by this not just the bit of land but, indirectly, everything.

I have shown so far, says the Natural Law Man, with fact to satisfy the Realist and evidence for the Historicist, that our sense of justice is at work in this matter of international conflict, both in our usually refraining from dispute and in the disputes that do arise. At the same time, I know that there is more to conflict than this. Our justice is not as it ought to be. The natural impulse of the young to justice needs to be trained, and the mature man guides himself with theory, by which I mean observation and reflection. The growth of many men is distorted, and of some is stunted by ignorance and stupidity about their own nature and that of the state. They do not realize that their nature is social and so they mistake what success is for men and states. Hostile passions towards others master them, and so they conflict.

I will give more detail about this, relating it to what I said in my opening general statement. I said then that the *raison d'être* of the state is such that every act of foreign policy, whether to one other state or to a group or to the whole world of states, should aim at the good of every state involved, with, as the ultimate aim, the achievement of conditions that are for the good of the citizens of them all.

Consider, in this light, the ordinary dealings of a state: it is negotiating say, a cultural agreement with another; it is taking a stand on monetary policy in a group of states to which it belongs; it is refusing to sign a world treaty on nuclear weapons. In such cases, as I have pointed out, the state does not deny to other states things that are theirs, only things that they want, and, accordingly, they do not say that it is unjust; but, in a broader understanding of the word 'justice', it may be unjust, that is, if its intention is to forward only its own interests and not the common good.

Consider, next, ordinary disputes between states. Sometimes, these are about the conditions under which men as individuals live. One state says to another: you are not protecting citizens of ours against mistreatment; your car-makers shall not sell their cars freely in our country; you shall no longer run the Anglo-Iranian Oil Company; we shall rule the Falkland Islanders, not you. Sometimes ordinary disputes between states are not only about the conditions under which men as individuals live but also about their relations as states. For example, when Iran nationalized the AIOC, this affected not only the individual shareholders, the employees, all who traded with the company, and all its competitors, but also the Iranians and the British as states, in that the Iranians saw control of the company as a matter of their national honour, the British, as a matter of their national security. Sometimes, the dispute affects men only as states; for example, the Indians on discovering that the Chinese had built a road across the remote, empty Aksai Chin.

In such disputes, one side or both may act without regard to justice; they cry 'justice', but dishonestly. Alternatively (and this seems more common), they want justice, but they have a half-developed idea of what justice is; they want 'justice for themselves', not for both sides, the common good. Then again, they may honestly seek the common good, but, differing about what it is, they may disbelieve in the honesty of the other side. States are ever ready to reach for the accusation that the opponent's motives are bad, for example, that its rulers are working up a foreign dispute because this will buttress their popularity at home. As though, even if this were true, it would dispose of the justice of the matter! States should start, on the contrary, from the position that the dispute is a mutual predicament, arising from the fact that justice in human affairs is not always self-evident, and has to be worked out. They should be slow to take obstinacy and anger on the other side as evidence of illwill and irrationality. Disputes between hypocrites and villains are easy to settle; the Realist is correct in claiming that, if everybody were a Realist, the world would be a peaceful place; it is disputes between men of goodwill and good sense that are hard.

States in disputes often fail to recognize that their thinking is controlled by theory of a bad sort. With the Historicist, they have a bias towards believing that a traditional situation is right, whatever it may be, or at any rate that radical change is always wrong. Alternatively, with the Rationalist, their minds are full of abstract constructs called 'society', 'state', 'nation', 'colonialism', 'revolution', and so on, and they incant these to justify change. Both the one and the other fail to begin with the conditions under which particular individual men are living and to ask whether the change of a frontier or of possession, or of a rule, or of whatever the matter is, would improve conditions for them or not.

The interests of men as individuals do not, I recognize, add up to their interests as states. The same is true of their honour; they have a national honour. States easily underestimate this in assessing their opponents. With the Rationalist, they understand something of individual honour, namely, human dignity as an aspect of human rights, but national honour they dismiss as an aberration. Alternatively, with the Realist, they reduce it to another kind of interest. Interests are easy to grasp; honour takes insight; both should be considered in disputes about the common good. All the time, though, in the uncertainties, the statesman should keep in view the good of men as individuals. National honour, like national interest, like the state itself, aims at that, and does not exist for its own sake.

I have consented to discussing disputes in terms of interests and honour but I think that I have made clear that what is essential is the good. In the end, states in disputes should be willing to give things up for the common good. I do not mean, as does the Rationalist, things that they merely think they want, things that they will soon find to be surpassed in value in a higher harmony of interests with the opponent; but things that really advance their prosperity and power and their reputation for power as a separate state; and which they should give up because their true interest and honour are to be found in a community of states and in the achievement of the common good. In the course of a dispute, each side feels under pressure; force may be used; damage and suffering and humiliation harden opposition. The right counter to this embitterment is at every turn to find a way to show desire for the good of the other state, ingenuity in this, and honesty.

At this point in our discussion, the Natural Law Man continues, I shall classify disputes further. The mark of a professional in every science is that he classifies; but also that, in the human sciences, he is content to be rough and brief.[4] I have been speaking so far of ordinary disputes of a bilateral kind (that is, between two states or groups of states) about territory or other possessions or a rule or a matter of that sort. I said something in my opening general statement about distributive justice within groups (where a good or burden has to be shared out), and so, in effect, about distributive disputes. This topic will recur in a world setting among rich and poor countries when we come to discuss commerce. There too we shall touch on rules of trade and economic management among groups of states and world-wide; these have so far been the main area of

[4] Aristotle, *Nicomachean Ethics*, 1094[b].

multilateral disputes. Multilateral disputes may never kill many people because organizing multilateral war may be beyond human ability. I realize, though, that the underlying issues are the most deadly that there are; more people die by starvation and epidemic disease and natural disasters and can die by chaos than die by war. I shall not enter the large field of the internal disputes of states, for example, about the constitution within nation-states, or about independence within imperial states; but we shall see something of the secondary disputes between states that arise from this source when we discuss intervention.

What remains is tensions between states and the expressive and symbolic disputes that ensue. Such disputes are the most prominent in world politics; for example, in the twentieth century, those between Nazi Germany and the Western powers, and between the Western powers and the Soviet Union in the Cold War, or, in South Asia, those between India and Pakistan. At first sight, the theorist of justice can have little to say here. For a tension signifies that one side or both have neglected the reason for the existence of states, namely, to seek the common good of their citizens, and, in collaboration with one another, the common good of them all. One or both are threatening the other unjustly. Therefore, it seems that in the disputes that arise, the only operative virtues are prudence, courage, and self-control; justice is irrelevant. For it would be stupid in disputes with an unjust state to expect that it will do justice to you, and equally stupid to do justice to it, conceding to it things that can strengthen it against you; as Socrates said, no one returns a madman's axe to him.[5] Moreover, the disputes will not be resolved by justice but by ending the tension from which they sprang.

On the other hand, it may be said that, though resistance to an unjust state is right, to resist on unjust grounds cannot be so. It is wrong for statesmen to ask their citizens to be ready to go to war and die in defence of a position which is bad as regards the individual men and the states concerned. Though the Realist insists in such cases on the necessity of resistance for prestige, balance of power, strategy, and so on, the fact is that resistance,

[5] Plato, *The Republic*, 331ᶜ.

by being unjust, is not truly prudent. For example, for Britain and France to have resisted Germany's remilitarization of the Rhineland in 1936 would have been wrong. It is well-known that the United States in the Cold War with the Soviet Union and China sometimes took up positions which seemed expedient in terms of the global struggle but which, by being unjust in local terms, perpetuated the tension, and in the climactic case, Vietnam, proved indefensible.

I conclude that, as a general rule, it is right to do justice even to a state whose ambitions must be resisted, wrong to resist an unjust state by injustice; but that, in some cases, the prudent man decides that what would be just should be admitted to the enemy state and to the other states concerned, but that doing it should be held in abeyance, and the reasons for this given.

I wish to end my remarks with a philosophical question. I have said that the ordinary disputes of the world are the world's conflict about justice. I believe that claims made in justice can be made intelligible to men from the other end of the earth and accepted by them as indeed just. I believe, moreover, that this has always been so. I am not sure what the Historicist believes. At one point, he says that men can listen to all voices across time and place; but, at another, that men can only hear those within their tradition of thought; and this suggests that a claim can only be accepted as just if the political tradition within which it is made is accepted. I ask the Historicist to make his thought clear.

Not so fast, the Rationalist interposes; philosophical questions bring chapters to a close and I have some points to make before that happens; three, to be exact.

To make my first point, I must remind you of my basic position: what we are given at the start of our lives is not a world to be discovered, but minds that proceed according to certain concepts to construct a world. So the central point as regards conflict is not that states should set out to try to discover justice, but that they should pursue their interests according to certain procedures. In this way, a political world is constructed.

Between states, as within them, talk of justice is a mere battle of words, inane and inflammatory. If there is any method in it at all, it is an effort to deduce the right conditions for men to live under from fundamental characteristics of human beings; and no one agrees about this. The laws of the world can only be known by the gods, if such there be; they cannot be known by men. In Rousseau's words 'we have not got the measure of this immense machine, we cannot calculate its relationships; we know neither its first laws nor its final cause; we do not know ourselves'.[6] The only sense in talk of justice is procedural justice; that is, justice is what results from fair procedures. Only let interest be set beside interest and discussed fairly, and the outcome will be the best that men can do. That is 'good' enough.

A political world is not constructed by power, as the Realist thinks; power is destructive or at most prevents destruction. There is no such thing as 'power politics'; the phrase is contradictory; power at best maintains the opportunity for politics, at worst destroys politics. What I mean by fair procedures is respect for the basic principles of relations between states, namely, freedom and equality, and, entailed in these, precisely the avoidance of the use of power, that is, of constraint and coercion and, above all, of force. There must be change in the world but it must be 'peaceful change'.

The ideal, as I said in my general statement, is a world federation of states, agreed upon submitting disputes that cannot be settled by diplomacy to adjudication or arbitration. States should work continually in this direction by reaching agreements to this effect, bilaterally or in regional or other groups. Short of this ideal, states should proceed by negotiation, assisted by good offices and mediation and fact-finding by other states, and by the expression of world opinion in international organizations.

Slow, uncertain, contested, rhetorical, acrimonious, and, in one word, inefficient as these procedures are, my second point is that to abandon them in favour of pressures and force is always worse. Recourse to power is an offence against reason and a mistake about interests. Often it simply does not work; the possibility of the use of power creates an excited atmosphere among policy-makers that impairs rational calculation; the opponent turns out to be able to mobilize more or less equal counter-power, and the dispute simply becomes more disruptive

---

[6] *Profession de Foi du Vicaire Savoyard*, pt. 1, ch. 2.

of actual and prospective co-operation, more damaging to wider interests, more costly in material, suffering and lives, more embittered, and more and more difficult to settle. National honour (in contrast to the individual honour of statesmen and other men) seems to me to be an irrational feeling; but so long as it exists in many nations and so long as coercion is considered the worst of insults, and defeat the worst humiliation, so long will the use of power still further reinforce the obstinacy of opponents. Interests prevail over so-called national honour in the end, I think, but the end is further postponed.

I admit that often a power-using state calculates correctly; it wins the dispute by the threat or use of power; but its people always pay a greater cost to their interests than the value of the thing they have won, as well as the supreme cost that they have descended to the level of brutes. For if opponents will look at their interests long enough and widely enough in negotiation with each other, they will usually find that they each would gain more by co-operation with the other than they would win by simply taking the thing in dispute. Iceland might have gained more by co-operating with the British and the rest than by excluding them from its waters; the Soviet Union would surely have gained more by co-operation with the United States after the Second World War than it gained by seizing mastery of Central Europe; India and Pakistan cheated themselves of great mutual gains by their fruitless quarrel. There is always the wider consideration that the people of a state benefit, if not directly, then indirectly, from the progress in prosperity of the people of the other state. Most widely of all, every state has an interest, even to its cost in a particular matter, in supporting a general rule against the use of power. From all these viewpoints, the interests of states confirm the rationality of staying within peaceful procedures.

Let me now summarize how I stand towards the Realist and her 'power'. I am willing to agree with her that constraint is important in human affairs, and especially in inter-state affairs; states are constrained from starting coercion by calculation of the likely costs, including those that opponents have the power to inflict on them; power prevents destruction. But the Realist thinks that a state can sometimes initiate coercion to its advantage; and I say that it never can. Further, the Realist, while she thinks that conflict usually leads to loss, also thinks that co-operation in peaceful affairs only sometimes leads to greater gain; but I say that it always does. Such is the harmony of interests among men. The Realist theory is that some men win and others lose; the Rationalist, that all win or all lose.

If this is the rationality of inter-state relations, why do states often take to coercion culminating in force and war? Sometimes, it is through misperception; they fail to look long enough and widely enough into their interests; or they perceive the opponent as threatening when he is only so because of his misperception of them. These clouds of incomprehension around a dispute can be dispersed if diplomatists curb their Realist bias, and international society has intelligent arrangements for negotiation and media-tion. The opponents come to see their 'conflict as a problem to be solved and not as a contest to be won'.[7]

Sometimes states are mistaken in the deeper way that they really believe that they can advance their cause by coercion and even war. This is because they are controlled by tyrants or ideologues or religious fanatics; these think they will win or the creed will win, no matter that their subjects, as individuals, will lose. Concerning this, I make my third point. Many believe that Rationalism is the theory of mild-mannered optimists who are not only reluctant to use force but are bad at it and should be replaced by Realist hard-men whenever times turn rough in world affairs. I point out, therefore, that a Rationalist believes in power as a counter to power, force as a counter to force, only as that, regretfully as that, but strongly as that.

You often cannot know which kind of state is facing you in a conflict: one that is muddled about its interests, as you may be about yours, or an aggressor. Whichever you suspect it to be makes no difference; you should negotiate with it tirelessly and, all the while, have defensive power. Once the state facing you takes to coercion, the situation changes: to negotiate in an atmosphere of coercion with a state that is using this senseless means is absurd; reason is now faced with unreason; you must now direct the whole of your energy to defence, that is, to resistance, or, where prudent, to coercion against coercion, and, if unavoidable, to making war on the war-maker, all with

[7] J. W. Burton, *Conflict and Communication* (London, 1969), 157.

the announced aim of bringing the irrational state back to peaceful procedures.

I recognize the dilemmas that arise in applying this principle. Secretary Acheson's motto in the Cold War between the Western Alliance and the Soviet Union was 'negotiation from strength'. The Soviet Union denounced this as capitalist imperialism's search for 'positions of strength' from which to dictate to the socialist camp; in other words, Realism. I think myself that the idea was Rationalism; but Rationalism that prudently recognized current circumstances. The phrase soothed the feelings of those Americans and those Western allies who believed that a negotiated agreement with the Soviet Union must be possible, who believed that the Soviet Union had interests that should be respected (as it certainly had) but also (irrationally) that an agreement with it could be worked out while it was still a state that practised coercion.

'Negotiation from strength', a true maxim among the peaceful, becomes contradictory when the peaceful are faced with an aggressor; it means now negotiating away the strength that makes negotiation possible. The Natural Law Man noted this earlier in his metaphysical fashion; don't do justice to the unjust. The supreme case is negotiation for disarmament. That the world should be disarmed is the final hope of a Rationalist in politics; but he means by this disarmament of the mind; 'wars begin in the minds of men'; he hopes to hear men proclaim: 'There shall be no war.' He is not so foolish, whatever his detractors say, as to think that the hope can be realized simply by negotiation. Among peace-loving states, negotiations to reduce arms are merely the working out in practice of what has already been achieved in the mind. Among hostile powers, it is an absurdity: 'only because we are armed can we be brought to negotiate; so let us negotiate to be disarmed'.

I realize that sometimes, in prudence, hopeless negotiations are necessary to appease public opinion; none the less Rationalist principles remain clear; I am not sure that the same can be said of Realism. In the *détente* of the 1970s between the Soviet Union and the United States, Secretary Kissinger deplored a tendency in the West to see *détente* 'not as a balancing of national interests and negotiations on the basis of strategic realities but rather as an exercise in strenuous goodwill, in which one removes by understanding the suspiciousness of a nation that is assumed to have no other motive to attack'.[8] I do not find the logic of that judgement clear.

About the Realist's attack on another method of statecraft, economic sanctions: she concentrates exclusively on their weaknesses as an instrument of coercion and says nothing of their strengths as an expression of international society's support for certain principles. I accept that here too there are practical dilemmas: in a given case, is more gained by expressing disapproval of a state or by maintaining contact with its people? Do you demonstrate to an opponent his interest in trade better by continuing it or by cutting it off? Are the gains worth the cost that you are abetting the already powerful and deplorable tendency in international society towards the politicization of commerce? But, to conclude: all theories of world politics face problems of prudence in application; the basic rationality of Rationalism is unaffected.

'Yes and no.' It is the Natural Law Man who speaks. The Realist keeps quiet, calculating that her work will be done for her.

The fact that the final goal of the Rationalist, the settlement of great international conflicts by adjudication and arbitration, has always been dismissed by practical men, the Natural Law Man continues, surely tells us something. It confirms, I contend, that the Rationalist thinks in abstractions, not realities. He thinks that states are persons; not, to be sure, organic persons, as in nationalism, but constructed, 'fictitious' persons. He therefore thinks that their disputes, like those of natural persons or corporations, ought in reason to be soluble by legal procedures. But states are not persons, and threats and injuries are not legal crimes, territory is not real estate, the independence of states is not that of corporations, treaties are not just contracts. When persons come before courts, the conditions under which they live, that is the laws, are taken as broadly settled, and the problem is to apply these to the case. When states are in conflict, the conditions under which people live are the issue, that is, frontiers, independent statehood, the rules of international trade, and so on. In short, the conflict lies not at the legal level

---

[8] K. A. Myers (ed.), *NATO: The Next Thirty Years* (Boulder, Colo., 1980), 10.

of human life but at the political. If a domestic analogy must be found for states in foreign policy, they are best compared, not with litigants, but with political parties trying to legislate. The Rationalist's own contention that the solution to international conflict lies in the recognition of a higher harmony of interests suggests that the heart of the matter is political, not legal. In Kant's federation, the procedures would be worked by politicians, not lawyers.

So negotiation, mediation, and so on are not a temporary, second-best expedient; they are all that we shall ever have. The question is how negotiation works to solve disputes. I say that it never works simply by setting out the conflicting demands and reasoning about them until a harmony of interests is revealed. Either it works by power: one side coerces the other into giving way or both strike a bargain for fear of some third party; or it works by the acceptance by both sides that they are a community, and that they should be prepared to make concessions for the common good.

Much as I believe in negotiation, I also believe that the Rationalist is unrealistic in saying that the initiation of coercion is always wrong. No polity, national or international, can work without the ultimate sanction of force, however far in the background. Without it, possessors may simply sit complacently in possession, protected by the social doctrine: 'no rebellion', 'no invasion'. I am inclined to agree with the Rationalist that he is not a revolutionary, at most a rebel sometimes, no jacobin. He has a marked tenderness for authority and possession. Perhaps this comes from his theory that these are attributes of individual men and states, prior to national and international society, and that society was formed to reinforce them. In natural law, authority and possession exist in community, and are disposable according to the common good. Prevailing conditions may embody unjust force. I do not say with the Realist that the threat of the initiation of counter-force is the only solution; but I do say that it helps to concentrate the minds of some men on the common good. To go into international negotiations announcing that you will in no circumstances use force is stupid.

I readily concede to the Rationalist that, once others start coercion, he is no faint-heart; he is the most ruthless and implacable user of force that there is. His slogan becomes: 'no negotiation with the men of violence'. He refuses to communicate with those he is fighting on the grounds that he must not seem to legitimize their cause or condone their methods. He breaks off diplomatic relations with the opponent state, and launches with all his energy into the organization of massive, far-flung, armed and rigid containment of the criminal. He would like to make total war on the enemy state, bombing it into unconditional surrender, purging it of its tyrants, ideologists, and fanatics, and so restoring it to peaceful procedures. Only prudence, not principle, restrains him, making him in the end succumb and negotiate with men he denied he would ever have any dealings with.

My view is that starting war is usually unjust but sometimes just, and that the banning of all offensive war in twentieth-century international law did not lessen war but merely increased hypocrisy. I have in mind the automatic relabelling of all wars 'defensive' wars or with some other euphemism, and the self-righteousness of possessors who went into battle saying that they were 'defending international law'. Probably India was right to seize Goa; what was wrong was the previous lecturing of the world about non-violence that this pin-prick deflated. Probably no Australian immigration policy would justify force; but not certainly. Many people adduce nuclear weapons as proof that men must abandon war; but this is not realistic. Men will not be driven from war by fear; they will simply find new forms of war that are war, not obliteration. I applaud the Rationalist's vision of a world in which the institution of war is abolished; but I mean by this a world in which there are in fact no wars; the potential for war will always remain, for the common good, in human nature.

A word about the news media. Those who work in them are self-conscious, as has always been the way with each new profession, but not reflective. Their role in international conflict is large (I do not say, their influence), but they offer few thoughts on it. Until they do, and debate on the matter starts, I can only say the obvious. The Realist holds that, in an international dispute, the news media must confirm the public's belief that 'our' case is completely right and that 'their' case is utterly wrong. The Rationalist thinks that the media's duty is cosmopolitan; even though they are nationally organized, they should present fact and reason, confident that this is in the national interest. Natural Law asks more: fact and reason alone never produce a solution; newsmen should go so far as to claim that their duty is to the common good of both sides. If the media and all statesmen and citizens are committed to this and to discussion in terms of this, they will bring the conflict to an end.

Time's up, says the Historicist; you have now made perfectly clear that your theory, like the Rationalist's and the Realist's and the Fideist's is subject to time. 'Seek the common good' or 'work out the harmony of interests' or 'organize power' or 'do the will of God' gives us no advice about what to do when we are in a conflict. These phrases speak only when the conflict is over. Natural Law says that, if disputants reached a solution without coercion, they were committed to the common good; if they did not, they were not. Rationalism and Realism are similar. Fideism says that, if the Armada sinks, that was the will of God, and if it floats, that was the will of God also. Such guide-lines do not guide. Theories are at most theories of history. Theories are hindsight.

What the will of God is depends on the spirit of an age. I do not mean that God says the same thing differently in changing times. I mean that the will of God changes over time. The concept 'the will of God' has altered entirely in recent centuries into something less personal: Reason or Reality. The content of these terms is not fixed either but varies with the spirit in a given age. Reason as the basis of the world is not for us today what it was for the Renaissance or the Enlightenment. Most recently, some have revived Natural Law with its common good. The explanation is that we are nowadays casting around for new lines of action; 'nation' and 'state' and 'proletariat' are perhaps giving way to 'world'; in the past, we heard the voice of all other traditions, but only notionally; now we perhaps really hear them; a world tradition may be emerging; and 'Natural Law' may be chosen as the most apt concept, world-wide. But, if that happens, what 'Natural Law' means will not be found by us or be exactly constructed by us. It will come to mean something among us, and we shall see, when we reflect on the world's experience, what that is.

I warn those that are impatient of such philosophizing and

wish to hurry to the practicalities of world conflict that they too need to understand history. Take the supreme aspect of conflict today, nuclear deterrence. It is, the others have said, a tissue of Rationalist theory, disconnected from real war, the latest answer of the men of peaceful procedures to the men of violence; it is madness. The only way that we can defend our consciences, our morale, our very reason in this situation is by reflecting that nuclear deterrence is not anyone's intention but developed historically.

The substance of the world's conflicts, tensions, and disputes is history. The Rationalist, the Natural Law Man, the Realist, and the Fideist are alike makers of chaos with their abstract justice and their disparagement of the traditions of national and international life in the name of reason or the good or power or the faith. Right, I say, is historical, given by the past, prescriptive, and to be developed in this same spirit into the future. The antagonists in a conflict understand it so. Ask them what they mean by 'ours' and 'theirs', and you will be given a history. To this will be added, the tale of 'our' sufferings at 'their' hands. The essence of every conflict, Americans against Russians, Israelis against Palestinians, Thais against Vietnamese, is two conflicting views of the past. Statesmen, citizens, and media men involved in a dispute, whether as antagonists or third parties, need to understand this.

I return to my contention that the decisive kind of practice is philosophy. To endure conflict we need to understand what it is. Since we are historical, we cannot help seeing the past as some sort of story. We should try to see the story completely. In the tragedy of the conflicting rights and the crimes of states, we can see a spirit that has a higher right and judges them.[9] As in Schiller's poem, we can see that in life there is hope and enjoyment and that those who choose the one should not desire the other. About this, 'World history is the world court of judgement.'[10]

---

[9] Hegel, *Philosophy of Right*, sect. 340.
[10] 'Resignation', closing verses.

8

Alliances

THE Realist says: when there was one man in the world, peace was invented; when there were two men, conflict; when there were three men, alliances. Alliances are a human habit in everyday conversations and in great world conflicts. They cannot be numbered in their variety of purpose, intensity, and organization. I will give you some general guidance.

The vital alliances are those directed at the balance of power. You must subordinate all your lesser alliances and manœuvres to these. There are big problems. I need only give as an example the question nowadays of whether the Franco-German alliance, the core of the European Community, could become the main balance-of-power alliance of these two powers, or whether it is necessarily subordinate to their alliance with the United States.

The underlying problem is how to identify your enemies correctly. You might think that the best way is to list your interests in order of importance, and then consider who is threatening them. In practice, ascertaining interests and enemies is one inseparable process, and the best focus is upon the enemies. For, except in the broadest terms, a state's interests are not definite; they are fluid, they can run in one direction or another, they can be rechannelled. More certain than interests are will and power. You should ask who has most ambition to expand and ability to do so. That state, one way or another, will do you most harm.

States easily misjudge this, and fail to form the right alliances in good time. They think that the obvious enemy is the real enemy. Usually they look to the past with the Historicist: the English continue to fight the Spaniards and the Dutch for many years after the rise of France. At best, states see the present situation, with little regard to the future. They are so locked in a pattern of enmities that they do not appreciate the imminence of a menace to them all, and combine to meet it.

'We have no eternal allies and we have no perpetual enemies. Our interests are eternal and perpetual, and those interests it is our duty to follow.'[1] Palmerston should have said 'our concern for our interests is eternal', but his words were exactly right as regards allies and enemies. Alliances ought to be short-term and changeable, made with a view to some specific emerging danger, maintained through a war, when that is necessary, and ended when the danger is over. In November 1979, a Pakistani mob burned the United States embassy; a month later, the two states were allies; in between, the Soviet Union had invaded Afghanistan; the two states thus had the same enemy for a while.

Intertwined with alliances are guarantees. About them, let me say this: the area within which men guarantee one another is the state; to guarantee the people of another state is an error at the deepest level of political theory. I grant that sometimes a guarantee may be unavoidable, but only as a diplomatic expedient. For example, the only way of avoiding or settling a dispute about something may be to guarantee that nobody shall have it. The guarantee may have to be given with great protestations of its permanence; and, as a matter of fact, such arrangements often become relatively fixed landmarks in international diplomacy; none the less, you should always value a guarantee at current, not past, prices; it is worth one thing to the people who make it and another to those who are asked to implement it. Collective guarantees, for example, the Locarno Treaty, arise at one diplomatic juncture and collapse at another. Separate guarantees depend on the current interests of the guarantors, or rather, their current view of who is their enemy. If the 1887 Franco-German crisis had come to war, Britain would probably have abandoned Belgium because at the time it favoured the Germans and feared the French; Belgium was simply lucky in 1914 that Britain's view had changed. An English statesman said in the Munich Crisis of 1938: ' . . . it was not for Czechoslovakia that we should have been fighting if we had gone to war last week . . . It was not for Serbia that we fought

---

[1] Palmerston, House of Commons, 1 Mar. 1848, in *UK Parliamentary Debates*, 3rd series, vol. xcvii, col. 122.

in 1914. It was not even for Belgium, although it occasionally suited some people to say so. We were fighting then, as we should have been fighting last week, in order that one Great Power should not be allowed, in disregard of treaty obligations, of the laws of nations and the decrees of morality, to dominate by brutal force the continent of Europe.'[2] Disregard the humbug English style of the last sentence, and you have here the truth: no state fights for another.

If war comes, I have two thoughts to offer. Generally speaking, among a group of more or less equal states, neutrality is unwise; a state should ally with one side or the other; for if it does not, the victor is likely to attack it in its turn, and the defeated will not now ally with it. On the other hand, a state should, if possible, avoid allying with another more powerful than itself to attack a weaker; for if they win, it will become a satellite of the more powerful state.[3] Luck is needed, especially by lesser powers; in our time, Sweden has been lucky, Mussolini was unlucky as well as unwise. Woodrow Wilson steered successfully through the shoals in the early years of the First World War, and so did Franklin Roosevelt in the early stages of the Second. In the war, you should fight not simply militarily but politically, meaning, above all, with an eye to a favourable peace. You should make peace when the best moment comes to cash winnings or cut losses. The British and Russians were right in the Second World War, as Realists, to fear that their ally might make a separate peace with Germany.

I pause, says the Realist, to hear objections. You are out of date, says the Historicist. You recommend alliances that are superficial, changeable, and easily ended. Light-footed statecraft of that sort belongs to the eighteenth century; it was clogged in the nineteenth by popular nationalism, and immobilized entirely in the twentieth by ideological, cultural, and racial loyalties; it may come back in the future, but to discourse about it at the present time is irrelevant. Realism is a strange mixture: it is a picture of world politics as a tooth-and-claw state of nature, but also a picture of a Golden Age of civilized diplomacy. I do not

[2] Duff Cooper; see James Joll (ed.), *Britain and Europe, Pitt to Churchill, 1793–1940* (London, 1950), 338.

[3] Machiavelli, *The Prince*, ch. 21.

expect theories to be based on any evidence, but I had thought they claimed to be coherent.

More than that, they should be made by men of reason, says the Rationalist. Realism is the theory of the powerful and the fearful. Relations between men based on power and fear are unstable and explosive. On the Realist's own admission, balance of power requires continually shifting alliances and continuous readiness for war. The balance is not a certainty. It is cast up in fog and suspicion. It is always delicate, hair-triggered. It is a chimera[4] which threatens in tooth or tail; when the balance looks robust, because the two sides seem equal in strength, fear fastens on the opponent's hostile intentions; when the opponent's intentions seem pacific, fear switches to asserting that he has superior strength. One way or another, Realist soldiers and statesmen always argue that the safest policy for their state is not a balance in the sense of equality but in the sense of a superior margin of power. Both sides argue so. They start a race for superiority. They never finish, for they turn on each other and destroy each other in a great explosion. Allies are sucked into the vortex.

In other words, an alliance is a great wall that extends the area of rubble. Not just two states are ravaged but four or eight or sixteen or however many more are recruited by the Realist. Against all this, I contend that the ideal for states is not the alliance but the security association. The first fact about international relations is not fear but interest in peaceful procedures; the second fact is that most states, most of the time, realize this; and the third, that they are more powerful than those that do not. The problem is to find for these facts an organization. Broadly, this is a security association; but what exactly?

The League of Nations and the United Nations were tainted with Realism, as I pointed out in my general statement, in that they envisaged enforcement action upon members, and not simply defensive war against aggressors. This was a mistake. States are obliged in reason not to injure one another and to seek to form security associations in which this is understood among them; but such associations are worthless and unworkable unless they are freely formed by states, through insight into

[4] Richard Cobden, 'Russia', in *The Political Writings of Richard Cobden* (London, 1867), i. 258.

their rational interests, and freely continued. Similarly, a state is not obliged to defend another at risk to its interests; neutrality is a plain right of states; they may make alliances or not as they choose, according to their interests; only states that have freely bound themselves in a security association to defend one another against aggressors are so bound.

States that do this are not aiming to convert an aggressor to rationality by force; merely to make it desist and respect peaceful procedures. Their motive for defending one another is that the renunciation of force within an association requires common external defence and that interest in the prosperity of associates entails not simply non-injury to them but defence of them. In short, in the security association, as in the rational state, force has a place but it is not the foundation. The Realist state, in contrast, cannot cohere without the threat of foreigners; Realist alliances are held together only by their enemies; and the Realist version of a security association is an armed tyranny by the great powers.

The security-association principle is a rational ideal which states should always take as their guide in the conduct of foreign policy. The actual construction of a security association depends upon opportunity but also upon continuous effort. Some modern regional associations are an advance towards the goal. States must continue the search for appropriate organizational forms. Under the pressure of everyday business, they are tempted to postpone thinking about this. Again and again, the world has seen an outburst of organizational creativity only after the catastrophe of a great war, not in time to avert it.

The task is broadly twofold. A security association requires ever-increasing interdependence of the populations on all matters so that disputes between their states may be prevented or be more easily soluble, and so that, in disputes with outsiders, each will be restrained by all. Secondly, as regards relations with outsiders, that is, non-member states and other security associations, the task is to create confidence that the association seeks to defend itself, and not to attack. The association must overcome the Realist's security dilemma that what seems to it to be defensive capacity may seem to outsiders hostile; and it must do this by abandoning some of the age-old Realist ideas about what constitutes defence. The association must show that it does not seek a margin of superior power; that it is as interested in ensuring that others could resist it as that it could resist them; that it seeks the equality of mutual vulnerability, mutual assured destruction, mutual impotence to attack. The ABM Treaty of 1972, in which the United States and the Soviet Union restricted their defences against ballistic missiles, was a mistake because the United States made it with a state that was a proven aggressor; against such a state there can only be full-scale defence of the traditional kind, and the problem is to reassure others that the measures taken are not directed at them. But the ABM Treaty idea was exactly the kind of arrangement that is needed between states and associations that have declared 'there shall be no war' and have not dishonoured their declaration. In such ways they make the beginnings of an ever-widening security association, which they seek to bring in the course of time to the perfection of one great federation of all the states of the world.

Among the errors in that blueprint, the Realist replies, there is one in the very foundations. The basis of your security association is that the people of the separate states will form ever-wider and stronger links of interest so that they come to see the irrationality of force and the rationality of peaceful procedures. But it is false to think that men and states are held together in peaceful association by harmony of interests, or ever could be. It is as false as the Historicist's acceptance of a possible future harmony of cultural traditions and the emergence of a world culture, bringing world peace. Burke wrote, half right, half wrong: 'Men are not tied to one another by papers and seals. They are led to associate by resemblances, by conformities, by sympathies. It is with nations as with individuals. Nothing is so strong a tie of amity between nation and nation as correspondence in laws, customs, manners and habits of life.'[5] But this is fanciful. There are no permanent friendships, any more than there are permanent interests. The inveterate ambition and fear of men and states readily transforms perceptions of interests, disrupts an existing pattern, however strong, and converts the deepest cultural kinship into the deepest kind of enmity. The only force that can overcome this spirit and bind

[5] Edmund Burke, 'Regicide Peace', Letter I, in *Works*, new edn. (London, 1852), vol. v., p. 305.

states together is power, a situation of constraint, meaning, first of all, fear of hostile power; and that is the foundation of alliances.

I concede to the Historicist that what I have so far said about alliances applies better to other periods of history than to recent years. He should not exaggerate this. The heroic years of United States foreign policy after the Second World War ended in the 1970s with the abandonment of an ally. The 1970s offered a prize illustration of the truth about guarantees: Britain's inaction when Turkey invaded Cyprus. We should not let ourselves be so hypnotized by the current structure-mongering of Northern Hemisphere politics that we cannot see the slippery character of inter-state relations in most of the world, in Asia, Africa, and Latin America. Among the great powers, as among the small, there is much mobility of alignment without formal alliance. Consider the manœuvring by China, the Soviet Union, and the United States in recent years; quite worthy of the Golden Age.

Still, on the whole, it is true that the present is a bad time for classic alliance diplomacy. Fideism and ideology nowadays ruin all good statecraft; when Sadat of Egypt makes a separate peace with Israel, he is assassinated by fanatics. The old imperial order has disintegrated into 160 states, most of which are too democratic or chaotic to be capable of making an alliance worth having. The great powers that currently dictate the terms of world politics frown upon the classic alliance; the Soviet Union and the United States believe in structures, not mobility. So, I agree, the alliance that is characteristic of today is not the classic alliance. But neither is it, as the Russians like to say, an ideological fraternity, or, as the Americans think, a regional security association. It is a new kind of empire.

The characteristic alliance of today consists of one great power and a number of small powers. The asymmetry of power is enormous. The Organization of American States, the Atlantic Alliance, the Warsaw Pact, and so on, are formally multilateral; but essentially they are a collection of bilateral relationships between the great power and the small powers; they do not really differ from the bilateral alliances of the United States with Japan and South Korea, and the Soviet Union with Cuba and Vietnam. The small allies do not matter much to each other; the crucial relationship for each is with the great power. The great power, for its part, has little need of some of its allies, considerable need of others, and great need of them all taken together in terms of their forces in being, their economic resources, their strategic position, and the military facilities they provide. Still, in no case is the relationship indispensable to it. The great power attaches far less importance to any of its allies than does the ally to the great power. The great power could even, in the last resort, survive without all of them. The small powers could not defend themselves against more than two or three others. The great power could defend itself against the whole world somehow.

From these realities of the modern alliance, guide-lines follow. Consider, first, the guide-lines for the great power. At the core of the alliance is the fact that the great power is guaranteeing the small powers. From this comes such voluntary loyalty as the small powers feel but also danger to the great power. For the great power faces the dilemma that a total guarantee (that is, a promise of limitless support against any armed attack) is desirable in order to anchor a small power in its allegiance and to give a clear deterrent warning to the rival great power; but undesirable in that the great power is making a commitment that goes far beyond the intrinsic importance to it of the small power. Such a commitment would be a dubious policy at any time; when, as at present, it involves the risk of war with large-scale nuclear weapons, it is folly.

The temptation is to discount the danger on the grounds that the lesser states that the great power is guaranteeing are not so independent and therefore so dangerous as those of yesteryear, Austria–Hungary or Serbia, say, in 1914. Today's alliances are known to be quasi-empires; the small powers are not so much foreign states as provinces; they are part of the great power's economic system; their security is unmistakably a prestige matter for the great power. Its commitment is made still more inescapable by the stationing of its own troops on the territory of the small powers. In consequence of all this, it is argued, the great power must necessarily defend the small powers, and the alliance is safe because the rival great power knows this with complete certainty.

Such talk sounds modern but is in fact out of date. The

Atlantic Alliance and the Warsaw Pact, its imitator, though modern empires, are also heirs of the Grand Alliance of the Second World War and of the United Nations. They perpetuate old strategy, so that they are not likely to be the most efficient form of organization for a contemporary war, and the old idealism of indiscriminate mutual security guarantees. These traditional structures, with their entrenched loyalties and bureaucracies, should not be allowed to obscure the real question: is a total guarantee, even of states that are provinces of an empire, prudent?

Two facts give the answer. Provinces on the borders of an empire can embroil the centre, and, for all the caution of the nuclear age, will do so one day, if they believe that the centre must necessarily support them. The dynamics of human competitiveness ensure this. The centre is thus unwise to give a total guarantee. The second fact is that the principle of guarantee as the basis of international security is only valid if fulfilment of the guarantee is known by all to be automatic; but automaticity is impossible. This fact was clarified at the time of the very first experiment, that is, in the debate on Article X of the League Covenant between President Wilson and his Realist critics.[6] The subsequent increased dominance of the great powers in the United Nations and in the Atlantic Alliance and Warsaw Pact does not alter this fact. Indeed, the very text of the treaties confirms it. Automaticity in a crisis is the ideal; the reality is that each state would decide what to do for itself.

These being the facts, they should be avowed. The inherited idealism should be cleared away which muddles expectations, which binds and does not bind, which cannot give the security that would spring from certainty in advance about reactions in a crisis, and yet prevents the security that would spring from awareness that there would be free, prudent decision in the light of the circumstances. The guide-line for the great powers should be to seek a slow, skilful transformation of the present illusory principles and the military arrangements built upon them, promoting open acknowledgement throughout the alliances that the guarantee is not and never could be total. Rationalist structuralism, rigidity, automaticity, and the whole search for

---

[6] Henry Cabot Lodge, *The Senate and the League of Nations* (New York, 1925).

certainty as the key to international security signify immaturity in statecraft. The allegiance of the small powers and the deterrent force of the alliance should be maintained by impressive leadership, not by promises.

I turn to the brighter side of the security arrangements of the great powers, the control over the world that their alliances give them. The United States and Russia suffered in the past from the politics of Europe; they put an end to this in 1945; each took control of half. Each suppressed the old enmities of the region in a way that suited the other. Russia submerged the volcanoes of Central Europe and the Balkans under a glacier. The United States dwarfed the old giants of Western Europe. The two powers partitioned Germany. Even their rivalry helped them in that they invoked the danger from the other to frighten their alliances into obedience.

Their problem is how to weaken the other without forfeiting these benefits that they gain from his strength. To destroy the empire of another is an error if you cannot control the successor states yourself. The United States and the Soviet Union made this mistake at the time of the break-up of the European empires after the Second World War; we must wait to see whether they make it again in their policies to each other's empire. I hope that at least they will not be deluded by their own propaganda. They sometimes picture themselves as campaigning against the other to liberate the subject states from slavery; but their real task is to engineer the orderly and peaceful transfer of control over these states from the other to themselves. They should avoid any policy that creates difficulties for the other great power, the prospect of collapse, desperation, and consequent recourse to violence; on the contrary, they should seek ways to help the other so that it can see a secure and prosperous, if non-imperial, future for itself. This process, to be smooth, must be imperceptible. That is a further reason why the rigidity and formality of the great imperial alliances should be reduced. The movement of the small states from one hegemony to the other becomes less apparent and therefore easier.

In short, as Khrushchev put it, the policy of the great powers towards each other should not be a hostile 'We will kill you', but the friendly offer of a service, 'We will bury you'. Even this phrase is too blunt; the motives of the policy of helpfulness to the rival should be disguised in Rationalist propaganda of some sort. The important difficulty, as I have already implied, is that, as your policy succeeds, as *détente* progresses into apparent *entente*, as your rival becomes prosperous and secure and less interested in dominating the world around him, fear of him subsides in your own empire, and this force for unity and order is lost. Allies are always an ill-assorted lot, quarrelsome and unco-operative; usually this is superficial and to be treated with tolerance; they are troublesome because they resent the fact that they need you. Real difficulty begins if they do not need you.

A false solution is that of the Rationalist, namely, to increase the unity of the alliance in a wholly new direction, economic integration; for example, through the old Organization for European Economic Co-operation and the present European Community, and, imitating them in form, the Council for Mutual Economic Assistance. This is false because an economic structure, piled on the military organization, increases the overtness of empire that blocks imperceptible movement of states out of the rival empire. In any case, the idea is based on a fallacy. The allies will not form an economic association primarily for economic reasons; they are, like all states, mercantilist; they do not accept the politically naïve theory of free trade; even if they did, the place to pursue free trade would not be in a limited association of states but in the whole world market. The Rationalist must admit that. The allies will form an economic association really for political reasons, that is, power. The great power commands them to form one, or they come together voluntarily in order to make a balance of power against him. The Soviet Union ordered the formation of the Council for Mutual Economic Assistance. The European Community was in part ordered by the United States, in part voluntarily formed so that old Europe could rival the new superpowers. None of this is in the best interests of a superpower.

The best plan for a hegemon in economic affairs is to have separate bilateral relations with each of its allies and among them. Any unavoidable multilateralism, for example in international monetary arrangements, should be centred on itself. Politically, bilateralism is safer for the great power than promoting association. The allies have no real objection to it; they need the great power's market more than they need one another's or than it needs theirs. Economically, to plunder the allies, as the Soviet Union once did in Eastern Europe, may be unwise, but bilateral relations can be managed to the great power's moderate advantage and should be.

This is desirable if only to offset the fact that the great power is likely to have to carry a heavier burden than the others of the military cost of the alliance. The Rationalist notion that the allies should pay proportionately equal amounts because they have an equal interest in joint defence is wishful thinking. The Natural Law Man's idea that alliances should be conducted for the common good of the citizens of the countries concerned and should be paid for according to distributive justice among them is even more naïve. The facts are that the allies will be guided by two calculations: how much must the great power necessarily spend in its own interests, and, in consequence, how much of a 'free ride' can they have;[7] and how much independence, influence and prestige within the alliance do they wish to purchase by military effort.

Some people suppose that a good way to reduce the overall cost of an alliance is joint weapons production. This is doubtful economically, as the Rationalist would agree, and is politically and militarily unrealistic. The right course for the great power is to leave each ally to make the specialized weaponry suitable for the kind of warfare it should wage in its circumstances, and supply the standard weaponry, as far as possible, itself. This mixture of national independence and great-power centralism will satisfy the allies well enough. In this, as in all economic matters, and, indeed, every aspect of the alliance, the great power's maxim should be not the unity of all but the unity of each with the centre. The symbol of imperial power is the turbine, not the wheel. This, if fear fails, is the principle of control.

I have considered modern-style alliances from the viewpoint of great powers. To see them as small states do, just turn the telescope around. Membership brings gains and losses to small states in security, economy, and prestige, and so does non-membership; they must calculate in current conditions and

[7] Mancur Olson, Jr., and Richard Zeckhauser, 'An Economic Theory of Alliances', *Review of Economics and Statistics*, 48(3) (Aug. 1966), 266–79.

recalculate as these change; a fashion for permanent, structured alliances came to a climax in the mid-twentieth century under the influence of Rationalism, and so did, in reaction, a movement among the small states for non-alignment; the twenty-first century may see the world of classic alliances restored. There is one fixed point about any kind of alliance in any century: it never looks the same to a small power and a great. A small power sees a local conflict in local terms, that is, the effect on itself and its region; the great power sees a local conflict in world terms, the possible effect on its world rivalry with other great powers; because they see the conflict differently, they are doubly opposed when they are enemies and at cross-purposes even when they are allies. A small power wants the alliance only locally; a great power wants support globally. Both need the brains to see the relationship with the other's eyes, but the small power most, because it is the weaker.

Here the Realist pauses again for objections. The Historicist insists that we hear the Realist nowadays only notionally, not really. Doubtless her theory describes much of the behaviour of today's world; but it does not express how we think, our ideal, or, put best, truth in our time. One day, she may be right, as she has been in times past; but not always; and not now.

You are both wrong, says the Rationalist: we must have a theory that is always valid; but Realism is always false. The Realist state and empire and alliance, being mere power structures, when the strong man dies, the state crumbles, when energy fails, the empire breaks up, when the enemy departs, the alliance disappears; the state of nature returns; where is permanent security for men in all this? My state and empire and security association are stable; they have deep foundations; they are built upon interdependence among men in society; they consist of law, within which the harmony progresses, defended by power. My security association is, in other words, a group of states that are constitutional, both at home and also internationally, in that they observe a constitution of peaceful procedures towards one another. This is a strong, enduring structure. Here is permanence and security.

The characteristic alliance of today is the Atlantic Alliance; not an empire but an alliance that is half-way to being a security association. To equate the Atlantic Alliance with the

Warsaw Pact is absurd. The Atlantic Alliance consists of states in which men are free and equal, and which, despite the superior power of the United States, are unprecedentedly free and equal as partners. If the Alliance progresses in the interdependence of its peoples, if each member state continues watchful of its national constitution, and if all of them co-operate to build an alliance constitution such that their conflicts can be resolved and their common purposes forwarded effectively, security will be achieved within the association and so will greater strength and security than at present in relations with the rest of the world. That this should be done in the North Atlantic region and in the other regions of the world and among states grouped according to principles other than the regional is the Rationalist vision of progress in world politics.

A case of double vision, the Realist rejoins; one eye is on constitutionalism and the other on power. Power demands that a state be willing to ally with any other state; constitutionalism forbids a state to ally with tyrants. The member states of the Atlantic Alliance have been spared this dilemma because a dominant power, the United States, has ensured that all of them are constitutional; it did this amid the ruins of old Germany in 1945 and by long pressure on the politics of France and Italy and Spain; give it more time with Greeks and Turks. Elsewhere, beyond the reach of imperial power, the dilemma is acute. Remember, please, that the purpose of the Rationalist state is to defend the interests of its citizens as they toil towards the mirage of security associations and a world federation. On the one hand, it should not ally with a tyranny because the alliance will have no foundation in society; tyrants are men of mere power, unpredictable, perhaps aggressive; their subjects, while accepting the alliance as defending national independence, will loathe it as helping the tyrant; the alliance will be unstable, impermanent, insecure; it will be, in short, in every way an affront to the principle of constitutionalism within and between states. But, on the other hand, the tyranny has at least some power; an alliance with it can help defend the Rationalist state; so an alliance with it is rational.

The Rationalist resolves the contradiction in practice by giving priority to power and postponing constitutionalism. He voices his dislike and misgivings enough to irritate the tyrant, but allies with him all the same. He excuses himself on the grounds that protecting the independence of the tyrannical state is at least a start towards constitutionalism; if it were to lose its independence to a powerful aggressor tyranny, its progress would be heavily retarded. Only by accepting the odious ally now can the Rationalist help to produce the decent associate of the future.

The Realist concludes like this: whatever the Rationalist's dreams for tomorrow, in practice he acts today like a Realist. He agonizes but he allies with anybody. So too does the Natural Law Man; his excuse is derived from the double-effect principle; if he allies with a murderous regime, this is to defend the common good, not the murders. So too does the Fideist; his excuse is that he is not truly allying with the infidels; he is making use of them. Whatever the reasoning, all in practice say with Winston Churchill, at the time of Britain's alliance with Stalin's Soviet Union, 'If Hitler invaded Hell, I would make at least a favourable reference to the Devil in the House of Commons.'[8] For the fact is that, in international relations, the search for power necessarily has priority. A Realist has no liking for tyrants. Machiavelli prefers a republic to a Borgia. Moreover, as Raymond Aron wrote, 'in the twentieth century, a great power weakens itself if it refuses to serve an idea'.[9] A great power thus does well to be a constitutional state and to proclaim this for imitation by the world. It does well to introduce the courtesies of constitutionalism into its alliances and into international relations generally. But it must not lose sight of realities. The constitutional principle belongs to the domestic life of states. The principle of relations between independent states, including alliances, will always be power.

The Rationalist has the last word: it is true that I ally with tyrants; but tyrannies, as even the Realist goes some way to admitting, are not a necessary feature of the human condition; alliances with them are merely a prudent expedient to which I am forced from time to time. Constitutionalism is the ideal, and it is a valid one, and to be worked towards. A constitution is the framework of that association which is the state, and it could be

---

[8] *The Second World War*, vol. iii, ch. 20.
[9] 'Une Philosophie de la politique étrangère', in *Revue Française de Science Politique*, 3(1) (Jan. 1953), 91.

the framework of associations of states. I grant that states are less sociable than individual men, and less inclined to admit the freedom and equality of other states, because they are unequal in power, and so less willing to commit themselves to an association of peaceful procedures and mutual defence. The Fideist thinks that the only force strong enough to overcome this selfishness of states is the Faith; that is, the amalgamation of the separate states into one community of the Faithful. The Natural Law Man relies on natural restraint of the sovereign mentality, so that citizens and statesmen aim at the common good of all. Both these conceptions are false, I say, because in condemning selfishness among states they go to the opposite extreme of demanding altruism. It is Rationalism that holds to the mean for men and states, co-operative individualism. What is needed is the reinforcement of the rationality of peaceful procedures between states by the integration of the interests of peoples. This is the basis of constitutionalism within states and could be the basis in relations between states, harder though it is to achieve there. Politics is not divided, as the Realist thinks, between domestic and foreign. There is one world.

9

Intervention

WHENEVER in world politics I hear the cry 'Intervention!' or 'Non-intervention!', says the Historicist, I am sure that those who raise it will turn out to be in the grip of a theory. Take the Realist, for example. On first hearing, she sounds gratifyingly dismissive of theory, and sensitive to history; but listen carefully. When a dispute breaks out in a foreign state that affects my state, says the Realist, I do not waste time by trying to define such concepts as 'non-intervention' in the 'internal' affairs of 'independent', 'sovereign' states, still less by trying to guide policy by them. I look at the political map; on this map, the important features are the lines of power running between capital city and countryside and beyond into neighbouring states and the world at large; legal frontiers and correspondingly the legalism 'non-intervention' matter only to the extent that people of importance in the dispute say they do. Even used politically, the concept is vague; as Talleyrand said, non-intervention 'is a metaphysical and politic word that means just about the same as intervention'.[1] To do nothing in politics is to do something. Non-intervention respects the outward 'sovereignty' of a state, while perhaps permitting the real content to collapse.

I am equally untroubled, the Realist continues, by the opposite theory that states sometimes have a duty to intervene in other states in the cause of universal human rights. To be sure, I always prefer a prosperous polity to an indigent tyranny; I wish well to all states in this respect; but, in order to succeed, they need a foundation of well-organized power; and it is not the business of my state to go around the world trying to provide this for others. Sometimes, my state will engage in 'nation-building' in some region of the world; but it will always

---

[1] 'C'est un mot métaphysique, et politique, qui signifie à peu près le même chose qu'intervention.' See Herbert Butterfield and Martin Wight, *Diplomatic Investigations* (London, 1966), 115.

do so with an eye to its own needs, and these will never be the same as the needs of the nations concerned. For example, in the 1950s, the Soviet Union and the United States, for their own purposes, gave economic aid to the Southern countries; this helped create military dictatorships and large bureaucracies, but this was not the same as strong government. Until countries achieve this for themselves or have it forced upon them by outright invasion and absorption, the outsider is foolish to worry himself or them about human rights.

The only good reason for concern with human rights abroad is propaganda: an opponent state may be able to embarrass you on the matter or you may be able to embarrass him. In the usual way with propaganda, this requires the existence of people who genuinely believe in the value of campaigning for human rights around the world. These people are the audience and they also provide the necessary camouflage. Under the Carter administration in the United States, following the Helsinki Accords with the Soviet Union, 'Conservatives, who had become increasingly suspicious of *détente* wanted to use human rights as ammunition in an ideological confrontation with the Soviet Union, while liberals saw human rights as a means of atonement for past United States support of authoritarian regimes.'[2] These winds of opinion were just right for launching a propaganda attack on the Soviet Union.

Returning to the substance of our topic, a decision whether or not to intervene in a foreign state should be taken without preconceptions and solely in the light of the particular circumstances prevailing. I have some maxims to offer as guide-lines.

First, an intervention must always be presented as defensive. If you are a small power, your action will alarm neighbouring states; if you are a great power, it will alarm the world. 'Is this aggrandizement? Who will be next?', and so on. Reassurance must be given. A great power can easily do this when it is intervening in a state within its sphere of influence. Its opponents will make a propaganda uproar over the affair, but in reality, no one is much alarmed. The great power is only defending what it already has; the sovereignty of the target state was limited already. Neither states that want to expand nor those on the

[2] William Hazleton, 'Morality and National Security, A No-Win Situation for the Carter Administration', *International Relations*, 7(3) (May 1982), 2100.

defensive try seriously to roll back an established sphere of influence. Eighteenth-century Europe tried to save Poland so long as it was a bulwark against Russia; once it had been partitioned, Europe troubled no more, except sentimentally. When the peacemakers of 1919 revived the dead state, the result was a generation of bloodshed, until it disappeared again under Russian control. Ordinarily and rightly, no one struggles for the independence of a state for its own sake except itself. States accept a powerful established order. They look for advances in fluid areas.

When a great power intervenes outside its sphere of influence or a small power intervenes anywhere, it must present its action in some other fashion as defensive. The Soviet Union was unusually neglectful of this when it intervened in Afghanistan in 1979; perhaps it thought that the area was not fluid, and that the world considered Afghanistan to be within its sphere. The usual tactic is to present your intervention as counter-intervention. In times when the rhetoric of international politics is ideological, this is easy: the activities of a Communist Party in a state can be denounced as tantamount to intervention by the Soviet Union; the profiteering oligarchy of a state is an arm of the American capitalist octopus; you are simply counter-intervening. At other times, a great or small intervening power will have to present the target state as in some other way a threat to its security. Helpful here is the fact that there is usually some sort of truth in this.

My second maxim, the Realist continues, is a warning that the people that interveners most easily fool are themselves. Statesmen, news media, and public are quick to jump to the conclusion that a dispute in a foreign state that seems to matter to them really matters to them. They read history and experience arbitrarily, without the guidance of power analysis. If they have scarcely heard of the state, they assume that the dispute must have the same importance as a similar dispute they remember somewhere else. If they have close connections with the state, they suppose that what is happening there now is a continuation of what happened there before. The monarchies of Europe, remembering 1789 in France, believe that they are all endangered by revolution in Spain in 1820. Everyone should read Castlereagh's Cabinet minute of the time for its warning against intervening upon 'abstract and speculative principles of precaution'.[3]

In the grip of abstract and speculative principles, the United States intervened continually for a generation after 1945. In doing so, it experienced the fact that an intervention can become the most intractable problem in politics. An intervention has not just some but all the most difficult characteristics of politics. You are in a foreign country; the matter is essentially civilian, not military; warfare may be of the guerrilla kind; you are operating with an ally; the aim of the operation is to achieve his interest, not (immediately speaking) yours; he, if anyone, has legitimacy in the eyes of the population, not you; he has, in consequence, much control over you. Above all, if you have great power, you cannot use it; for if you do, you alter the problem but do not solve it. You either turn the country into a desert or a local war into a regional or world war, or an intervention into imperial control of a repressed, disaffected, and stagnant satellite. The United States avoided this last hazard; the Soviet Union in Eastern Europe did not.

Always, continues the Realist, expect counter-intervention. The sight of a state exerting and perhaps extending its power invariably provokes other states to do the same. Their reaction may be forceful or merely propagandistic, brutally direct or subtle, indirect and unexpected; this depends on their opportunities; but some reaction there will be, adding to the cost and length of the operation. There is no escaping this hostility even where there is ideological agreement. The powers were united in 1820 in their detestation of the Spanish revolt, but they could not agree to any one of them marching an army into Spain. When France did so, Canning intervened; he resolved that 'if France had Spain, it should not be Spain "*with the Indies*". I called the New World into existence to redress the balance of the Old.'[4] The foundations of the Monroe Doctrine against outside intervention in Latin America were hereby laid. Ideological differences exacerbate the hostility of the powers to unilateral intervention but always fundamentally their anxiety is about power.

---

[3] 5 May 1820. See Kenneth Bourne, *The Foreign Policy of Victorian England, 1830–1902* (Oxford, 1970), 198–207.

[4] Harold Temperley, *The Foreign Policy of Canning, 1822–27* (London, 1925), 584.

Finally, says the Realist, never expect gratitude. The benefits from the intervention or counter-intervention have to lie in the struggle itself or in the victory; what happens afterwards cannot be counted on. The faction that you have helped to win power will continue to be your ally only to the extent that it continues to need you. Ideological brotherhood makes no difference to these realities. A story told of the Austrian statesman Schwarzenberg is *ben trovato*: resentful that his country should be indebted to Russia for intervening in Hungary in 1849, he said, 'The world will be astonished at the extent of our ingratitude.' When four years later Russia was attacked by Britain and France, Austria did nothing to help Russia and, indeed, threatened to join its attackers.

Now, says the Historicist, I will give you my judgement on these guide-lines offered to you by the Realist about intervention: they are superficially attractive but basically fraudulent. Their down-to-earth dismissal of theory conceals a theory; their appeals to the evidence of history are an abuse of history. For consider the basis of Realist maxims. They may appear to the unwary to be factually based, empirical, derived by some inductive process from a study of history, and systematically tested. But no such process is possible. History does not generate maxims. The maxims are derived from the Realist's theory that the nature of politics is a struggle for power.

Besides this, the Realist's maxims have another failing. They may appear to give her decisive guidance in the situations that face her, but what really happens is that in any given situation she has an array of relevant but contradictory maxims, and she has to decide in the end between them. For example, a splendid rule in political action is: 'Go as far as you can see, and then see how far you can go'; but, on the other hand, you have Lloyd George's dictum, 'Nothing is more fatal than to try to leap a chasm in two stages.' So the Realist has to decide; and, having made her decision, she propounds the chosen maxim to her fellow committee members as though it were the one self-evident guide to what ought to be done.

The Realist uses history in an arbitrary way to reinforce what she has decided. Thus, if she has made up her mind to advise against an intervention, she invokes Castlereagh's warning against proceeding on 'abstract and speculative principles of

precaution' and cites Canning's counter-intervention that strip-
ped Spain of Latin America. She would have liked to add that
history teaches that it is foolish to intervene in a revolt in such a
country as Spain when the army supports it and the people hate
you; only she could not, because this is what the French did,
and succeeded easily.

The reputation of Machiavelli and his like as historically
based political theorists is spurious. Their historical method is
in complete opposition to the true, the Historicist method.
They make of history a ventriloquist's dummy for their own
voices. 'What you call the mind of the past', says Faust, 'is at
bottom the mind of these gentlemen with the past mirrored in
it. What a sight! One look will do! A refuse-bin, a lumber-room,
at best a play about princes with excellent pragmatic maxims,
well-suited to the mouths of puppets.'[5] The true historical
method is, recognizing the continuity of human mind, to bring
the mind of the past to consciousness in one's own. The past is
then not exploited but forms the mind. At the moment of action
in politics, the past should not be used but forgotten. The mind
should make the future freely.

I come next, says the Historicist, to the Natural Law Man
and the Rationalist. While the Realist's views had an attractive
appearance with a theory concealed beneath, these two have
their theories in full view, with nothing beneath whatever. Each
has a theory of non-intervention and a theory of intervention.
All are without foundation.

A fair summary of the Natural Law Man's theory of non-
intervention is this: men have no natural right as individuals to
correct each other's conduct; they have such a right only as a
community and in the respects required by the common good.
The right is exercised by those to whom they give the authority
to do so: legislators, judges, and so on. Hence, no one from
outside a country has a right to correct the conduct of those
within it, that is, their acts, laws, systems, and ideas, by
invasion or conquest or taking sides in their disputes or the like.
The whole world, it is true, is a single community, but it does
not have a world authority; it is divided into countries, with

⁵ Johann Wolfgang von Goethe, *Faust*, pt. 1, ll. 577–85.

state authorities. These are in charge of a state. Outsiders have no authority.

The Rationalist's version has an individualist starting-point, but the same conclusion: non-intervention. Men are free and equal, they are self-determining, they have no right to impose their views on others. When they contract to form a state, that state is independent and equal and self-determining. No other state may presume to control its affairs by dictatorial interference of any sort.

Now, says the Historicist, I point out that both these theories are literally baseless. They tell us that we must not interfere in an independent state, but they do not tell us how an independent state comes to be independent. The Natural Law Man simply says that the world is divided into separate states; but how, on what basis? The Rationalist says that some men contract together to set up an independent state; but why these men and not those? In other words, what makes some people insiders, entitled to authority, and others outsiders, who must not interfere? This problem is spotlighted whenever in current politics a new state struggles to come to birth, that is, to secede from an existing state or empire. A number of men declare: 'We have decided that we shall henceforth be a separate state.' But in virtue of what are they an exclusive group so that they are entitled to make this decision by themselves?

Surely the Natural Law Man ought to say, in fidelity to his own basic principles, that the way the world is divided, the creation of new states and the amalgamation of old ones, should be decided by all who are affected, according to their best judgement of the common good of all. This would amount to saying that, on Natural Law principles, the whole world and especially neighbouring states and compatriots are entitled to intervene in the creation of states; and, from this, it surely follows that they have a right of intervention of some sort ever afterwards. What the world creates, the world can supervise. Consider, for example, the states of Latin America. Long before their resistance to United States intervention in the twentieth century, long before Canning and Monroe protected them from European intervention in the nineteenth, they began life by conquering the native kingdoms of the Indies. One argument that they used was that outsiders sometimes have a duty to take over backward states for their own good.[6] Is not this argument valid as regards some of these states themselves today?

The Rationalist, for his part, always attempts to evade historical questions. He is concerned with the timeless rationality of the social contract, not with explaining how rational men could have achieved it originally or have expected later generations to be automatically bound by it. The historical process of the original creation of a world of separate states is of little interest to him. The essential point for him is that free and equal men are entitled to segregate themselves on whatever basis they choose and make a state together. They had this natural right of self-determination in the beginning, they continue to have it today, and they will always have it. The logic of Rationalism leads in the end to the view that, if a group of men wish to secede from a state and set up a separate state, and their fellow citizens seek to prevent this, the rest of the world should consider intervening on behalf of the would-be seceders. For the principle of human independence is at stake at the most fundamental level.

At this point, a Rationalist usually draws back. Secession and the possibility of having to support it open his eyes to the enormity of saying that men, in the making of their states, are to be considered free to do as they like. There has to be some stronger reason for the fearful disruption of secession than the mere fiat of 'free' men. Would that, having attained this insight into secession, the Rationalist would then see the truth about existing states! To say that they consist of men who are 'free and equal' and that for this reason outsiders may not interfere is fantasy. Men who live in barbaric squalor are not free and equal in relation to outsiders who do not.

The Rationalist holds that men are all free and equal ultimately on the grounds that they are all rational. But rationality is historical; it differs according to time and place; to say that the people of a barbarous state are rational, exactly as we are rational, and that therefore we may not interfere with their ways is, I repeat, fanciful. Each culture has its own tradition of rationality. This fact is sometimes taken to be grounds for a rule of non-intervention: 'We have our ways, they have theirs, we

---

[6] Francisco de Vitoria, *De Indis*, pt. 3, 8th title.

have no right to interfere.' But this too is fallacious. For the
ways of many cultures include interfering in others that they
believe are barbaric; I think that this is a suspect impulse for
reasons that I gave in the second of my general statements; still, if
this is the way of a culture, who has the right to forbid it? What
could be the basis of a supracultural rule of non-intervention?

Liberal thought in the last century approved the absorption
of lower by higher, backward peoples by more advanced.
Absorption was better for Basque and Breton, Welshman and
Scot, thought Mill, than 'to sulk on his own rocks, the half-savage
relic of past times, revolving in his own little mental orbit,
without participation or interest in the general movement of the
world'.[7] Beyond Europe, most peoples were classified as 'barbarian' or 'savage'; they should take orders from the 'civilized'
states until they had progressed sufficiently to be free and
equal; meanwhile, they did not count in arguments about the
principle of non-intervention in independent states.

Throughout, the basic question about that principle survived:
among the civilized states, and, by our day, among all states
(since none may now be called 'barbarian' or 'savage') those
that think themselves more civilized have an impulse to interfere
in the ways of those they think less civilized; and why should they
not do so? Some liberals of the last century sought an answer in
their alliance with nationalism: the unit for independent statehood should be 'the nation'; members of a nation are entitled to
separate themselves, to make a state, and to participate in its
affairs; non-nationals are disqualified and should not intervene.
The difficulty about this is how to provide a rational definition
of a nation, of which men are in, which out. Here, failure has
been total.

Inevitably; for nations are not a construct of Rationalist
reason, but of reason that works itself out in history. Each
nation has been formed by a unique series of circumstances,
actions, and sufferings and continues to be shaped and reshaped,
always questionable and conflictory. State frontiers and legal
citizenship and convictions about who is and is not entitled to
take part in the affairs of the nation canalize this turbulence;
but sometimes the channels are flooded and breached and

[7] John Stuart Mill, *Representative Government*, ch. 16.

swept away, and, when the flood recedes, a new land and nation is uncovered, wider or smaller, different in who are its people. There can be no root rule of non-intervention because nations have no root frontiers. When we face a conflict in a foreign state, we have no guide in deciding what to do except understanding of the character and the beliefs of the adversaries, that is, their history. When the situation is not so much a definite conflict in a foreign state as that we detest its customs and regime and politics, we should remember that, if we intervene, either we must obliterate like a flood, or be willing to work for many years, such is the obstinate endurance of the customs of a people.

I will say more about that in a minute, the Historicist continues; for I now turn to the fact that the Natural Law Man and the Rationalist have not only a theory of non-intervention but also a theory of intervention.

The Natural Law Man's theory is this: though we have no authority over other states, we have a duty to defend innocent people from being killed. The division of the human community into separate states does not mean that we abandon our fellow men to any treatment that their fellow citizens may choose to inflict on.them. The acts, laws, systems, ideas, and disputes of the people of another state are their business alone, but the killing of some of them by others is not.[8] Killing imposes an obligation on us, not simply to argument as do wrong customs, but to coercion in defence of those being killed. The sharpest form of killing is slaughter. The widest is the continuous repression of life, that is, the continuous exclusion by one group of another from the common good, the denial to them of the political, civil, and economic rights that the citizens of a state should accord to one another: despot or oligarchs destroy the livelihood of the people; tribe subjugates tribe; colour discriminates against colour; majority persecutes minority; the metropolis of a nation or empire exploits the provinces. Such cases face outsiders with great problems of prudence; none the less, to find some way to intervene is an obligation.

The Rationalist version is as follows. Though men, being free and equal, may not impose their views on each other, there is an

---

[8] Vitoria, *De Indis*, pt. 3, 5th title.

obvious exception: they each have a natural right to enforce
respect for their freedom and equality, and this means specifically
their human rights to life, bodily security, freedom of worship and
speech, and so on. They come together to create a government
to protect these rights, each transferring his natural right of
enforcement to it. Suppose, now, the social contract is broken,
and the government fails in its duty or abuses its power.
Suppose, with Grotius, that the people are suffering tyranny,
with Vattel and Kant that they are rebelling, and there is civil
war. Cases range from a tyranny over a whole people to
oppression by some of the people of others, for example, in
plural states and empires. In all such cases, what should be the
attitude of outside states to the oppression and to rebellion or
secession?

Rationalists all answer that intervention, while not obligatory,
is permissible. They differ only on why. Some invoke the
natural right to enforce respect for human rights; for this
reason, outside states may coerce a tyrant. Others argue that,
states being independent and equal, they may never presume to
censure each other's internal conduct; but if a state has collapsed
in civil war, so that there are two rival governments, then
outsiders may give rein to their sympathy and intervene on the
side of freedom.[9]

My comment on these theories, says the Historicist, is as before
that they are useless because they lack historical foundation.
They float like balloons in an airy, abstract way over the world.
They have no anchorage in any particular time and place. The
struggle of Bohemia against the Empire in Grotius's day was
not the same as its struggle in Masaryk's day; the meaning of
'freedom', 'rights', 'the common good' was very different; and
no one can believe that 'intervention' was the same enterprise
for Frederick and the Winter Queen as for President Wilson. If
I am right in this for Bohemia, a single tradition over time, how
much the more over place for all the nations of the world!

Let me bring this philosophizing to a practical point; the ways
of a nation develop in time and place; they cannot be changed
by what these shallow theorists call 'intervention'. The most
that foreign intervention against a tyranny can achieve is to

[9] Grotius, *De Jure Belli ac Pacis*, bk. 2, ch. 20, sect. 40; ch. 25, sects. 1, 8; Emmerich de
Vattel, *Le Droit des gens*, bk. 2, ch. 4; Kant, 'Perpetual Peace', sect. 1 art. 5.

change the person of the tyrant. This may be valuable; some tyrants are worse than others from the point of view of the country and of other states. But any change more profound depends on the evolution of the country. A tyranny is a culture. The Natural Law Man and the Rationalist seem to suppose that underneath every tyrant lies an imprisoned population, full of the spirit of the common good or human rights, longing to be released. But tyrant and people are united in indifference to such ideals. Until the people change, the intervener merely removes one set of oppressors to make way for another. The sign that the country has evolved, that the culture has changed, and that the people are ready for freedom is that they themselves drive out the tyrant and do not replace him. Freedom cannot be given to them. They can only achieve it for themselves.

The judgement is sometimes made that a given people is ready for freedom but is crushed by the means of repression available to the modern tyrannical state; alternatively, that it has proved that it is ready for freedom by rising in rebellion or secession; intervention to support it is therefore well based. I smell theory defending itself with special pleading. The judgement may turn out to be true, but more likely not. I except only one great class of cases, that is, where there is strong evidence that a people is capable of free institutions and is being denied this by a tyranny that would not survive but for the intervention of a foreign power. In such cases, counter-intervention may be judicious, in order to create a balance of foreign forces within which, so far as possible, the people can decide its government for itself.[10]

In sum says the Historicist, the Natural Law Man and the Rationalist ought usually to be deterred from intervention by sensitivity to the history of the nation in question. What in fact deters them is prudence: they judge that, on the whole, they will do more harm than good. In addition, what saves the Rationalist is a fundamental aspect of his theories.

Whereas the Natural Law Man is absolutely obliged to take some form of action against oppression in a foreign country, subject only to prudence, the Rationalist is merely permitted to do so if he chooses. For the basis of politics for the Rationalist is that

[10] Mill, 'A Few Words on Non-Intervention', in *Dissertations and Discussions* (London, 1875), iii. 153–78.

men are individuals, pursuing their own interests. Rationally, they must not injure any other human being; they must defend those with whom they have contracted to form a state; but as to defending or in any way helping other human beings, they must do so only if their own interests allow it. They have at most a conditional obligation. The decision is theirs. This being so, the Rationalist continually discusses intervening for human rights in other countries but rarely does it. The interests of his state usually combine with prudence to restrain him. With heavy heart, he usually retreats from his theory of intervention to his theory of the independence of states and non-intervention.

The only occasion on which the Rationalist state can give full rein to its sympathy for oppressed people is when it is basically intervening in its own interests. It helps 'human rights', 'freedom', and 'constitutional government' in the course of helping itself. The most common case concerns security. In Rationalist theory, a state has the right in all circumstances to defend itself against injury, and this sometimes justifies intervention in another state. The protection of citizens and business corporations at risk in the turmoil of a foreign state may require it, and so, above all, may national security. Suppose with Mill that your state is menaced by another; you are a constitutional state; it is unconstitutional and under pressure from a popular party; you may help that party.[11] Alternatively (and this is how the United States saw its policy for twenty years following the Truman Doctrine of 1947) the turmoil within the foreign state seems likely to lead to the kind of government there that seeks to overthrow your kind of government. A rival great power (the Soviet Union) may have intervened to assist the process, or, at any rate, with that effect. The rival may even be seeking a regime subservient to itself or anyway that is the likely result. In other words, what is afoot is 'indirect aggression' by a great power, imperialism. This is a threat to the independence not only of the target state but of all states, including your own. You must resist by intervention or counter-intervention.

A dilemma arises for the Rationalist if the party threatening to win in a foreign country and to form an aggressive or subservient regime there is the popular party. It cannot be a constitutional party because, in accordance with Rationalist

---

[11] Mill, 'A Few Words on Non-Intervention', p. 175.

theory, constitutionalists are never aggressive or willingly subservient to foreign powers; none the less it may be the party in
this backward country that most nearly represents the will and
interests of the people. Sadly, in such circumstances, the principle
of the independence of states has to take priority over the
principle of popular will and interest. Reluctantly, intervention
against the popular party may have to be undertaken in the
name of the independence of the state. For independence is a
prerequisite of progress towards the true will and interests of
the people and their eventual constitutionalism as free and
equal men. Still more important, the independence of your
state and of all states must be secured against dangerous
regimes.

The question of intervention for human rights shades into
the question of humanitarian intervention to end great and
prolonged slaughter in foreign countries. Here, the Rationalist
has the same permission from his theory to intervene, the same
sympathetic impulse to do so, and the same regard for his own
interest, inhibiting him in practice. The Natural Law Man has
the same obligation as always to find some prudent form of
intervention, and now, nothing holding him back from the most
drastic form, the use of force. For group must be defended
against group in another country, and not now against the
diffuse deadliness of tyranny, but against a narrower, clearer
attack: massacre, genocide, civil war. The aim is not now to
change a society but simply to stop a terrible event.

Much of the violence of the world is little noticed. We cannot
get the facts, or our minds cannot take in the scale of the evil, or
we turn away because we can do nothing. The biggest case, the
Nazi genocide of the Jews, developed to full fury after world war
had started. After that war, the new Communist regime in
China killed several million people it did not want. The same
happened in 1975 in Cambodia. In Indonesia in 1965, the army
reacted to an attempted *coup d'état* by killing many hundreds of
thousands of Communists. The Pakistan military regime in
1971 killed still more people in its attempt to stop the secession
of Bangladesh. In the Nigerian civil war, which went on for
three years in the 1960s, about one million people died. Lesser
killings, still often running into tens of thousands, happen all
the time somewhere in the world.

In the Natural Law Man's view, outsiders could sometimes act in such cases. They could stop the killing and take the country under administration temporarily. Organizing this is one of the duties of states. The practical problems are hard and require much debate: for example, the rival merits of setting up mechanisms for collective intervention or of reaching tacit understandings among the powers; the appropriate roles of world and region and of great, medium, and small powers; conventions on information, timing, extent of authority, terminus, repetition; and so on.

The main obstacle, which prevents even thought about these problems, is, according to the Natural Law Man, the prejudice of states. This consists of their current fears and suspicions of one another (for ·example, ideological, post-imperial, and so on) but it runs deeper than this into their understanding of statehood. They turn away from the natural belief that they exist as separate states for the common good of the human community and that therefore they have an obligation to the people of other states in life-or-death situations. Their ideas are distorted by Fideism or Realism or Rationalism so that they think they exist only for their own ends: the Faith, or Power, or the National Interest. Their citizens assume with great bravery that they should, if necessary, die defending their country, but equally assume that they should not be sent to die to save the lives of foreigners. So long as these are the dominant ideas among states, intervention in a foreign country is not likely to be disinterested, and, even to the extent that it is, no other state will believe this. Here is the final inhibition on action by states. Ever ready to denounce the motives of another for intervening in some pitiable country, the certain prospect that they themselves would be denounced completes their own discouragement from action. The case for apathy in the face of killing seems conclusive. The exceptional interventions such as those in Bangladesh, Cambodia, and Uganda in the 1970s were glorious and also shameful; shameful not on the part of the interveners, India, Vietnam, and Tanzania, not on the part of the states that denounced them, but on the part of all of them because of their common, pusillanimous ideas about the responsibilities of statehood.

My comment on this, says the Historicist, is that, like all

Natural Law thought, it is based on a contradiction: intervention in defence of other human beings, dying in distant parts of the world, is said to be a natural law of humanity, and yet the fact is acknowledged that people do not do it. In Natural Law thought, a truth to be true must always be true; so why, at the beginning of history, did tribes not intervene, and why today do states not? It is no use saying that their natural ideas have always been distorted by other ideas; a truth to be true must be true sometimes; otherwise, it is just a fantasy. I think myself that it is possible that the world will organize itself for humanitarian intervention. The nineteenth century had the idea of 'the civilized powers' intervening. In our time, the idea of 'world' may become real, and intervention to stop great suffering may be part of this. If people want this, let them argue for it; but bringing in a theory that intervention is and always has been natural is no help at all.

As a way of summarizing the errors I have been censuring, I will comment on Marxism. For Marxism is not an independent theory of intervention, any more than it is of international politics generally, but an amalgam of the errors of Natural Law, Rationalism, Realism, and Fideism. Marxism consists, in the first place, of the universalism of Natural Law and Rationalism; not, of course, as to content; it dismisses 'the common good' and 'human rights' as bourgeois deceits; but as to the underlying notion that there are truths about social organization that are valid for all societies everywhere. It recognizes as a weakness of Natural Law and Rationalist theories their timeless, static quality and so includes a historical ingredient, the idea of the development of societies; but not, of course, a genuine ingredient; there is no respect for the history of societies; they must all progress according to a single theory.

Marxism suffers from the same sort of contradiction as Natural Law: it offers a law of history, but also says that people will not keep this law unless you stir them up to do so. Like Natural Law and Rationalism, it preaches that men ought to intervene in distant parts of the world or anyway are permitted to do so. However, as soon as Marxists are saddled with responsibility for running the foreign policy of a state, the biggest element in their ideas becomes Realism: they intervene or not as seems best for the survival or expansion of their state. Marxism turns out to mean in practice whatever the state operating it says it is. As Meinecke said of the principles of the French Revolution, universal ideas are always in reality somebody's nationalism.[12] At the same time, Marxists make bad Realists. Their ignorance of the history of anywhere, which is the result of their preoccupation with theory, means that they do not understand the people among whom they are intervening, and are soon much disliked by them. Yet this and all the other exposures of the true nature of Marxism do not lead to its demise. People recoil from its practical defects, but continue none the less to work tirelessly on the theory. For the final ingredient in Marxism is Fideism. People want it as a faith.

I come in this way, says the Historicist, to my final opponent, the Fideist. Let me make plain that I have no quarrel with customary religion. I see the part played in the history of nations by their national religions and by religious beliefs in the sufferings and struggles of the proletariat. Religious attitudes are equally evident among those who nowadays think in terms of 'international community' and 'world'. At the present time, many men repudiate formal creeds but are none the less religious. Man's deepest determinant, unconscious mind, is the outcome of 'immemorial existential situations'; the men of today are descended from *homo religiosus*, and in all their ways cannot escape this history.[13]

What I attack is Fideism because it sets truth against custom. It claims contact with an eternity beyond history. It purports to bring into the development of nation, proletariat, and world a transcendent to be used to control that development. It is the most virulent form of the delusion that men can know timeless universals. It leads not merely to errors of statecraft and periodic revolutionary outbursts of unreason, as do the theories of the Natural Law Man, the Rationalist, and the Realist, but to the continuous disruption or degradation of human community. For if a society once turns from the development of its customary religion to the reform of that religion by appeals to eternal truth, the question at once arises, whose revelation of eternal

---

[12] Quoted in Richard W. Sterling, *Ethics in a World of Power: The Political Ideas of Friedrich Meinecke* (Princeton, NJ., 1958), 71.

[13] Mircea Eliade, *The Sacred and the Profane*, trans. Willard R. Trask (London, 1959), 209.

truth is the valid one, and the society may have to prepare for civil war. Or if a society at one end of the world is visited by a universal religion from the other, China, say, by Rome, the outcome is either superficial compatibility, with underlying imperviousness to the alien mentality, or the weakening of the traditional system of morality. Another historical possibility is a society united in its belief in a transcendent religion, a society in which men are distracted from human community by an other-worldly love, and an original eruption of energy subsides into languor and memories of past greatness.

In the energetic phase of a universal religion, it is supremely disruptive in world politics because it is totally interventionist. It does not give a mere occasional licence to intervene; claiming to transcend the significance of independent statehood altogether, it gives continuous licence. Within the Camp of the Faithful, within Christendom, say, or the *dar al-Islam*, states have strictly speaking no internal affairs; the Faithful everywhere expect to take a hand in politics anywhere from the Escorial to Magdeburg or Tunis to Baghdad. Outside the Camp of the Faithful, states, being infidel, have no claim to respect; missionaries will come to teach them, not to learn; diplomatists, to conspire, not negotiate; and a complete campaign of subversion will continue until the time has come for conquest. So extreme are the pretensions of Fideism that the word 'intervention' loses all meaning in the amalgamation of domestic and foreign politics into one undifferentiated chaos.

The Historicist concludes: one final word against all my opponents. If they have any truth at all, if their abstract, universal, timeless verities have any roots in the world, it is in a world that is gone. Theories are based on past facts, faiths refer to past revelations. They thus have a powerfully conservative effect on the mind. Old dogma impedes intelligence in grasping the problems of the future. The phenomena fossilized in theories of 'independence', 'sovereignty', 'intervention', and 'non-intervention' are actually changing continuously. So are wider, related phenomena. The frontiers of states are crossed not only by intervention but by world social interaction. New forms of interaction are multiplying in world society. The damage that each centre of change can do to the rest is growing. States try to protect themselves, demanding that other states control the change, or setting up their own controls. Whether as regards intervention or this broader form of incursion, new thought is continually needed on the idea of a frontier, that is, on the relationship of one to all, a part to a whole, on what each has a right to and what is an injury; and, following from that, on desirable new techniques of international control. What is least needed in this process is fixed ideas, theories, and creeds; what is most needed is the sense of continuing a long history of human creativity.

The Fideist has the right of reply, and says this: the Historicist calls me the arch-interventionist. Not so! Is it I that make the desert that he names 'world social interaction'? Is it I that abet the penetration of all frontiers by free trade, investment, monetary movement, migration, drugs, by aggressive technologies, fashionable styles, moral modernity, pollution, and disease that smash down all differences between traditional cultures and reduce the world to a single, homogeneous, lewd, and ugly degradation? No, it is the Realist who abets this, and the Natural Law Man with his simple idea of a community of mankind, and, above all, the Rationalist with his vision of a world-wide cosmopolis. The Historicist neither encourages nor discourages, but gives us no defence.

For my part, all that I seek to spread over the whole world is a single spirit, the Holy Law. I desire, unlike the others, the preservation of the variety of cultures and nations. The affairs of the peoples of the world should not be managed by shallow internationalists, but entrusted to men accustomed by tradition. So the family, the village, the town, tribe, nation, and culture will be defended against the false freedom that permits invasion by what destroys, golden, worthless, sand, death. They will also have a far greater defence. The forces that I have listed that penetrate all frontiers, the hectic commerce of the world, have a single source: not just greed, not just materialism, but more Satanic yet, Man's assertion of himself, facing ultimate despair. The Law rebukes this proud spirit, and replaces it with joy.

Our life is organized by frontiers. Who must be asked to the wedding; who may and may not do this trade; who may take part in our *coup d'état*, and who may only write a book about it? A German scholar of language wrote, 'At the beginning stands

the hedge.'[14] Everyone knew, long before the Historicist joined
our company two centuries or so ago, that our frontiers are vital
and yet always uncertain, contentious, and changing, because
man can speak to man, culture to culture, tradition to tradition,
society to society, across them. The question is: when in this
process should men be dictatorial, use force? The Historicist
condemns the Realist for her pawky maxims and the Natural
Law Man and the Rationalist for their theories. He himself
gives us no guidance. When we have followed in all our affairs
our national tradition and are now face to face with another
tradition, and the question is killing, he gives us no guidance.
He gives us only understanding when the killing is over,
hindsight, a sense of tragedy, history.

The Historicist condemns the Natural Law Man and the
Realist and the Rationalist as to all their thought for claiming
that it is valid across time and space; but his arrogance of
reason is still higher. For these three say that, when a man acts,
he does so sometimes reasonably and sometimes not; he handles
skilfully or stupidly the history of a matter and the universal
truths bearing on it. The three of them disagree on what these
truths are, but they agree, as does any sane person, that a man
acts sometimes reasonably, sometimes not. The Historicist is
not content with this; he says that there is a longer perspective
in which, whatever a man does, he acts reasonably. Historicism
has its universal truth, valid across time and place: good and
evil are reconciled in the rationality of history.

Pride is the source of this philosophy, and diabolical are its
effects. Men no longer have final responsibility for their acts,
good or ill, and the dignity that goes with this; what they do is
superficially done by them but finally by forces of history,
biological and spiritual and social, that surpass them. Their
reaction to this philosophy has been exhilaration, frenzy, cruelty,
and destruction unimaginable, and despair. I say, for my part,
that we cannot understand our history. As individuals' 'scarcely
anyone is clever enough to recognize all the harm that he has
done'.[15] As communities, we cannot claim to see how the good
and evil that we do is reconciled. Men cannot forgive themselves;
only God.

[14] Jost Trier, 'Zaun und Mannring', *Beiträge zur Geschichte der deutschen Sprache und Literatur*, 66 (1942), 232–64.   [15] La Rochefoucauld, *Maximes*, 269.

10

War

How can the sufferings of war be justified? Think of the
soldiers:

> Lines of grey, muttering faces, masked with fear,
> They leave their trenches, going over the top,
> While time ticks blank and busy on their wrists,
> And hope, with furtive eyes and grappling fists,
> Flounders in mud. O Jesus, make it stop.[1]

Think of the bereaved. When the bomber pilot was killed,
'his mother was distraught with grief and kept on sobbing,
"We'll never get over it, we'll never get over it." At last her
husband turned to her. "No", he said, "we'll never get over it.
But we will get used to it" '[2] Think of the corruption of the
whole of society that follows from war. There can be no
justification in reason for all this affliction (it is the Fideist who
speaks), only in Faith. Nothing can sustain the soldier, console
the bereaved, maintain the strength of society but crusade.
'War is a crusade or it is a crime. There is no half-way house.'[3]
Only pacifism or Faith have true understandings of war.

Consider first, the Fideist says, not our own wars but the way
in which we inflame the wars of others. Since the Second World
War, there have been scores of lesser wars, with many millions
dead. This was made possible by arms exports from the United
States, the Soviet Union, Britain, France, and other states. Let
us see the foolishness of reason in this matter: how it justifies
this trade; how it destroys the justification; how it would
restrict the trade, but cannot do so on its own principles.

Sometimes put forward as a justification of the arms trade by
Britons and Frenchmen, and certainly their strongest motive, is

---

[1] Siegfried Sassoon, 'Attack'.
[2] Roderick Strange, *The Catholic Faith* (Oxford, 1986), 28.
[3] I think R. H. Tawney said this but I cannot find where.

their own security and wealth. For, they say, they need a national arms industry to protect their countries; and this industry, like many others, must be large to be economic, and so it must have export markets. Also, arms exports give employment, and they help greatly with the balance of payments of the nation.

These arguments are false even in reason. There is no economic reason why arms exports should not be phased out of national employment and the balance of payments. Rather than maintain separate national arms industries, the Atlantic Alliance and Warsaw Pact countries might each create amongst themselves a single large industry and market. Especially those who talk of an Atlantic or European community should seize on this possibility. Certainly it is the proper course for the Camp of the Faithful. Whatever the solutions to these problems, one truth is as plain to moral reason as to Faith: they should not be solved at the cost of others. To think that your own security and wealth justify selling deadly weapons to others is damnable.

Governments offer a higher-sounding justification: the customer states demand the arms; they are independent states, entitled to make their own decisions about the quantity of arms that they need for their security; they denounce any talk of limitation by the supplier states as paternalism, even imperialism; hence, arms exports are morally blameless. There is an irony in this governmental justification of the arms trade. It is exactly the justification given in earlier generations by the private arms dealers. Governments took control of the arms trade after the Second World War precisely to end the scandal of 'the merchants of death'. In the event, they have taken over the argument of the merchants along with their business.

The argument amounts to this: we are entitled to sell arms to people to whatever extent suits us because they are entitled to kill each other to whatever extent suits them. The relationship of the Northern states of the world towards the Southern states that their reasoning has led them into may be summarized as follows. The Northern states gave up their godless empires, which at least created a kind of peace and order, *pax Babylonis*. They substituted a multitude of independent states in the name of freedom, equality, and economic progress. They now watch the collapse of freedom, equality, and economic progress, while busily selling the armaments which complete the destruction of peace and order. The darkness that they have made is blackest over Jerusalem. The 'city of peace' is the centre of war.

Each pleads: 'If our country were to limit its sale of arms, competitors would step in and increase their supply. Initially, existing competitors would do this; what Britain did not sell, the French would. Supposing, later, that all exporters were to agree on restraint, the result would simply be increased production in the customer countries. The only effect of our self-denial would be to promote the proliferation of armaments industries in the world, and, furthermore, at great economic cost. For the reason for trade, including the arms trade, is that it is the cheapest way of satisfying demand. New armaments industries that sprang up as a result of restraint of international trade would be a waste of resources. The hope of the naïve that less expenditure by the Southern countries on arms imports would lead to more expenditure on peaceful economic progress is doubly doomed to disappointment.'

This apparently reasonable plea by arms exporters is rebutted even by reason. There are, to be sure, group wrongs, that is, wrongs that all agents should stop doing collectively because if any one of them stopped separately, he would suffer injustice. But the arms trade is not of this kind. It is a separate wrong, that is, a wrong which each agent ought to stop doing, irrespective of what the others choose to do; for, though he might suffer temporary inconvenience, he would not suffer injustice. No one defends drug-selling with the plea that other drug-sellers would step in or that the customers would concoct their own drugs inefficiently. Why then have some the effrontery to seek to justify arms-selling in this way?

Besides, it is not inevitable that, if our country sells less, others will fill the gap. The clever economic arguments presume that the level of demand for arms in the world is given; but this is not true. The level of demand is created by the intensity of competitive salesmanship. More profoundly, it depends on the degree of prestige accorded internationally to the military dimension of politics and to armaments. The Northern countries, especially the United States and the Soviet Union, are the leaders of opinion in this. If they militarize the character of international politics in innumerable ways culminating in an obsession with the military balance between them, they must expect the prestige of militarism to climb in the rest of the world and the demand for armaments to soar. The liberal notion is too simple that armaments cause conflicts; and equally simple is the notion that the conflicts of the world are given and determine the level of armaments. Fascinating to men is the glitter of the sword and the fame of battle; decisive among them is what counts as manliness. Those who have the supreme power of war or peace in the world settle that.

Under the torrent of arms exports, beneath the selfishness and greed and sordid pleading, there is a small justifiable international arms trade. In any imaginable world, there must be provision for gift or sale of arms to allies and for purchase by neutrals. In the world envisioned by the Faithful, control of the arms trade would be in clean and honest hands, and the guide-line would be to ban commercial motives and to consider only whether arms sent to these or those people would advance the cause of the Faith. The world prescribed by the men of reason is, at first sight, similar: governments shall regulate arms exports, not according to commercial considerations, but political. So, for example, each of the North Atlantic arms exporters has laid down guide-lines for itself: arms designed for internal repression are not to be supplied to tyrannies; arms for external security are to be supplied in ways and amounts which do not worsen conflicts, that maintain a balance between enemies, and so on.

Also, from time to time, these countries have discussed common restraint and have attempted discussions on restraint with the Soviet Union. Let us acknowledge the sincerity of these efforts. At the same time, let us acknowledge that they could not possibly have any effect. They could not succeed even in theory. Natural law theory asserts a principle that opposes selfishness and greed, the principle of the common good; but natural law theory is completely inoperable amongst sinful, fallen men. Rationalist theory purports to harness and harmonize selfishness. But selfish men cannot curb their own selfishness unilaterally, irrespective of what the others do; so the drive to national, commercial, or political gain can never be curbed by unilateral national guide-lines. The selfish men must make an international agreement on restraint; but if they did, they could not keep it; for one or other of them would eventually see superior gain in breaking the agreement, and the others would rationally have to follow. Rationalism, on its own principles, can never confine the arms trade to a size that Rationalism thinks justifiable.

I will now leave the subject of arms, the Fideist continues, for the yet greater one, war itself. My message will be the same. I will show how the efforts of reason to confine war to what is reasonable are contradictory and break down in confusion and are utter foolishness.

First, the Natural Law Man. He offers us a set of ideas known as the 'just war'. While war is always an evil and usually wrong, sometimes it is the only way of stopping injustice. The conditions that must be satisfied are, first, that you have proper authority to make war. Ordinarily, this means that you have been recruited to fight by the legitimate government of your state, but the matter is complex where there is a government-in-exile, or an international guerrilla campaign, or a rebellion, or a situation of lawlessness. You must, next, have a just cause: that is, a wrong is being done, for example, you or others are suffering tyranny, or another state is infringing your state's independence, unjustly seizing its territories, injuring your fellow citizens, wrongly refusing trade in the commodities of the earth, obstinately insulating its own citizens from intercourse with the outside world. You must, thirdly, have right intention; that is, you must intend justice and peace and nothing else. There must be no using pretexts to satisfy ambition or the desire for revenge. There must be a strong likelihood that the wrong can be righted by force, no pride or recklessness, no disproportion between the likely destruction and the wrong suffered, no hatred of the enemy, and no cruelty in ways of fighting him.

If a war satisfies these conditions, it is a just war. There is no certainty, on this matter, only opinion. Still for citizens and statesmen to question themselves under the three headings exerts a pressure on them to be just. Most of the time, people agree on what is just, so most of the time they are at peace. The fact that, when they go to war, both sides proclaim that their war is just does not show that the concept is inane; on the contrary, this is an acknowledgement of its importance.

This Natural Law reasoning is very fine, no doubt, declares

the Fideist, but there is one obvious flaw: each side decides for itself that its war is a just war and not a war of selfishness, greed, error, or folly. This is surely intolerable in reason! People can plausibly claim to decide what is just in a matter concerning third parties when they act as judge, arbitrator, counsellor, or wise friend to one of the parties. But how can people claim to decide this in their own case? And, above all, with enough certainty to go killing other people! Let reason call war by whatever name it pleases but, in very reason, let it not call war 'justice'!

The Natural Law Men know this weakness in their doctrine. They try to put it in the best possible light. They demand that a belligerent be no mere belligerent but enact a higher, impartial role. Among the Romans and successor imperialists, the role was that of peacemaker:

> Roman, remember by your strength to rule
> Earth's peoples—for your arts are to be these:
> To pacify, to impose the rule of law,
> To spare the conquered, battle down the proud.[4]

In Christendom, the higher role that the belligerent should enact was that of a judge; a just war was a judicial punitive war against foreign malefactors. You might have expected the Natural Law tradition to teach that the justice that states should seek in war is the same as in their domestic politics, that is, the common good; but, so far, Augustine's idea of the state and justice has persisted as regards war: states, if they are not to be robbers, should act like judges.[5]

This myth of war is powerful so long as there is only one state, Rome, as one judge surrounded by barbarians. Even when there are many states, the myth continues strong so long as the states see themselves as one community in succession to Rome and as Christendom. For then, underlying the diversity of their laws, there is a single justice; and so in any conflict, one side is wrong and the other side right; and, in war, one is a malefactor and the other is a judge, acting on behalf of the community. When the sense of community fades, the myth is perpetuated

[4] Virgil, *Aeneid*, vi. 851, trans. R. Fitzgerald (New York, 1983).
[5] Michael Donelan, 'Grotius and the Image of War', *Millennium*, 12(3) (Autumn 1983) 233–43.

only because no one can think of anything better.[6] When a world of sovereign secular states emerges, when judicial authority is derived from separate, natural right, not from the community, the myth collapses under the absurdity of having to picture a set of judges all making war in judgement on one another.

All this is to discuss the myth as myth. But I go further, says the Fideist; it is a lie. It is at best a noble lie, a desperate attempt by Augustine to clothe the nakedness of the infidel state, and by his successors to dignify the so-called Christian kings. For the truth is that the Romans made war and created their empire by using a series of blatant pretexts. The *pax romana* was just, not in the motives of the Romans, but only in that God made use of the Romans to break the pride of the nations. The kings of Christendom made war in selfishness and greed, dressed up in legalism, not as judges. The Vicar of Christ, that should have ruled them, degenerated into their rival. The ideal of judicial impartiality in one's own cause was an impossible one. The condition of modern states is still worse. They lack even a myth, a common ideal of war. They make endless wars crying 'justice', while knowing that they can give no account of what justice among states might be.

I will elaborate this point; I will discuss the modern conception of how reason can justify fighting a war, the Rationalist concep- . tion. In the eighteenth century, the Rationalist dismissed the myth that war is a judicial act. He did so, not on my grounds that it is a lie, concealing selfishness and greed, but on the grounds that, states being free and equal, they cannot presume to judge one another. He felt obliged simply to say of states going to war that each should consult its conscience scrupulously, with such aid as it could get from legal writers and, having decided that its cause was just, should respect the fact that its opponent had decided the same. However, the Rationalist was discontented by the freedom that this gave to states to act irrationally, that is, to settle disputes by force, and in the twentieth century he unveiled his desired restriction: a state should never begin a war, it should only respond. Only defensive war was legitimate; aggressive war was always wrong, and was to be condemned as 'aggression'. The Rationalist resurrected

---

[6] Francisco Suárez, 'De Caritate', Disputatio 13, 'De Bello', sect. 4, in *De Triplici Virtute Theologica*.

the judicial myth to this extent, that those who committed aggression should be put on trial at Nuremberg or Tokyo.

I ask: is this reasonable in reason's own terms? The attacker, always in the wrong? The defender, always in the right? To be sure, the Rationalist means that the attacker is always wrong in that he has taken to the use of force; right and wrong may lie differently as regards the substance of the conflict; but this should be settled by peaceful procedures. I answer reason with reason; I recall what the Natural Law Man said of peaceful procedures, that adjudication between states is a delusion, and that negotiation is equally so if the possessor of a disputed thing can merely sit complacently in possession, chanting 'No force, force is wrong.' I say more, I recall the cynical words of the Realist on this matter, and I denounce Rationalism as not merely unreasonable, but as a wicked, self-interested lie. For at any given period in world politics, some states are on top and some are on the bottom, the selfishness and greed of some is victorious, that of others, momentarily defeated. So what the Rationalist view comes down to is that the world shall be stopped with certain robbers in the ascendant. When, say, the Roman Empire or the British Empire or the Rationalist Northern states are dominant and satisfied with their loot and wish only peace, the Iron Age of war shall end, and the Golden Age of peaceful procedures shall begin. Golden for some!

The Rationalist's attempt to justify his wars amounts, I say, to this: states may fight in defence of themselves and others, even if their cause is a bad one, in the name of an ideal of peaceful procedures that is irrational. This is the thought with which the soldier is to face his death, the bereaved are to console one another, and the society is to fortify itself against the moral corruption of war! But I will move on; for it is obvious that the Rationalist's thought is at its shallowest as regards *ius ad bellum*, the right to go to war. I will follow him into deeper waters, his efforts to limit the violence once warfare has begun.

The Rationalist separates this matter of *ius in bello* completely from *ius ad bellum*. He rejects the Natural Law Man's talk of just cause in going to war, and, in most respects, his judicial punitive myth, not only on the grounds that they are inane as between independent states and encourage aggression but also because they imply that the enemy is a criminal, and so reinforce ruthlessness and cruelty in warfare against him. Whatever the rights and wrongs of the outbreak of a war, the Rationalist says, the belligerents must keep within limits in fighting each other. A state, even if fighting a defensive war and even if, therefore, its opponent is proceeding illegitimately, must disregard this fact in considering how to make war against him. All belligerents must obey rules of warfare under which some sufferings inflicted on the enemy are justifiable, others are not.

Let us see how reasonable the Rationalist's rules are. His efforts mainly have led to a structure of laws of war in the nineteenth and twentieth centuries, very elaborate compared with the religious and military codes of earlier times. Today's international humanitarian law of armed conflict has a Geneva stream, which seeks to protect the sick and wounded and prisoners of war and civilians, and a Hague stream, which seeks to regulate the weaponry and conduct of land, sea, and air fighting. I do not wish to disparage this immense, dedicated effort; I acknowledge great successes, especially at Geneva; but I point out how little overall the flood of legal wordage has done to damp down the flames of war. The peace movement has been surpassed by an overwhelming war movement. Armed forces have grown to millions, and use all the resources of advancing technology to kill each other. Civilians have been made targets of blockade and bombardment in yet more millions. States have agreed few laws regulating weaponry and methods of fighting, and those few they have swept aside at will in the heat of war.

The explanation of the increased destructiveness of modern warfare is, at first sight, the progress of technology, the means to mobilize ourselves and to destroy each other. But technology is not our master; it is driven by our ideas. Our weapons are diabolical, but the Devil is not in them but in ourselves. A submarine is, at first, only a toy with an unknown, open future; what permits us to use it as a weapon against warships, an act at first considered abominable, and later to use it to sink merchant-men and passenger liners without warning, once unthinkably disgraceful, is a change in ideas of what is permissible in war. We design bombs which destroy cities because we have come to think that killing civilians is an acceptable way of winning.

The change in our ideas towards extremism has been fuelled in the past two centuries by nationalism and ideological hatred. These are why war has become worse. The point I wish to stress is that the war movement meets no true resistance from Rationalist reason, only words; for Rationalist reason does not sustain the mentality of restraint that is fundamental to the limitation of warfare, ensuring that some weapons and methods of warfare will never be invented or, if invented, not used. Rationalist reason seeks to control us by laws when it has lost control in our minds.

Consider what the Rationalist offers men as the reason for restraint in warfare. He offers the idea of a contract. Amidst the irrationality of war, rational, self-interested men will at least want to limit the risk, where possible; they will agree not to attack one another with weapons and methods that are unnecessary to winning and are merely destructive; they will make a contract to that effect called the laws of war. As the fighting, so the moment of victory and defeat is governed by a contract, the moment when the beaten soldiers crawl from their holes, asking quarter: 'We will stop fighting, if you will spare us.' The Rationalist appeals, besides the contract of self-interest, to the sentiment of humanity: suffering that is unnecessary to winning the war is merely cruel, inhumane, and to be banned.

The Rationalist's idea of restraint in war as a contract is the extension into war of the idea of the state as a contract; so let us first follow him into these further depths. Eighteenth-century Rationalism meant by the state as a contract the particular kind of contractual association called a partnership. Look how this weakens restraint in war! For, in a partnership, every partner is accountable for the acts of every other; so in a state that is a partnership, every citizen is accountable for what the soldiers do; all therefore may be attacked, civilians as well as soldiers. Or suppose we are ruled by a modern Rationalist who conceives of the state as another kind of association, a corporation. The restraint on war is yet weaker. The corporate person is fighting; so the corporate person, civilians as much as soldiers, may be targeted; and the corporate person is responsible for the horrors committed, which is to say, all of us in general and none of us in particular. Wherever Rationalists harbour a punitive instinct towards aggressors, restraint is totally abandoned. In the Anglo-

Saxon tradition of thought, a corporate person can do wrong.
Germany can do wrong; bomb all Germans, indiscriminately.
In the Continental tradition, a corporate person cannot do
wrong; so whatever Germany does cannot be wrong.

So much for Rationalism's ideas of the state as a restraint on
extremism in warfare. As to its laws of war based on contract
and humanity, they are a wall of paper against barbarism. For
they forbid only what is unnecessary and merely destructive
and cruel. Every new possibility opened up by technology will
be represented as helpful to the prosecution of war and therefore
as necessary. The argument in committees of statesmen and
soldiers is inexorable: 'We would be unreasonable if we failed to
explore this possible new method of attack, if we bound our
hands against it by an international agreement, if amid the
exigencies of war we kept an agreement made in peace.' Those
who try to oppose this argument have no basis; they are
incoherent and sentimental. Restraint in war and laws of war
are the self-interest of states; therefore, self-interest can override
them. Humanity in warfare is what is left when necessity has
had its due; and that is, if necessary, nothing.

The Rationalists are also utilitarians. They can make rules but
only provisionally; in the end, they must calculate; in warfare,
they must count which methods will leave fewest people dead
and make the war shortest. So if bombing civilians in 1939 will
prevent a repetition of the trench warfare of 1914, they must do
this. If obliterating Hiroshima will remove the need for a
frontal assault on Japan, they must do this. Very reasonable;
except that by not prohibiting any method of warfare absolutely,
the utilitarian simply chooses among the obviously available
methods and does not search far for alternatives. By not
prohibiting any enormity absolutely, the utilitarian state is
proclaiming that the quality of people's lives does not matter,
only the quantity.

Rationalism, with the resources I have described, utility and
contract of mutual interest with the enemy and a humanitar-
ianism which is not an absolute restraint but only a residual
that operates when necessity has had its due, Rationalism, I
say, cannot with these resources restrain the furious war-
making of wrathful Man, and least of all in the days of nationalism
and ideology and other such causes which will surely arise in

the future. These enthusiasms contain within themselves no principles of restraint; nation or party or cause are the highest value; and anything must be done in their service. Rousseau argued that, war being between groups, not individual men, only the appointed agents of the group, the soldiers, may attack and be attacked, not the ordinary individual men, the ordinary citizens.[7] But this makes of the group a bloodless abstraction; and every nationalist or party loyalist or member of a movement knows that, whatever the nation or the party or the movement is, it is not a bloodless abstraction! It is an organism in which each is a cell, receiving his values and his ideas and the growth of his prosperity from the whole. In war, it is a united agent of destruction, and a single target to be destroyed; it faces life or death; restraint in fighting is cowardice or treachery. This demonic spirit strikes down Rationalism with a single contemptuous blow as it marches on its enemy.

Let us now see how that other man of reason, the Natural Law Man, withstands Apollyon. Let us see how solid is the basis that he offers for restraint in warfare. He had some influence in the peace movement of the nineteenth and twentieth centuries and in the elaboration of laws of war. I say that the incoherence of his ideas about warfare completes the explanation of why the peace movement failed.

At first sight, Natural Law thought, compared with Rationalism, is strong against barbarism. For it does not separate justice in going to war from justice in warfare; the first provides a foundation for the second. Even as we may only go to war against those who have wrongly attacked us, so, in warfare, we may only kill those who are doing the attacking. To start a war against the innocent is to defy the first principle of thought, namely, that life is good and may only be taken in defence of that good. In the course of warfare, to kill the innocent intentionally is the same defiance of the same principle. The principle is absolute. The Israelis said of their warfare in Lebanon in 1982: 'The circumstances of combat require the combatants to be tough . . . but the end never justifies the means and basic ethical and human values must be maintained in the use of arms.'[8] A state that

---

[7] *The Social Contract*, ch. 4.
[8] Kahan Commission Report, pub. 9 Feb. 1983.

defends itself by intentionally killing the innocent is defending nothing.

What counts under the principle is injurious action, not feelings; you may kill soldiers, albeit they have no ill will towards you, but not the old men in the coffee shops, full of hatred. Because warfare is done by humans, it is a social act and results in inflicting suffering not only on the combatants but on society more widely. The lives of non-combatants are dislocated; they suffer bereavement; they are killed. What is demanded by the principle is that this be undesired and unintended and not out of proportion to the military target attacked. Deciding who is a combatant and who is a non-combatant cannot be exact; roughly those whose activities are intelligible only in that a war is being fought are combatants; there is room for argument about whether some categories of people are combatants or not; but roughly most people in time of war, for all the talk of total mobilization, continue their peaceful jobs and are non-combatants. Towards both combatants and non-combatants, a final requirement is minimum force. Your aim is to stop an attack, not to kill people. This is the reason, not some supposed contract, why you must spare those who surrender, provided that they are harmless. All three requirements, discrimination, proportion, and minimum force, must control not only your warfare but the previous planning of your warfare: the design of your weapons, the disposition of your resources, the strategies you foresee, and the tactics you teach your soldiers.

These guide-lines for justice in warfare follow in the Natural Law Man's thought, as I have said, from justice in going to war, but, to express the intimacy of the connection even better, we can say that they are simply aspects of right intention. They simply detail how in war you should intend nothing but justice and peace, not killing, suffering, or destruction. The Natural Law Man may concede that the traditional picture of right intention, as judicial and punitive, reinforced ruthlessness towards the guilty, the enemy combatants, but he can argue that, on the other hand, it reinforced respect for the innocent, the non-combatants. In any case, other pictures were available in the past (notably that the two sides were like litigants and should respect each other accordingly) and still others may develop in the future (such as the idea that right intention is to seek the common good).

Reasonable as all this is, the Fideist continues, it contains a fatal contradiction. Right intention forbids hatred of the enemy; but reason knows no way of rousing the spirit of its citizens and soldiers to battle but hatred. What drives a soldier to endure at Thermopylae and in the mud of Flanders, or a sailor in Arctic waters, is loyalty to his side and hatred of the enemy; not perhaps as persons; for these he may have fellow-feeling; but collectively as 'the enemy'. Nothing else strengthens the heart of a mother who has lost one son as a second is recruited. To enrol and sustain a society at war, the news media must be mobilized to fuel anger. Reason cannot move anyone to anything, least of all to war. The roles of judge or litigant or champion of the common good are feeble inspiration. Reason cannot substitute for hatred. Reason must hate if it is to fight. There is no reason in war.

War must in reason be unrighteous. War belongs to the realm of darkness beyond the frontier of the realm of peace, to the *dar al-harb*, to the Realist realm of necessity. A man can at best say this: 'one does not cease to be a moral being when one takes up arms, even if required by military necessity to commit immoral acts. There are other tribunals to which one may be called to account.'[9] In the darkness, there is only one tribunal at which to answer and find mercy; in the necessary sinfulness, only one redemption.

Of the whole of the moral life, of the whole of politics, a man can at best say: 'I live for others.' What makes the others worth this? Of war, one can at best say: 'I die for others.' Why?

Others are worth living and dying for because they are God's. Men have value insofar as they live and die for the will of God, fighting for the cause of the Kingdom. Here is courage for the soldier, consolation for the bereaved, strength for society. Here, and only here, is justification for the killing that I do in war. My war is a holy war.

In our time, the men of reason offer a final defence of their doctrines: 'We can at least be sure that one war was rational, a just war: the struggle against Hitler and Nazism.' False! I do

[9] Michael Howard, in Howard (ed.), *Restraints on War* (Oxford, 1979), 14.

not deny that this war had to be fought; but do not call it a reasonable, just war. The causes lay not in Germany but in the whole of the West. It was a civil war of the West of which all were guilty in some degree. There were men of blood on all sides. Even the Historicist sees the folly of reason in seeking to justify one side as righteous and to condemn the other side as criminal. Hedge and ring are primordial, before good and evil. What is done in history is not done by this state or that, but is an interaction. Reason, he says, should not try to pass judgement on war but rather to understand it. War is to be understood as a time of testing of states. The cries of justice that each state raises are a tragic clash of right against right.[10]

The Historicist is correct, but he should speak of a clash of wrong against wrong. The interaction of history is one of sinfulness. Both sides in a war are sinful. There is only one way in which one side can be singled out as justified, and that is by shifting our understanding of a war to a level that transcends the human. Hitler can only be singled out as uniquely responsible and damnable if he is understood as an instrument of Satan. The nations that rose up against him were righteous in that their war against him was a crusade.

For those that die, a war is the end of the world. Their dying can only be lifted up from squalor, and the sufferings of a war be justified if the war shares in the Apocalypse. It is the onset of Armageddon, fought by the angels. It foreshadows the coming of the Imam, the Mahdi, the Prince of Peace. It is The Day. 'When that day comes, I shall set myself to destroy all the nations that fight against Jerusalem.'[11] This was the chant of the Crusaders. 'The nation and kingdom that refuse to serve you shall perish, such nations shall be utterly ruined.'[12] The world shall be made by this war the New Jerusalem.

A war is the beginning of the Last Judgement. When we, the people of the Faith, decide that we must go to war, we are not judges in our own cause. We offer our lives in what we believe to be God's cause. Judgement belongs to that higher level of understanding that surpasses men. Only God knows how far the cause is truly his, truly holy, and he will declare this in the Last Days. Meanwhile, we fight as sinners. The sufferings of

[10] Shlomo Avineri, *Hegel's Theory of the Modern State* (Cambridge, 1972), ch. 10.
[11] Zechariah 12: 9. [12] Isaiah 60: 12.

war are God's judgement on our enemy and also on us. We are forgiven the sufferings we inflict on our enemies because this is the punishment of God for their sinfulness. We too suffer because we are sinful. Augustine's idea of war as a judicial act is in the end the idea of the Divine Judge punishing all the nations.[13] Babylon is, in the end, not the protector of Israel (*utimur et nos pace Babylonis*); it is the executioner of divine justice upon Israel: 'I mean to disperse you throughout the nations, to scatter you in foreign countries, and to take your foulness from you. I shall be dishonoured by you in the opinion of the nations; and so you will learn that I am God.'[14]

The sufferings of war can never be justified, only sanctified; there is no justice in war, only holiness. The Latin Christians taught that war to be holy must conform to the natural principles of just war; the Crusades were a recapturing. The Orthodox Christians fought holy wars of defence. But I say that every war fought on behalf of the Camp of the Faithful, even one begun by it, as is sometimes expedient, is holy. The Faithful, when commanded, gather for war against the infidel or for rebellion against King of Spain, Pope of Rome, Queen of England, or any such that bow down to the Beast. They must fight until the Faith is supreme over fleshly idolatry, the Law is observed, and men are truly at peace and can truly prosper.

As to methods of warfare, the Faithful respect legal doctrines and military codes but their supreme guide is the spirit of God, which is a spirit of holy anger and of mercy. Reason, I have shown, talks of mercy but, in practice, is all anger. Faith reconciles mercy and anger thus: the storm of war shall be God's storm. Reason says that the old, the weak, and the children should not die, but it cannot protect them. Faith accepts that they will die; they share the guilt of all men and are visited in war by the anger of God. Reason says that soldiers that surrender and are harmless should be spared. Faith respects the military code that grants no quarter to those who have been offered mercy and have chosen to fight on. Faith executes them in holy anger. The Crusaders, after terrible sufferings, conquered and massacred. Cromwell wrote of Drogheda: 'I am persuaded that this is a righteous judgement of God upon these barbarous

[13] *De Civitate Dei*, bk. 1, ch. 1; bk. 5, ch. 23.
[14] Ezekiel 22: 15–16.

wretches, who have imbued their hands in so much innocent
blood; and that it will tend to prevent the effusion of blood for
the future, which are the satisfactory grounds to such actions,
which otherwise cannot but work remorse and regret.'[15] Faith
kills in order to give warning to others and thus show mercy to
them. It spares soldier and civilian if there is no divine cause to
destroy them. Those that survive the storm stand silent before
the mercy of God.

I will end this discourse on the foolishness of reason and the
need for Faith by speaking of the worst kind of war that Satan
has so far unleashed.

When the Terrorist strikes, the Rationalist hurries to suspend
his feud with the Natural Law Man about *ius ad bellum*, and,
together with him, demands to know from the Terrorist: 'How
can you claim for your use of force proper authority; or just cause;
or right intention?' The debate that follows from these questions
seems to the men of reason to destroy the credentials of many a
Terrorist, whether rebel group or repressive government.

Sometimes, though, the Terrorist satisfies the men of reason
on these questions; they support his war; they call him by some
more friendly name, such as 'freedom fighter' or 'national
security state'. The question to him then is: 'How can you
justify that aspect of your war which is distinctive, namely, the
particular kind of force that you use?' The Terrorist's reply is
crushing: 'I do not need to reason with you about this; for I only
do what you yourselves, the men of reason, do.'

The Terrorist kills clandestinely political opponents and
policemen and soldiers. He blows up old men and women and
children. But the Rationalist does these things too in his wars,
when he thinks it necessary. That is, he applauds partisans,
saboteurs, commandos, and all kinds of raiders, and men who
attempt tyrannicide. He bombs cities. His defence policy includes
nuclear deterrence, and this might lead him to kill many
millions of old men and women and children. He will avoid
these things if he can, but he will do them if necessary.

The Natural Law Man is trapped in a contradiction fully as
great: if a state relies on nuclear deterrence, it violates the
principles of just war; but if it renounces nuclear deterrence, it

[15] *The Writings and Speeches of Oliver Cromwell*, ed. W. C. Abbott (Cambridge, Mass.,
1939), ii. 127.

leaves itself defenceless against injustice. Perhaps, in the coming years, the Natural Law Man will develop new weapons that will remove this contradiction; even so, the disease discovered in his just-war doctrine will not be cured; once a doctrine has shown such a contradiction, it cannot survive.

The Natural Law Man tries to evade the contradiction by using the distinction between separate and group wrongs. Nuclear deterrence is wrong but it is not a separate wrong by each individual state, to be ended by it unilaterally; it is a group wrong of the community of states, to be ended by them multilaterally. I reply that, separate or group, nuclear deterrence remains a wrong. It remains an injustice that, however temporarily, just-war doctrine permits if injustice is not to be victorious. Nuclear weapons are the suicidal climax of the wicked centuries-old competition for power of the secular state. They are, at the same time, the catastrophe of its reasoning.

Terror, in all its forms, the burnt flesh of Algiers or Hiroshima, is the mark of the Beast. Beings that commit such acts cannot find salvation in reason but in one way only. They can be as a 'brand plucked from the burning' if what they do, however terrible, is done in the spirit of the Faith. They then see that the suffering that they inflict and endure is divine judgement upon men and their states, even to the total destruction of the world. It is Apocalypse.

Finally, the Realist speaks. I applaud your exposure of the shallowness of the Rationalist and the Natural Law Man, she says to the Fideist. You match the scale of the problem of war, as they do not. Heine writes somewhere: 'Being Greek is a young man's game. One grows up to be a Jew.'

Where I disagree with you is this: what is it to be a Jew? To be a Jewish state, anyway, is to be, I say, not a faith but a power. Among all the struggles of small countries in every corner of the world, why is the conflict over Palestine so important in everyone's eyes? Explanations in terms of strategy and economics and great-power politics are all true, but they are not fully intelligible unless we notice a special quality in Palestine. Faith is of the right scale to be that quality, I grant you; but the quality is, in fact, power. Unlike most of the other small countries of the world, Israel has a coherence that men's eyes can focus on; it is a power. And it is so, not as you, the Fideist, would argue, because of a faith, but because it is a people that, after centuries of dispersion, has at last organized itself into a Realist state.

Fideism, for its part, destroys states. It was the Fideism of Aurangzeb that began the fall of Mogul India by turning Muslim and Hindu against each other. Europe in the Middle Ages would have torn itself to pieces in religious wars if Christianity had not been tamed by the power of the Papacy, 'the ghost of the deceased Roman Empire sitting crowned upon the grave thereof'.[16] With the decline of the Papacy, Europe set about exterminating itself in a century of wars of religion. The Fideist should learn to take as his watchword like everyone else: 'We too must keep the peace of Babylon.'

Our salvation lies in Realism about going to war and, if war comes, in continued Realism in fighting it. The mark of the truly professional soldier is that he follows the rule 'economy of effort'. This, not moral and legal theorizing, is the sure guideline that should be expressed in tactical and strategic manuals and codes of military law. Use resources of lives and material sparingly. Do not kill or be killed needlessly. This is the true principle of restraint in warfare. The generals that fought the Battle of the Somme were not wicked or law-breaking; they were (to use their sort of phrase) just 'damn bad soldiers'.

Guerrilla warfare is a tactic to be considered neutrally and coolly like any other, and so is terror and government terror. Usually the assassination of rulers and commanders, the clandestine killing of soldiers and policemen, and the blowing up of city dwellers and the terrorizing of peasants is inefficient. Sometimes it is not. This is not the proper sphere for ethics and law, and still less for religious fanaticism, for Zealots, Hashishins, and their sort. What is needed is clinical precision. To be sure, what is also needed is propaganda that is sensitive to the muddled emotions and (yes, the Fideist is right) 'the double standards' of popular opinion about terror. The United States Air Force campaign against North Vietnam in the 1960s, 'Rolling Thunder', was aimed with exemplary professionalism at military targets, but the propaganda battle about it was lost.

---

[16] Thomas Hobbes, *Leviathan*, ch. 47.

The professional soldier's economy of force is admittedly only a principle of restraint in using the resources allotted to him. He is not at all restrained in demanding more resources from the nation; he always wants more men and more guns, more force of any sort; and (this is the crucial point) more and more. In MacArthur's words: 'War's very object is victory, not prolonged indecision. In war there is no substitute for victory.'[17] The intrinsic nature of war is Absolute War.[18]

In practice, there are restraints on the total commitment of all resources, and the most important of these is political control. If necessary, Truman must dismiss MacArthur. War must be handled from first to last with careful calculation in the widest possible national perspective. The sale of arms to other states and groups must be under close political control. A Realist, being a mercantilist, experiences no radical tension, as does the Rationalist, between commercial greed and political qualms; all commerce should be supervised politically, and the arms trade is simply a prominent item in this task. As a state should only begin a war for the preservation or advancement of its power and only when it is highly likely to be successful, so it should only continue a war for so long as this is the case. Its statesmen must master the competitive spiral of war; must be skilled in leading the opponent to believe that they will commit all the resources necessary to win, when in fact they have set themselves strict limits according to the worth of the stake; must resist the temptation to reinforce failure; and must be ready to cut losses, to present defeat acceptably, and to turn to new opportunities.

The Realist concludes: I am not so much prescribing to states the kind of restraint in war that I have sketched, as describing what states, on the whole, have always tried to do and will always try to do. They do not always succeed; sometimes a state is destroyed; but still this cautious, self-serving, self-preserving handling of war is the best that states can do; and it will probably suffice in the future, as it has in the past, to keep the world in one piece. Debating nuclear deterrence in such words as 'irrational' or 'immoral' is unrealistic; nuclear deterrence is necessary, at present anyway; and, like everything that is

[17] To the US Congress, 19 Apr. 1951.
[18] Karl von Clausewitz, *On War*, bk. 8, chs. 2, 3.

necessary in human life, it must and can, with luck, be managed. The intention of a Realist behind nuclear deterrence is conditional in a double sense: he intends to retaliate if the enemy attacks but he intends only to do so if this will not lead to Apocalypse. Nuclear deterrence embodies the old irony of the human condition: fear of the worst makes us better. Nuclear weapons reinforce Realism. The Fideist sees nuclear weapons as the sign of the Great Beast. So they are. They are the sign of Leviathan over the world.

11

Commerce

I am glad to be the main speaker, says the Rationalist, for our last, best topic: world commerce. I propose as our starting-point the following vision. Imagine a world in which goods, services, money, knowledge, ideas, skills, and the people that possess them are allowed to cross all frontiers peacefully in freedom.

In other words, says the Fideist, a world market economy. I will tell you what I think of a market economy: it is a cattle-market kept by pigs. The relationship that it establishes between men is price, profit, and wage. Their labour is bought. The price paid bears no relation to their worth as people.

The market economy needs rich men: its dynamic is the pursuit of wealth; but rich men are pigs. When their nose is not in the trough, it is in the air. If their wealth does not ruin them, it ruins their children.

The market economy exalts material success. Discovery is its other dynamic, the continual search for new wants, a hunger that is never satisfied.

A market economy is no doubt a necessary relationship between men; the Marxists were utopians; but if it is the fundamental relationship, it is degrading. What has the Rationalist to offer in addition? According to him, a society, Britain, say, is 'a civil society—a set of people associated in no other essential way than their subjection to British law'.[1] What is this law? The ring around the market. No wonder that men turn to ideologists for the deeper understanding of social life that Rationalism denies them! Rationalism clears the way for revolutionism, nationalism, collectivism, socialism, and who can foretell what next!

A market economy should be a godly economy, a market

[1] Kenneth Minogue, *The Times*, 3 Nov. 1987.

society should be God's society. The swinish stampede of world commerce should be transformed into a market in which cows and pigs are lifted up by him to be no longer animals but men, his servants. In such a society, though we relate to one another by price, wage, and profit, the fundamental relationship is our worth in the service of the Law of God. We take a decent subsistence for ourselves in a modest gradation; and ensure this for our fellows throughout the Camp of the Faithful; and devote the remainder of our lives, freely, without reward, to achievements of knowledge, creation, and action that give delight to men and glory to God. People say that it is the arts that dignify men and raise them above the level of animals. But history witnesses that if the arts of a society do not centre on religious art, they degenerate. All life depends on God.

The Rationalist replies: you are making the common mistake of supposing that by world commerce I mean only world production and trade in a world market. I had best state some fundamentals.

Many human activities are aimed at producing goods. Many others are aimed at earning our daily bread. All these activities are bought and sold on the market. Every activity is in some way economic.

But to see our activities only in this aspect is an impoverishment. Being a lawyer or a flute-player or a footballer satisfies us in more ways than that it earns us our food. Equally, business activity is satisfying not only because of its product but also for the display of skill and enterprise.

Business is not a 'material' pursuit in contrast to 'ideal' or 'spiritual'. This contrast, used by the Fideist, is a dualist disease of Western thought. Business is, in one way or another, science, technology, aesthetics, ethics, politics, and religion. It draws on every part of the heart and mind. There is nothing left out as belonging to some higher sphere. Perhaps our best moments in life are given to us by the musician and the athlete; none the less, a man's choice to work in business may be rational; if it is rational, he is as good a man as the musician or athlete.

Price, profit, and wage are only one of the relationships between men in business. If they are taken to be the most important relationship, that is, no doubt, degrading; but they should not be. They are indicators of the level of demand for products and skills in the market. They are impersonal. They are independent of the will of the people in the business. They say little about their worth.

The most important relationship between men in business is freedom. To be free to reason about a product or a service or how a job should be organized, to back your opinion with work or money, to be answerable, to be proved wrong or right, is to have dignity as a man and worth as a person. Freedom is the condition in which we can create things and be satisfied, which is to say, be prosperous.

Business is part of all our activities. By binding ourselves as a society to no more than a ring of laws, we make a great freedom in which we can join whichever others we please, in whatever activities we choose: a school for our children, a pension fund, football, or flute-playing. A civil society, though it has no common plan or purpose, is, none the less, in the rich variety of its achievement, a great work of art. Production and trade make everything possible; and not as a mere ancillary but as an integral part. Our bodies are part of ourselves, and, in the same way, the countryside and streets are part of the place we love; the aeroplane, of the journey; the furniture, of the home; the flute, of the music.

The freedom that the employee, employer, investor, scientist, and technologist need for dignity, worth, satisfaction, and creativity is equally needed by the musician, the athlete, the lawyer, the official, the journalist, and the politician. The culmination of freedom for all of them is the right to come and go, to make one's life where one thinks best, to show one's skills wherever one chooses, to buy and sell wherever one wills, to reason with and benefit from all other minds, and, in sum, to enjoy the world at its widest without frontiers. This is a vision far from being realized, always needing prudent derogations, never to be fully realized, but always the rational vision to guide us. In this vision, the business commerce of the world is inseparable from the wider commerce; it should not be overvalued or undervalued in its contribution to the whole. Every kind of commerce requires the freedom of every other.

The Realist comments: what human beings most want is not freedom but security; military, against foreigners; civil, against frauds and thugs; economic, against misfortune. Freedom is in some ways helpful, in other ways, not. The state must do whatever is necessary for defence and order; legally, not arbitrarily, but not timidly either; for only so can commerce flourish, because only so is there security of person and property; men can 'make their fortune'. The state must be the chief organizer of prosperity because this is necessary to authority over its subjects; also, to avoid being overshadowed by private holders of great economic influence. The state must impose taxes to finance modern massive investment in research and development. It must protect the frontiers of the country against migration that unsettles the citizenry; against outflow of capital when this benefits only foreign economies; against exports beyond what are needed to finance imports; and against imports that disrupt domestic industry and increase dependence on other states and weaken defence capacity.

Some people think that Realism is out of date, that it belongs to the states-system as it was two centuries ago before the onset of world industrialization. This is nonsense. I was at home in the politics of peasant societies; I am at home in the politics of industrial societies; and I will still be home if what lies ahead of us is the politics of kindred and dynasty. Monarchy, oligarchy, democracy, dictatorship, tyranny, and chaos are all one to me in being equally subject to my political theory.

I believe in every kind of security, the pursuit of prosperity as well as the pursuit of power. The state was the great promoter of industrialization long before the nineteenth century, through the twentieth century, and to the present day. It was impelled by the necessities of war and military strength, but, inseparably, by concern for the welfare of the people. The free market economy has a great defect: every movement within it is the most intelligent possible but the machine as a whole is blind, careering headlong, uncontrolled, to no one knows where; to depression, unemployment, the decimation of industries, and the destruction of communities, and so the undermining of the authority and defences of the state; or to the suffocation of the world by prosperity of a kind that no one wants. Therefore, I believe in state planning, economic management, and protection.

Though power and prosperity are inseparable, power, at moments of choice, must come first. The state is the pre-condition of society. The origin of the belief that Realism is obsolete is the vision of a world in which the state is dwindling in favour of world society under the impact of international industrialization. This was nonsense in the nineteenth century, when liberals and Marxists deluded themselves into seeing world affairs as the rise of a cosmopolitan, commercial bourgeoisie, matched by a world-wide proletariat; and it remains nonsense when contemporary liberals picture the states-system submerged by a rising tide of 'transnationalism'; and it always will be nonsense. The state is the first need; what changes is its scale, tribal, national, imperial, regional, perhaps world, or perhaps some smaller form again.

In the present states-system of many independent states, order, secure commerce, and hence prosperity, come from a superpower giving orders or from the great powers as a group co-ordinating. Manchester in the nineteenth century and Chicago in the twentieth thought that, but for the malign interference of states, a world market economy would emerge naturally and ensure our peace and prosperity. Nothing of the sort! The international economy is not self-equilibrating. If there is no control, what happens is the 1930s.[2]

Keeping order in the international economy requires economic power but, backing this, military power. Whether at home or in the world, whether we are talking of business commerce or the wider commerce of art and science and thought, military power is the first need. 'People', 'assembly', 'opinion', 'law', 'teaching', 'ethics', 'house', 'game' presuppose armed 'manring'.[3] The court of Urbino was the creation of a soldier. The soldier has the highest worth of all men; he is versed in the arts; but willingness to be killed is higher than any art. We acknowledge this; as Johnson said: 'Every man thinks meanly of himself for not having been a soldier.' To call society a work of art, as the Rationalist did, contradicts his own theories; it is the state that can be a work of art. The state is, moreover, the necessary patron of the arts. When the pharaoh, the caesar, the pope, the king, the governments, local and national, of the world, do not reward the arts, no one else does. I noticed the other day that the Hallé Orchestra needs £300,000 or it must disband. I wonder whether, under the present tight-fisted British government, the business-

---

[2] Charles P. Kindleberger, *The World in Depression* (Harmondsworth, 1973).
[3] See ch. 9, n. 14.

men of Manchester will give the money. Not religion, but civic pride, state pride, is the impetus of the arts. From first to last, from the lowest matter to the highest, it is the state that guarantees our life.

The Rationalist replies: the state should be strong but light. Society should be provisional and open and ready for change. This is true supremely as regards military security. 'Defence is of much more importance than opulence,'[4] I agree; but this does not mean that the state should structure industry to defence needs and maintain particular arms producers. For the structure and the producers will always be out of date; the state finances the survival of an organization and a conception of weaponry that won the last war and fails in the next. You yourself seemed to see this in your opening statement. The better way is to let industry develop according to market forces; and for the government to monitor industry's changing technology and how warfare is changing; and subordinate its procurement plans to that.

In other words, the state should not presume to tell society how to defend itself; society will show the state, if it will only look. I say the same of the arts: let them develop as each of us chooses; let the poor man help 'Preserve Urbino for the Nation', if he wants to; the rich man finance a football team. State patronage presumes to tell society what it should want; it represses the ideas of rich and poor; if Manchester does not save the Hallé, that is because it has been taught to leave support of the arts to the state.

The state is not a single Prince but a group person, and thus is a stupid patron of the arts; 'a camel is a horse designed by a committee'. The Muses are women and do not like group persons. The Ducessa presides over the discussions at Urbino, not the soldier. The soldier is part of a group person: he gives his life, not as an individual, but as a comrade in an army. We need and praise him, and yet, as part of a group person, his principle of life is in tension with the principle of civil society, as we see frequently all over the world.

The state is a bad organizer of 'social security' and an incompetent planner of industry. I gave the theoretical reasons in my opening statement; witness in the Western countries the

[4] Adam Smith, *The Wealth of Nations*, bk. 4, ch. 2.

otiose siphoning of welfare monies out of one of the citizen's pockets back into the other; witness, as to planning, in France, the steel industry; in Britain, cars, nuclear energy, silicon chips; in India, the misallocation by Delhi of all the nation's investment. The Realist argues that private enterprise will not fund the biggest industries or the colossal investment in research and development needed for the future. What this means is that private enterprise is bad at breeding white elephants; that the nations must engage in a furious competition to build the most advanced pyramids; and that the future must at all costs happen fast and gigantically. Why?

In many countries in our time, the planned promotion of manufacturing industries in the name of modernity, prosperity, and defence, has led to the neglect or depression or even the destruction of agriculture. Government and city ruin the farmers. In other countries, agriculture has been subsidized and protected in the name of defence and tradition: *pas d'agriculture, pas de patrie*. The agriculture that has developed makes a mockery of this argument, for it is an industrial agriculture that disfigures the land and relies on imported oil and chemicals, and all at enormous cost to the citizenry. The farmers ruin the country.

Protectionism in any branch of business is costly to other businesses and to consumers, and risks creating in the country a pattern of production that is inefficient whether for civil purposes or for defence. 'The infant industry' grows up spoiled and misshapen and incapable of competing in the world. Where this is not so, where a state develops an efficient industry behind protective barriers, it is not developing a competitor that fits into world industry, that creates but harmonizes; it is breeding a tiger behind bars that, uncaged, makes havoc.

To increase the economic and welfare functions of the state in order to enhance its authority in the eyes of its citizens is absurd. You curtail their freedom without giving them efficiency. You promote the growth not of ordinary persons but of a heartless and corrupt group person. By loading on to the state huge responsibilities in which it fails, you weaken respect for it in the discharge of its small but vital proper duty.

This duty is to defend men's world-wide commerce: that is, to punish the sporadic delinquency of ordinary persons; to check the standing tendency of group persons, such as business corporations, to abuse their strength, whether singly or in international combinations; and to stop aggressor states. The state does this by enlisting the co-operation of the majority of persons, corporations, and states in the making and maintenance of rules. The principle behind these is maximum equal freedom. Thus, international business should be, as under the GATT, multilaterally regulated, non-discriminatory, and free.

I do not question the need at any given time for prudent modifications of freedom and equality. Sidgwick argued in nineteenth-century Britain that the ideal of free migration had to be qualified by considerations of patriotic cohesion, the effect on the state's efforts to raise the condition of the poor, and cultural and political stability.[5] These are not permanent principles, in my opinion. Raising the condition of the poor is not a proper task for the state, especially not at the expense of the foreign poor. Still, I admit that prudence will always demand utilitarian frontier controls of some sort. I insist only that, when immigrants are admitted, they should be given equal citizenship and not be made a helot class.

In prudence, there is need to control the speed of change in business. The decline of some industries has to be eased by subsidies, protection, payments for retraining, and so on. And correspondingly the rapid rise of others has to be braked by export restraints or the like. But let us never delude ourselves that such measures can amount to 'the rational planning of industry'. They are piecemeal, hit-or-miss, and as likely as not to do long-term harm, offsetting any short-term good. They are merely a necessary expedient to quiet the interested or ignorant clamour of some section or other of the population. The measures should be minimum, temporary, not covert but known 'at home and abroad, and agreed by all affected, nationally and internationally.

A final example of necessary prudential action: rescue operations for broken-down Realists and other economic incompetents; that is, for states that have ruined their economy by attempting to plan it in peacetime as in war, as the Soviet Union did for sixty years, and that have seen their mistake; or for governments that have incurred, in the name of promoting economic development, enormous international debts that they cannot pay, as did some

---

[5] Henry Sidgwick, *Elements of Politics* (London, 1881), 295–6.

Latin American governments in the 1970s (governments, be it
noted, not the wretched people of the countries) and that can be
persuaded to reform their financial ways. However, I emphasize
that these operations and all prudential actions of the sort I have
been discussing should be minimum; for they are exceptional,
pragmatical, of limited rationality, and thus likely to be decided
by the push and pull of power.

Rules, on the other hand, need not be the product of power.
States do not create order by imposing rules, as the Realist
thinks; order springs from human harmony of interests; rule-
making is only the detailing and proclamation of what is
inherent. The international economy does not need a hegemon.
Britain, in its time, and the United States later, did not dictate an
order; rather they presided over one, by associating themselves
with the interests of many other states, in conformity with some
widely agreed norms of rationality. Because the basis of order is
harmony and rationality, not arbitrary will, states can achieve
equality in rule-making, despite great differences in power. The
Southern countries of the world can make their voices heard in
decisions on international commerce, not by attempts at coercion
or by forming coalitions against the Northern countries, but by
mobilizing the common interest that exists between their producers and Northern consumers, and indeed between their
producers and Northern producers who wish to invest where
costs are least. The international order will work as smoothly as
possible if only the required rules are made to permit the people
of the world to pursue their interests world-wide freely.

To sum up: governments have enough to do, at home and
internationally, making rules to prevent us injuring each other,
without telling us further how to be prosperous. The victory of
this principle in Western Europe and North America over the
last 200 years and the defeat of Realism, with its state planning and welfare and mercantilism, has transformed the life
of the people of that region. In 1700, the majority of them, as
in the rest of the world, lived always close to hunger; their lives
were 'poor, nasty, brutish, and short'. They now live in luxury
undreamt of by princes. I see no reason to think that this
phenomenon is abnormal, confined to a few areas of the world
for a short period of history. The whole world can enjoy the
same prosperity if it will follow the same principles.

And the whole world can enjoy peace. The Realist state is hostile to others, not only in its ideas, but in its organization. Its planned, managed, and protected economy, its monolithic welfare organization, and its industries controlled according to defence, create a society that is centralized, conservative, and closed to easy inter-penetration with other societies, and incapable of one day shifting its frontiers to form a wider society with them. The Realist laughs at the vision of a states-system transformed by the spirit of commerce. Cobden was disappointed in 1856; liberals and Marxists alike in 1914; reason is never fully implemented; there will always be setbacks. The last word, though, is that our minds are such that creation is superior to destruction, wealth to poverty, the arts to brutality, harmony to discord. World society is more powerful than separate states.

The Historicist speaks: your notion that the West became rich and peaceful because it followed the theory of free trade and that the rest of the world could do the same is false and the enemy of your hopes. Western people certainly sought 'wealth' and 'peace' and 'freedom'; but these words were 'essentially contested concepts';[6] their meaning had to be established in action; they were controversial, imprecise, improvised, continually evolving, which is to say, historical; their only continuity of meaning was some agreement among the disputants about past experience. 'Freedom', 'wealth', and 'peace' are not theories but histories.

We should dismiss from practical politics the Rationalist vision of a world society of free commerce. I am not for it or against it; I say only that it is a fantasy. The meanings of the concepts with which the Rationalist constructs the vision have not been established in action, and so the vision is meaningless. To tell a statesman that trade and migration and so on should basically be 'free' but subject to 'prudent controls' is vacuous and useless to him. Visualize, if you will, 'free trade in cloth'; it is a mere abstraction; so try again, visualizing it as a real activity of real people; you will soon see that your vision is constructed of the assumptions and convictions and practices of your particular time and place. For example, you assume that 'free trade in cloth' includes the right of anyone to engage

---

[6] W. B. Gallie, *Philosophy and the Historical Understanding* (London, 1964), ch. 8.

in the cloth trade; but other societies have not assumed this. You used to assume that free trade in cloth is compatible with preference by governments and consumers for national goods over imports, but, after much controversy, you no longer assume this. As to assumptions about what 'prudent controls' must obviously include, the great differences between society and society over time and place are plain. So what a statesman needs to know in a controversy is what his countrymen mean when they use the phrases 'free trade' and 'prudent controls' or analogous concepts in non-Western societies. In seeking this knowledge, he should first try to understand what his countrymen have experienced. Then he has to argue.

I have been told that I give no guidance in the argument. I give the only guidance worth having, a historically formed free mind. I say, for the last time, that theories are deadly and, in the case of the Rationalist, deadly to the cause that he has most at heart, freedom. Beginning as a liberal in the eighteenth century, he was a collectivist by the twentieth. For, as the Fideist said, mere freedom under the law atomizes men and leaves them defenceless against tyrants; and equality has no rational stopping-point as it proceeds from equal freedom under equal laws, through equality of opportunity, to equality of the resources with which one begins life, and so to equality of 'life-chances', and finally to enforced equality in wealth. The underlying tenet of Rationalism, I remind you, is that we cannot know the world and must construct it. This means that there is no reason why light rules around society in one century should not be remade into heavy rules in another; and why state intervention in the market, originally confined to defence purposes, should not extend to any other form of welfare by planning, economic management, and protection.[7] I say, for my part, that we indeed cannot know the world as observers; we have no standpoint outside the world; so theories about it are arbitrary. We know the world because we are within it. We know it by experience, the historical experience of our tradition, nation, class, profession, that we have learned, and by our own. No one can claim a special status for his ideas. All must argue. This is how, equally and freely, we make the future.

[7] James Mayall, 'The Liberal Economy', in Mayall (ed.), *The Community of States* (London, 1982).

The decisive voice in the debate is that of world historical individuals whose genius lies precisely in their freedom from theory. Theories are static, and visions are tranquil and unchanging, but the world is turbulent and dynamic. The main mass influence shaping the future is the people of the leading nations. The role of authors is to help shape the mind of the people in each day's debate and then, for the most part, to be forgotten. Keynes's *Means to Prosperity* is the best kind of book to aspire to write, not his *General Theory*. A few authors demand the attention of many generations, but they should be read for their genius, not for their doctrines. They should be treated as great contributors to the tradition, as revered opponents, not as masters. Smith himself is not a Smithian; Marx, a Marxist; Keynes, a Keynesian. They remain free.

I warned earlier against making history into theory. I give here as an example how the data of 1861–1913 make a Phillips Curve that spans 1914–67 and then collapses. I warn equally against theoretical traditions. They are not true traditions, for, in them, author, statesman, or businessman does not simply try to understand his predecessors before arguing with them and doing something new; he joins a school of thought; his contribution to some problem is not his brains but received methods, ideas, and arguments, merely recycled. Economists are needed in our debates, but their economics is at present a misleading way of thought. They should imitate, say, Sismondi, who was helped by history to break free of orthodoxy.

I say the same of higher matters. Defence is debated continuously in all countries, but usually only at the margins. For all argue from inherited, fixed positions of Army, Navy, or Air Force, and all are united in sharing basic assumptions about how the nation's defence should be organized. The organization was laid down by the great men of the last heroic age (the last Great War, the Revolution, or the like) and is received doctrine for their successors. It is their traditional theory.

The arts are currently controlled by a Rationalist tradition, Modernism. Authors no longer simply write novels and poetry; they are constrained by academic theories of literature. Architecture in the twentieth century has been dominated by theories that deliberately broke with architectural tradition. Painters have learnt to paint not a picture but a theory. Music was not renewed by serialism but subjected to it. Though ours is on the whole a Historicist age, the highest ground is the refuge of the Rationalists, and a barren place they have made of it. But times change. I am content to hope. The Rationalist is the main speaker on these matters now, but he was not a hundred years ago, and perhaps he will not be a hundred years hence.

The Rationalist replies: the arts are barren today because of Historicism. The theory from which they suffer is a historical theory, namely, that changing times are reflected in changing arts, and the twentieth century, being a radically new world, must have radically new forms of art. No book may be written, picture painted, building built, score composed, unless it is new. Academics, patrons, dealers, and customers hasten to support whatever is new because they are frightened by the story of their predecessors who did not. The correct name of the enemy is not Modernism but the Modern Movement.

Rationalist theories are friendly to creativity. We cannot know the world from an outside standpoint and not from within its history either. The world is made by a myriad hands and always changing. It is not to be comprehended totally and finally, whether as a whole or in any part. From this follows freedom: no one can claim a monopoly of insight into any matter and an exclusive right to control what is done. Society consists of rules that assert this fact and enforce it, and of freedom within them. Between rules of this sort and rules that pretend to organize the welfare of people in further respects, the difference is clear. The decline of eighteenth-century liberalism into twentieth-century collectivism is an interesting, sad story. It does not affect the logic of Rationalism.

I have some use for history. Keynes wrote, 'A study of the history of opinion is a necessary preliminary to the emancipation of the mind.'[8] The question is, what sort of mind do we think will solve a problem best: one that senses life as continual change and believes itself to have been formed by a past that it cannot impose on the future; or one that recognizes that human thought has some fixed concepts and procedures and that these yield some fixed principles. By using these in perception we develop theories that explain the problem and guide us in

---

[8] *The End of Laisser-Faire* (London, 1927), 16.

handling it; not dogmas, not verified, simply not falsified, provisional, open, and ready to change.[9]

My critics suppose that Rationalism is limitless faith in the power of reason. No.

The first fixed principle is that each of us is an individual and looks to his own interests. Each will not provide public goods; so all must do so through governments. Each will not observe public goods; he takes care of his own property, and separate ownership is often the best way to exploit many of the resources of the world in everybody's interests, including those of future generations; but he will deplete and damage commons, as suits him; so we must take care of these by rules made by governments, nationally and internationally. There is, in other words, a kind of economic planning that is necessary, namely, one that aims to prevent injury by providing and protecting public goods and by stopping us when our projects inflict public ills or by making us pay.

A similar limit to reason is that, in pursuing each his own interests, we generate much of the information that others need for rational action, but not all of it. Markets provide of their own accord much statistical data, but not all that is necessary. Also, banks, left to themselves, may each lend to foreign governments more than they would if they knew how much all were lending; investors and producers may shun long-term investments because they have too little security about the future market that all will make for all; the various agents in the economy may create excess demand leading to inflation because each does not know the intentions of the others. Governments, therefore, have a duty to promote good communication in an economy, without, however, assisting the tendency of businessmen to cartelize and collude. This duty extends to other aspects of society where the intentions of each of us are thwarted by ignorance of the intentions of all, for example, our use of our environment. If all try to enjoy a public pleasure, none does.[10] The duty also extends to the views and intentions of governments themselves. They should co-operate internationally to achieve not only maximum knowledge by each society of the others, but also maximum possible openness in affairs of state.

[9] Bryan Magee, *Popper* (London, 1973).
[10] Fred Hirsch, *Social Limits to Growth* (Cambridge, Mass., 1976).

Thirdly, what I have just said is the limit, or nearly so, of what governments can do in the management of the economy, nationally and internationally. The economy, as the Realist said, is not immediately in equilibrium; but nothing can change this. Between any free act and response, there is a moment of imbalance before harmony, and this, multiplied by millions, makes surges of action and reaction in the economy, rapid fluctuations over a day, and great movements over a decade or more from growth to recession and back again. Governments are tempted to try to enforce equilibrium, but their intervention merely deepens the movements of the economy into convulsions.

Governments today spend prodigiously on subsidies to in-dustry and agriculture. The money could be better spent by the people. Subsidies, apart from other distortions, commonly lead eventually to glut. Each country promotes a national car or ship industry which crash together in the end. The most plausible excuse is the wish to see full employment of manpower. True, when national factors of production are lying idle, the arguments against protection are weakened; but only superficially so. Fundamentally, the best we can do towards the maintenance of full employment of factors in countries that usually enjoy this and towards the smooth absorption of factors into the world economic system of those countries that as yet do not is to ensure the free development of the world market.

Governments are tempted to think that the economy is a machine that they ought to be able to adjust continually by the application of macro-economic theory. This is an error. Theory helps most on matters where men have a common purpose; but the economy is not such a matter; here the limits of theory and helpful action are quickly reached. Moreover, governments face a practical dilemma. If they operate a closed economy, they have the levers of control but the economy is inefficient; if they have an open economy, their efforts at control are frustrated by the foreigners; fast as the government pushes the economy one way, the market links with foreigners pull it another. You cannot control a society if you do not control its frontiers; or, to put the point better, if you do not know where its frontiers really are; or, to put it best, if you cannot know whether it has frontiers at all.

A big economy, such as that of the United States, backed by

military power, can, as the Realist implied, tyrannize over the international economy, managing affairs to the cost of the others. But such policies do not maximize world prosperity on the whole; and that is a loss to the United States or any other country because, when it considers all its forms of commerce with other societies, it cannot be sure who among the others are really foreigners or where its frontiers are or whether fundamentally it has frontiers at all.

A seductive line of thought is that the leading governments should co-ordinate their management of their national economies and develop joint international management. This is fallacious. It elevates the theoretical pretensions of which I spoke from a national to an international scale. It contradicts the most basic fact about states, that they are individuals, a society, not a community. Each state will demand policies that suit its own managerial purposes. Each will require some other state to be the self-sacrificing locomotive economy that hauls them all to prosperity.[11]

The task of governments internationally is not management but rule-making, aimed at keeping economies open, prohibiting national control policies, preventing injuries by other agents, regulating commons, detecting market blockages, and increasing communication. Such limited action will not guarantee equilibrium but it is the best that can be done. I do not deny, as I have said, that prudence will sometimes demand that governments make internationally agreed piecemeal interventions of one sort and another; but such devices, while perhaps easing one imbalance, will set up another.

If we want freedom and prosperity in world commerce, we must accept that the cost is rise and fall, change, movement, risk, enterprise, building, collapse, reconstruction. If we attempt state control of national economies, we curtail freedom and prosperity, and we pay the cost anyway; we get the 1930s. The claims of governments to spare us the cost, though disguised as rational economic thought, are in fact age-old Realist demagoguery with the aim of power, ending in collision with other states, and tyranny. We should hold to the tradition that manipulation makes men servile, rules make men free. By 'tradition', I do not

[11] Robert D. Putnam and Nicholas Rayne, *Hanging Together: Cooperation and Conflict in the Seven-Power Summits*, 2nd edn. (London, 1987).

mean a continually evolving understanding of what 'freedom' and 'prosperity' are. I mean something permanent and always handed on because it is rational.

My final point concerns the Historicist's allegation that Rationalism entails egalitarianism in wealth. I rebut this with several arguments, including my recognition of the limits of reason.

Marxists think that the rich are so by robbing the poor. On the contrary, the obvious truth is that the progress of some of us to great riches enriches the rest of us. A more sophisticated notion is that our inequality in wealth offends against distributive justice and that we ought to correct this by taxation and other means. One argument used is that the inequality arises in part from differences in our natural talents, and that these are arbitrary and ought to be compensated for. But this is a strange way of talking since without such differences we would not be rational agents with interests at all but clones. Another line of argument is that equally talented children should have equal education; equally sick people, equal medical care; everyone should have the basic means required for equal freedom to choose a way of life; and so on. We would all like to see such equality, I think, but that does not mean that it is a right, and that I should spend my money achieving it for other people. As I said in my original statement, an 'I' with interests is obliged not to injure another such 'I' but is not obliged to help him. The root argument is that my money is not really mine; it is available for equitable redistribution because it was produced in co-operation with the whole of society. But I paid for the co-operation of others through the market day by day; what remains to me belongs to me; it is not common property to be shared out. The 'National Product' is a nationalist or Realist fiction or merely statistical.

Anyway, how much should I and everybody else pay in this equitable redistribution? Should we be left with equal take-home pay? Why? Why not? There is no rational way of deciding. The Natural Law Man is the expert on distributive justice, and he knows very well that only in an association with a common purpose (a business company, say, or a group of traders setting up a market, or the state) have we a principle for sharing out burdens and benefits. Society as a whole has no common purpose. Reason has no grounds on which to choose a particular distributive principle and, moreover, would not know how to apply one. In other words, reason cannot improve upon the distribution brought about by people in a free market under law. I concede to the Realist the influence of luck on our different fortunes; but, as to justice, it can only amount to fair procedures, which is to say, in our dealings with one another in society, the market.[12]

If we treat our society as a machine, whether by attempting distributive justice or planning or economic management or by any other form of social engineering, a machine it may become. It will then be useless for anything but war. Sparta is not a joyful place or remembered for its arts. People may, alternatively, turn resentful or irresponsible, fractious and criminal. Our society will then again be joyless and ugly. If, on the other hand, we ensure that our joint action as a state lies lightly on us, each, having the free disposal of his wealth, great or small, may make something of it, and our society may be worth remembering.

As in our separate societies, so in world society, some people think that our aim ought to be to try to create greater equality of wealth. But, here too, this aim is not the right way to prosperity.

Some say we ought to create greater equality because the rich in world society are so by robbing the poor. I grant that the age of imperialism, like the whole of history, was full of great wrongs, including many episodes of forced labour. But no one can assert that the economies of the South would have developed better without the incursion of the North; or, looking wider than the economy, that the South lost on the whole by its commerce with Northern cultures. Conversely, we can surely say that the North gained by its commerce with Southern cultures; but we cannot say that its astounding economic progress depended on exploitation of the South.[13]

Putting the matter more theoretically, the proponents of the thesis that the rich exploit the poor commonly obscure an obvious distinction. They may be saying that exploitation

---

[12] James Buchanan, 'The Justice of Natural Liberty', in G. P. O. O'Driscoll, *Adam Smith and Modern Political Economy* (Ames, Ia., 1976); F. A. Hayek, *Law, Legislation and Liberty* (London, 1976), ii.

[13] Patrick O'Brien, 'Europe in the World Economy', in Hedley Bull and Adam Watson (eds.), *The Expansion of International Society* (Oxford, 1984); Arthur Lewis, *Some Aspects of Economic Development* (Accra, 1969), 15.

sometimes arises or that it necessarily arises. If the former, their
books deserve the closest reading, and, when found cogent,
corrective action should be taken. We worked out rules regulating
capitalism in domestic society and there is no reason why we
should not in world society. But if the contention is that
exploitation is inevitable, we need not read their long, hard
books. For what cannot be cured must be endured.

A more sophisticated argument, as in domestic society, is the
need for distributive justice. The candidates for distributive
justice are said to be countries; the inequality of 'rich countries'
and 'poor countries' needs to be corrected or compensated. For
example, it is said to be arbitrary that some countries have
great natural resources and others few.[14] Even a Rationalist is
momentarily awed by the vast inequalities here. It does seem
unfair that Brazil and Indonesia should be overwhelmingly
rich in resources while Britain and Japan are so poor. Perhaps
Brazil and Indonesia should compensate Britain and Japan.

A reverse line of argument is that it is unfair that Brazil and
Indonesia should mainly produce commodities and Britain
and Japan mainly manufactures, since the income from the
latter is inherently better and more stable. Poor commodity-
producing countries should be given grants in compensation
and should be helped to become manufacturing countries.

All such notions dissolve for a Rationalist when he reflects that
countries cannot be the subject of distributive justice. 'Brazil'
and 'Indonesia' have no resources; there are no manufacturing
'countries'; 'countries' are not unequal in wealth. The only
effect of such talk is to build up the Realist state. It is the Realist
state that can have sovereignty over natural resources; that can
engage in selective development of the economy in accordance
with its notion of how to promote power and prosperity; that
can receive the 'economic aid' of other states whenever their
own foreign-policy purposes suggest it; not 'countries', least of
all people.

The true subjects of distributive justice are people. It is
relevant to them whenever they are joined together in associations
with a common purpose. It is not relevant to them as world
society. For, as the world, they have no common purpose; there

---

[14] Charles R. Beitz, *Political Theory and International Relations* (Princeton, NJ, 1979), 136 ff.

is no common product to distribute; the co-operation involved in world commerce is requited in each transaction; there are no agreed principles of distribution. What people need in the South or anywhere else is freedom to make a living within the equal protection of the laws. Polemics about distributive justice and a duty to aid the economic development of Less Developed Countries achieve nothing but a political fog in which oppressors escape. Within Southern countries, the many who are ignorant and weak need governments that enforce their rights against the few that are cunning and strong. They need governments that cease to distort the economy in the name of 'national development' with the result that the people starve. In relations with the North, Southern people need rules of trade that neither penalize nor favour them but are equal for all everywhere. Such action does not aid Southern people to live, but allows them to live, and so to prosper.

I summarize Rationalism thus: human society is freedom within rules that bind all equally. Its foundation is a rational harmony of interests between strong and weak, intelligent and stupid, rich and poor. Because we often do not see this, force is needed; but more often we do see it. Society is never fully realized. In *The Wealth of Nations*, Adam Smith wrote: 'To expect, indeed, that the freedom of trade should ever be entirely restored in Great Britain is as absurd as to expect that an Oceana or Utopia should ever be established in it. Not only the prejudices of the public, but what is much more unconquerable, the private interests of many individuals, irresistibly oppose it.'[15] This being true of Britain, how much more so of the world! True of business, how much the more of the entire commerce of mankind! My vision is thus not a vision of history, of what ever was or ever will be, but of what in history is always reasonable and is on the whole dominant over error and achieves our prosperity.

The Natural Law Man makes the closing remarks: we see a natural progression in our experience and duty from self to family, friends, country, and world. The reverse progression lies still deeper in our nature, from the universal to the individual. A baby can be brought up in any culture. A man has in him the

---

[15] bk. 4, ch. 2.

structure of every language. Knowledge of mankind makes us a true homeland, a nation without hatred.

Our associations, from family to homeland, are required by the practical needs of our nature, but our nature also requires that they become more to us than a mere collection of people who jointly accept some reasonable rules and otherwise go about their separate business. Patriotism is more than loyalty to a constitution that protects our interests, and more than love of the streets or countryside that we come from: it is a kind of desire for community.

In the politics of our homeland, when there is friction and we are perplexed, when dispute threatens and even hatred, we look for advice to the opinions and practices of other countries. *Securus iudicat orbis terrarum.* But in the last resort we appeal to a profounder universal: Man. We say, for example, that we know naturally that we should avert ills from each other and seek the common good. On this ground, we contend in economic affairs that to help any of our countrymen who are in human need is an obligation and not simply a matter of prudence or optional benevolence.

Freedom within equal laws is a great achievement; but suppose the laws embody an idea such as absolute property? What Sismondi wrote of the nineteenth-century British applies today in Brazil: 'If the Marchioness of Stafford was entitled by law to replace the population of an entire province by 29 families of foreigners and some hundreds of thousands of sheep, they should hurry up and abolish such an odious law, both in respect of her and all the others in her position.'[16] We need in law-making our natural sense of the common good if we are to recognize cruel theories and traditions for what they are and challenge their utility and cut them down.

The market, the great circuit of our prosperity, depends not only on the law but also on the moral law, that is, on trust and therefore honesty. More than this, the market and the business company are, for all their freedom, a degrading relationship between men so long as the philosophy behind them is that each man is pursuing his own self-interest, and only providentially helping to maximize the wealth of all. To each of us, in this

---

[16] Quoted in John Prebble, *The Highland Clearances* (London, 1963), 119.

view, others are a mere necessity: our employees are treated as a cost; our customers exist for our benefit. The truth is that we fulfil our nature and so achieve dignity and satisfaction or consolation in our toil, if our philosophy is that a man works and a company works for the community.

Though the members of a business company, like any other association for a common purpose, have available to them general principles about how to distribute the burdens and benefits justly, they will only agree on how to apply them if there is a general spirit of the common good. Openness of information in company, market, and state affairs is very desirable; but it too can be achieved only to the extent that each can have confidence in the goodwill of the others. The provision of public goods, avoidance of public ills, care of public property, concern for commons, and regard for the republic itself are not achieved, and rationally cannot be, if each one respects the interest of all for only so long as he has his own separate interest in doing so.

As peace in the homeland depends on desire for the common good, so does peace between homelands. Our natural duty to help men in human need is not confined within frontiers but extends throughout the community of mankind; doing that duty requires us not to profit commercially from economic systems in foreign countries that cause destitution, to intervene to have these systems changed where we prudently can, not ourselves to operate oppressive national and international commercial rules and policies, and to give money and technical help. Which countries should do how much of these duties is a matter of distributive justice; that problem, like all the others that arise, will be handled amicably to the extent that states desire the common good.

The same can be said about the balance between the independence and interdependence of homelands. The world is divided for good practical reasons into separate countries with separate states; these cannot subsist as political, legal, and military entities, and satisfy the desire of their citizens for a sense of community, without some degree of economic self-sufficiency. A land that is merely a corner of a wider commercial system or is simply one great rice-field or coal-mine, however rich, is not a homeland; to be a homeland, it must contain many industries, skills, talents, and arts. Free world-wide commerce will not ensure this. Brazil says so today, Germany and America in the last century, Britain, France, and The Netherlands before them, and others back to the beginning of history. Freedom of commerce is a great vision, but not alone. It may maximize the good of the whole but not the good of all the parts of the whole, which is the common good. We must oversee our commerce, and act, even at economic cost, to ensure the diversity that we need. The question is how much diversity do we need, what degree of self-sufficiency. About that there will be differences of opinion between homelands, leading to friction and destruction, unless each proceeds in the spirit of the common good.

In all our politics, national and international, we are seeking to accommodate the fact that we belong to two communities, our homeland and mankind. We need to make rules and pursue policies and co-ordinate them internationally in that light. Mere freedom of commerce between societies and consequent inderdependence will not by itself lead to peace between states. Harmony of interests is not attained simply by rationality in bargaining. There must be awareness of community, desire for the common good.

How is this necessary quality in men and states to be achieved? Relax! It is programmed into us as a species. We have survived so far, and thus the only evidence available grounds optimism about the future, not pessimism. We know that we should avert ills from others and seek the common good. Philosophers debate the validity of human knowledge, but that is not a matter for men but for the gods. Men know what they know.

We often do not act on our knowledge through ignorance of facts, which is why we must attend to the international arrangements for the news media. We fail also through stupidity, arising from defects in our arrangements for political debate. Knowledge emerges through honest discussion. There are guide-lines in the discussion but we often disregard them. We refuse to reflect on our moral nature in the natural world; we are determined to be 'masters and possessors of nature';[17] we deny the existence of a natural law; we think that our

---

[17] René Descartes, *Discours de la Méthode*, pt. 6.

theories and traditions are enough; we invite the laughter of the gods.

The guide-lines of the natural law are too widely set to take us to our exact goal; we need a further kind of knowledge, that is, the virtues. They grow in us through education and practice and reflection. To the four that are basic, courage, self-mastery, justice, and prudence, I gladly add, since we are discussing commerce, generosity. We need to think that greed is ignoble; as rich men, that great differences between our wealth and that of the poor make great demands on us; that we should do more for our countrymen than relieve human needs; we should help them, say, when their industry collapses, to make another. We should feel that we, the rich and clever, are not free to leave our homeland to its poverty and corruption, and to migrate to some corner of the world that is rich and clever and honest like us. *Spartam nanctus es; hanc exorna.*[18]

Men will respect their community, its laws, its commons, and so on, if they think it is worth respecting. It must be a community devoted to excellence. Every man, whatever his trade, that averts ills and considers the common good, that has the virtues proper to a man, is as good as every other man. But not all trades are equally good, and not all the pursuits of happiness. The worst egalitarianism is that 'quantity of pleasure being equal, push-pin is as good as poetry';[19] the worst denial of what we know is that the difference between trash and gold is a matter of opinion. Our talent for this trade or that, businessman, athlete, flute-player, is not decided by us. Genius is not to our glory. The end of all our commerce is to pay for the best. That is our part in making 'a city common to gods and men'.[20]

---

[18] 'You have been given Sparta; make the best of it' (Graeco-Roman proverb).

[19] Jeremy Bentham, *Works*, ed. John Bowring (London, 1839), ii. 253.

[20] Cicero, *De Finibus*, iii. xix. 64.

Bibliography

INTRODUCTION

FORSYTH, Murray, and KEENS-SOPER, Maurice (eds.), *A Guide to the Political Classics* (Oxford, 1988).
MARITAIN, Jacques, *Moral Philosophy*, trans. Marshall Sutler and Others (London, 1964).
PASSMORE, John, *The Perfectibility of Man* (London, 1970).
QUINTON, Anthony (ed.), *Political Philosophy* (Oxford, 1967).
THOMSON, David (ed.), *Political Ideas* (Harmondsworth, 1966).
WOLIN, Sheldon, *Politics and Vision* (Boston, Mass., 1960).

CHAPTER 1. NATURAL LAW

BRIERLY, J. L., *The Basis of Obligation in International Law* (Oxford, 1958).
D'ENTRÈVES, A. P., *Natural Law*, 2nd edn. (London, 1970).
GALSTON, William A., *Justice and the Human Good* (Chicago, Ill., 1980).
SIGMUND, Paul, *Natural Law in Political Thought* (Washington, DC, 1971).
SIMON, Yves R., *The Tradition of Natural Law* (New York, 1967).
WEINREB, Lloyd, *Natural Law and Justice* (Cambridge, Mass., 1987).

CHAPTER 2. REALISM

ARON, Raymond, *Peace and War*, trans. Richard Howard and Annette Baker Fox (London, 1966).
BEETHAM, David, *Max Weber and the Theory of Modern Politics*, 2nd edn. (Cambridge, 1985).
GOODIN, Robert, *The Politics of Rational Man* (New York, 1976).
JOUVENEL, Bertrand de, *Power*, trans. J. F. Huntington (London, 1945).
MCNEILL, William, *The Pursuit of Power* (Chicago, Ill., 1982).
OSGOOD, Robert E., and TUCKER, Robert W. *Force, Order and Justice* (Baltimore, Md., 1967).

CHAPTER 3. FIDEISM

CARGILL THOMPSON, W. D. J., *The Political Thought of Martin Luther*
(Brighton, 1984).
HÖPFL, Haro, *The Christian Polity of John Calvin* (Cambridge, 1982).
MARKUS, R. A., *Saeculum, History and Society in the Theology of St.
Augustine* (Cambridge, 1970).
MARTIN, David, *Pacifism* (London, 1965).
WALZER, Michael, *The Revolution of the Saints* (London, 1966).
WATT, John A., *The Theory of Papal Monarchy in the 13th Century*
(London, 1966).

CHAPTER 4. RATIONALISM

BARRY, Brian, *Theories of Justice* (Berkeley, 1989).
GEWIRTH, Alan, *Reason and Morality* (Chicago, 1978).
HINSLEY, F. H. *Power and the Pursuit of Peace* (Cambridge, 1963).
HIRSCHMAN, Albert O., *The Passions and the Interests* (Princeton, NJ,
1983).
NARDIN, Terry, *Law, Morality and the Relations of States* (Princeton, NJ,
1983).
WILLIAMS, Howard, *Kant's Political Philosophy* (Oxford, 1983).

CHAPTER 5. HISTORICISM: 'NATION' AND 'STATE'

ACTON, John, 'Nationality', in *The History of Freedom and Other Essays*
(London, 1907).
DONAGAN, Alan and Barbara, *Philosophy of History* (New York, 1965).
MEINECKE, Friedrich, *Historism*, trans. J. E. Anderson (London,
1972).
PLAMENATZ, *On Alien Rule and Self-Government* (London, 1960).
WELLS, G. A. *Herder and After* (The Hague, 1959).
YEATS, W. B., 'Cathleen ni Hoolihan', in *Collected Plays*, 2nd edn.
(London, 1952).

CHAPTER 6. HISTORICISM: 'PROLETARIAT' AND 'WORLD'

BOBBIO, Norberto, *Which Socialism?*, trans. Robert Griffin (Cambridge,
1987).
BOZEMAN, Adda, *Culture and Politics in International History* (Princeton,
NJ, 1960).

JASPERS, Karl, *The Origin and Goal of History*, trans. Michael Bullock (London, 1953).

KENNAN, George F., *American Diplomacy, 1900–1950* (Chicago, Ill., 1951).

LINKLATER, Andrew, *Men and Citizens in the Theory of International Relations* (London, 1982).

LUKÁCS, Georg, *History and Class-Consciousness*, trans. R. Livingstone (London, 1971).

CHAPTER 7. CONFLICT

BARTH, Karl, *Against the Stream*, trans. E. M. Delacour and Stanley Goodman (London, 1954).

BURNS, Edward McNall, *Ideas in Conflict*, British edn. (London, 1963).

SCHELLING, Thomas C., *Arms and Influence* (New Haven, Conn., 1966).

SCHIFFER, Walter, *The Legal Community of Mankind* (New York, 1954).

WALTZ, Kenneth N., *Man, the State and War* (New York, 1954).

WATSON, Adam, *Diplomacy* (London, 1982).

CHAPTER 8. ALLIANCES

BEATON, Leonard, *The Reform of Power* (London, 1972).

CLAUDE, Inis L., Jr., *Power and International Relations* (New York, 1962).

CROWE, Eyre, 'Memorandum on the Present State of Britain's Relations with France and Germany, 1 January 1907', in G. P. Gooch and Harold Temperley, *British Documents on the Origins of the War, 1898–1914* (London, 1928), iii. 397–420.

DEHIO, Ludwig, *The Precarious Balance, The Politics of Power in Europe, 1494–1945*, trans. Charles Fullman, rev. edn. (London, 1963).

JERVIS, Robert, LEBOW, Richard Ned, and STEIN, Janice Gross, *Psychology and Deterrence* (Baltimore, Md., 1985).

ZIMMERN, Alfred, *The League of Nations and the Rule of Law* (London, 1936).

CHAPTER 9. INTERVENTION

HOFFMANN, Stanley, *Duties beyond Borders* (Syracuse, NY, 1981).

KUPER, Leo, *The Prevention of Genocide* (New Haven, Conn., 1985).

MULDOON, James, *Popes, Lawyers and Infidels* (Liverpool, 1979).

O'BRIEN, Conor Cruise, *To Katanga and Back* (London, 1962).

TESÓN, Fernando, *Humanitarian Intervention* (Dobbs Ferry, NY, 1988).
VINCENT, R. J., *Nonintervention and International Order* (Princeton, NJ, 1974).

CHAPTER 10. WAR

BEST, Geoffrey, *Humanity in Warfare* (London, 1980).
FOTION, N., and ELFSTROM, G., *Military Ethics* (Boston, Mass., 1986).
GAGE, Nicholas, *Eleni* (New York, 1983).
O'BRIEN, William V., *The Conduct of Just and Limited War* (New York, 1981).
TUCKER, Robert W., *The Just War* (Baltimore, Md., 1960).
WALZER, Michael, *Just and Unjust Wars* (New York, 1977).

CHAPTER 11. COMMERCE

BHAGWATI, Jagdish, *Protectionism* (Cambridge, Mass., 1988).
BUCHANAN, Allen, *Ethics, Efficiency and the Market* (Oxford, 1985).
HUTCHINSON, T. W., *The Politics and Philosophy of Economics* (Oxford, 1981).
KEYNES, John Neville, *The Scope and Method of Political Economy* (London, 1890).
PANOFSKY, Erwin (ed.), *Abbot Suger on the Abbey Church of St Denis and its Art Treasures*, 2nd edn. (Princeton, NJ, 1979).
SCHUMPETER, Joseph A., *Capitalism, Socialism and Democracy* (New York, 1942).

Index

Abelard, Peter 46
ABM Treaty (1972) 126
Acheson, Dean 115
Acton, Lord 96
Afrikaners 55
alliances 16, 17, 18, 35, 49–50, 53, 71,
    121–36
Ambrose of Milan 11
Amos 40
Anabaptists 42
antinomianism 42, 46
Apocalypse 47, 55, 171, 174, 177
Aristotle 7, 8, 9, 12, 15, 16, 62, 109
armaments 31, 65
    arms-control 32
    disarmament 32, 115
    nuclear 28, 31, 32, 38, 95, 103, 118, 120,
        128, 167, 173, 176–7
    procurement 28, 64, 132, 183
    trade 157–61, 176
Aron, Raymond 135
arts and sciences 13, 14, 24, 49, 51, 55,
    87, 179–80, 182–3, 189–90, 201
Augustine of Canterbury 55
Augustine of Hippo 41, 42, 43, 47, 162,
    163, 172
Augustus, Emperor 25, 33
Aurangzeb 175

Babylon 43, 52, 54, 158, 172, 175
Barbarians 9, 10, 67, 70, 145, 162
Behaviouralism 22
Benedict of Nursia 40
Bentham, Jeremy 57, 60, 62, 201
Bernadotte, Count 1
Bernard of Clairvaux 46, 54
Bismarck, Prince 28, 34
Blum, Léon 87
Boniface VIII 45
Bridges, Robert 37
Buddhism 56
Bull, Hedley 30
Burke, Edmund 79, 96, 126
Burton, John 114
business 179–80
    companies 13, 24, 27, 64, 69, 184, 185,
        194, 198, 199

men 3, 28, 92, 96, 179–80, 182, 191,
    197
    see also group-person
Butterfield, Herbert 30, 137

Caesar, Julius 9
Calvin, John 41, 44, 46, 47
Canning, George 140, 142
Carr, E. H. 1
Carter, Jimmy 138
Castlereagh, Lord 31, 139, 141
Cavour, Count 1
Chateaubriand, François-René de 76
Christianity 3, 56, 74, 91, 154, 162, 163,
    172, 175
Church 41
    and State 42, 43, 61
Churchill, Winston 1, 34, 83, 135
Cicero 2, 9, 10, 57, 201
class 84–7, 93–5
Clausewitz, Karl von 28, 176
CMEA 131
Cobden, Richard 73, 187
commerce 14, 16, 19, 34–5, 48, 53, 69–
    70, 73, 131, 178–201
    see also arts and sciences; business;
        economy
community
    of the Faithful 40–2, 45–9, 55, 154,
        172, 179
    international, see state, society of states
    of mankind 10–12, 199, 200–1
    national 11–12, 19, 50, 79, 198, 199,
        201
conflict 16, 20, 27, 28, 51, 58, 59, 101–20,
    200
country 12, 15, 19, 65, 80, 81, 93, 101,
    138, 151, 158, 159, 184, 196, 199
crisis 103, 129
Cromwell, Oliver 172
crusade 10, 51, 53–4, 157, 171, 172
culture 3, 23, 80, 88, 126, 144, 148, 155–
    6, 195, 197

Dante Alighieri 20
Darwin, Charles 75
Descartes, René 200
Deuteronomy 48

Devil 40, 41, 47, 49, 51, 135, 155, 156, 165, 171, 173
Dilthey, Wilhelm 75, 76
diplomacy 15, 35–6, 52, 68, 70, 91, 105, 112, 114–15, 117, 131
discussion 8, 10, 13, 14, 19, 20–1, 26, 46, 48, 49, 56, 57, 62, 82–3, 90, 97, 188–9, 200
Disraeli, Benjamin 80
Dulles, John Foster 45, 51

Ecclesiastes 40
economics 81, 85, 87, 189
economy 13, 19, 50, 81, 91–2, 199
  communication 191
  development aid 71, 138, 196, 197, 199
  economic sanctions 103, 116
  free trade 70, 91, 131, 187–8
  government and 16, 19, 26, 63, 64, 70–1, 183–7, 188, 192–3, 199, 200
  market 63, 64, 91, 178–9, 181, 182, 183, 195, 198
  mercantilism and protectionism 34–5, 53, 70, 91, 131, 181, 184, 200
  money 48, 71, 131
  planning 26, 70, 87, 94, 184, 185
  rich and poor 2, 18, 26, 48, 53, 63, 71, 109, 178, 183, 185, 194, 195, 197, 198, 199, 201
  see also business; commerce; good, public; justice
Einstein, Albert 38, 75
Eliade, Mircea 153
Elizabeth I of England 51
environment 3, 69, 110, 154, 191, 193, 199, 200, 201
equality
  persons 13, 23, 57, 63–4, 83, 144, 185, 188, 194, 195
  states 34, 52, 67, 186, 196–7
Ethelbert of Kent 55
European Community 17, 18, 35, 96, 121, 131
Ezekiel 171, 172

faith (doctrine) 40–1, 44
  heresy 46, 51
  infidelity 39–41, 47, 51, 54
  see also virtue, faith
Fichte, Johann Gottlieb 29, 79
Fideism 3, 38–55, 179
  alliances 49–50, 53
  commerce 48, 50, 53, 178–9

conflict 49, 51–4, 101–2
diplomacy 52
international law 52
international organizations 49–51
intervention 50, 153–6
society of states 49, 52
war 156–74
world 49
force 15, 25, 27–8, 36, 42, 51, 53, 60, 68, 72, 114, 117, 125, 150, 156, 173
'Formula Concordiae' 41
fortune 37, 123, 177, 181, 195
Frederick II of Hohenstaufen 22
Frederick V, Elector Palatine 147
freedom
  persons 46, 57, 59, 60, 62, 63, 66, 75, 97, 144, 180, 185, 190, 198, 201
  states 16, 50, 66, 89, 125, 137–56, 199
Freud, Sigmund 76
frontier 9, 11, 24, 27, 29, 50, 54, 57, 70, 89, 106, 137, 145–6, 154, 155–6, 170, 178, 192, 193, 199

Gadamer, Hans-Georg 83
GATT 35, 91, 185
Gaulle, Charles de 24, 105
Gentz, Friedrich 1
Gibbon, Edward 56, 59
God 39–49, 50, 54, 56, 61, 119, 156, 170, 171, 172, 173, 179
  grace 40, 44, 45, 61
gods 14, 37, 39, 104, 112, 200–1
Goethe, Johann Wolfgang von 142
good 7, 13, 42, 60, 61, 201
  common 8, 10–14, 19, 20, 23, 69, 90, 104, 108, 109, 119, 146, 170, 198–200
  public 12, 13, 64, 191, 199
Gramsci, Antonio 30
Green, T. H. 8
Grotius (Hugo de Groot) 1, 65, 147
group-person 14, 23–4, 66–7, 69, 116, 166, 168, 183, 184
guarantee 122–3, 127, 129
Gustavus Adolphus 51

Hamilton, Alexander 26, 72
Hampshire, Stuart 25
harmony 11, 14, 46, 58, 59, 68, 90, 114, 117, 133, 186, 192, 197, 200
Hayek, F. A. 60, 63, 195
Hegel, G. W. F. 1, 75, 78, 87, 90, 93, 120, 171

Heine, Heinrich 174
Helsinki Accords (1975) 50
Herder, Johann Gottfried 75
Historicism 75–97, 142, 154
  alliances 123, 133
  commerce 91, 187–90
  conflict 119–20
  diplomacy 91
  international law 92
  international organizations 91, 94
  intervention 137, 141–55
  society of states 91
  war 88, 90, 171
  world 95–6, 119, 152, 187–9
history 39, 65, 76–7, 85, 96–7, 141–2,
  188–90
  economic 81, 87
  philosophy of 10, 39, 47, 55, 65, 73,
    74–5, 78, 79, 85, 93, 97, 120, 147,
    156, 171, 174
Hitler, Adolf 32, 135, 170, 171
Hobbes, Thomas 22, 23, 25, 31, 57, 90,
  102, 175
honour 8, 16, 32, 44, 91, 104, 105, 107,
  108, 113, 160, 198, 201
  dignity 8, 108, 180, 199
  prestige 16, 34, 102, 104
Howard, Michael 170
Hume, David 58, 59, 60, 68, 74
Hutcheson, Francis 62

Idealism 1, 22
IMF 18
intervention 16, 19–20, 34, 50, 66, 71,
  136–56
Isaiah 171
Islam 52, 56, 74, 154, 175

Jeremiah 52
John XXIII 13
John of Leyden 46
Johnson, Dr 182
Judaism 55, 74, 174
Judges 42
Jung, Carl Gustav 39
justice 8, 106, 109, 111, 120
  divine 40–1, 171–2
  international 17, 68, 104–12, 163–96,
    199
  in the state 12, 42, 47, 48, 58, 59, 111,
    194, 199
  see also law; virtue, justice; war

Kahan Commission (1983) 168
Kant, Immanuel 2, 38, 56, 57, 58, 59, 60,
  70, 72, 73, 74, 117, 147
Keynes, John Maynard 189, 190
Khrushchev, Nikita 31, 130
Kierkegaard, Sören 39
Kissinger, Henry 33, 115
Klopp, Onno 77
knowledge 8, 20–1, 56, 76–7, 107, 187,
  188, 191, 200
  see also discussion; economy,
    communication; opinion
Knox, Ronald 42

La Rochefoucauld, Duc de 156
law
  international 14, 19, 34, 35–6, 52, 67,
    68, 70, 71, 91, 92, 105, 112, 116, 118;
    see also war
  ius gentium 11, 19
  municipal 12, 47, 61, 62, 82, 175, 178,
    198
  revealed 40–1, 45–7, 49, 155, 172, 179
  see also Natural Law
League of Nations 72, 96, 124, 129
Lenin, V. I. 26, 86, 94, 95
liberalism 63, 70, 89, 145, 160, 182, 188,
  190
List, Friedrich 81
Lloyd George, David 141
Locarno, Treaty of 122
Locke, John 57, 58, 59, 61, 81
Lodge, Henry Cabot 129
Luke 54
Luther, Martin 43, 47
Lyell, Charles 75

MacArthur, Douglas 176
Machiavelli, Nicolò 37, 44, 90, 135, 142
Maistre, Joseph de 80
Mao Tse-tung 86
Marcus Aurelius 11
Martin, Lawrence 43
Marx, Karl 85, 86, 88, 93, 189
Marxism 26, 31, 49, 55, 84–8, 93–6,
  152–3, 179, 182, 194
  see also state, imperialism
Masaryk, Jan 147
Mazzini, Giuseppe 79, 96
Medici, Lorenzo de' 29
Meinecke, Friedrich 44, 153
Metternich, Prince 31
migration 50, 69, 118, 181, 185, 187, 201

military 3, 18, 27, 175, 182, 183, 189
Mill, John Stuart 60, 73, 145, 148, 149
millenniarism 42
Minogue, Kenneth 178
Möngke, Great Khan 56, 65
Monroe Doctrine 140, 143
morality 7, 23, 24–5, 27, 38, 44, 57, 82, 92–3, 170, 200
  see also honour; virtue
Morgenthau, Hans J. 1, 34, 90, 102
Mussolini, Benito 123

Napoléon I 32
nation 65, 79, 88, 92, 93, 96, 145, 147, 198
  nationalism 14, 23, 50, 55, 65, 80, 84, 88–9, 93, 116, 123, 145, 166, 168, 194
NATO 17, 127, 129, 133
Natural Law 7–21, 40, 104, 197, 200–1
  alliances 16, 17, 18
  commerce 14, 16, 19, 197–201
  conflict 16, 104–11
  diplomacy 15
  international law 11, 105, 116, 118
  international organizations 17, 151
  intervention 16, 19–20, 142–4, 146–8, 150–2
  society of states 12, 15
  war 15, 161–3, 168–70
  world 9–12, 20, 111, 151
nature
  human 8, 104, 111, 118, 197–8, 199, 200
  state of nature 22, 31, 60, 72, 123, 133
  see also environment; Natural Law; rights, natural
necessity 31–2, 37, 167, 170, 177
Nehru, Jawaharlal 88
Newman, John Henry 43
news media, *see* opinion
Niebuhr, Barthold Georg 78, 87
Niebuhr, Reinhold 43, 45
Nietszche, Friedrich 25, 76

Oakeshott, Michael 63
OAS 127
OEEC 131
opinion 190, 201
  international 20–1, 34, 112
  national 26, 49, 60, 82
  news media 21, 26, 49, 65, 82, 118, 120, 170, 200

propaganda 21, 34, 36, 54, 68, 138, 175
  see also discussion; knowledge
order
  international 20, 28–35, 51, 182, 186
  national 12, 24, 46, 79, 181, 195
Ortega y Gasset, José 79
Oxenstjerna, Count 51

Palmerston, Lord 122
Papacy 46, 163, 175
Pascal, Blaise 38
patriotism 12, 185, 198
Paul of Tarsus 40, 41
peace 1, 3, 27, 30, 43, 52, 54, 73, 103, 158, 172, 175, 187, 199
Pius V 51
Plato 9, 10, 11, 25, 38, 110
politics 2, 3, 62, 63, 64, 80, 91, 170, 198
Pol Pot 86
Popper, Karl 74, 191
power 9, 25, 36, 112, 182
  balance of power 29–31, 54, 110, 120, 121, 124
  personal 23, 25
  state 23–37, 112–14, 126, 181–2, 183–4
  see also force; honour
powers (great, medium, small) 25, 27, 28, 30–1, 33–4, 35, 120, 127–30, 132–3, 138, 174, 182
prestige, *see* honour
progress 87, 195

race 14, 50, 65, 66, 76, 77, 80, 83, 89, 123, 145, 150
Rainborow, Thomas 57
Ranke, Leopold von 77, 91
Rationalism 56–73, 191, 197
  alliances 18, 71, 124–6, 133–4, 135–6
  commerce 69–70, 73, 178–87, 190–7
  conflict 59, 111–16
  diplomacy 68, 112
  international law 68, 71–2, 112
  international organizations 68–73, 112, 124–6, 185, 186, 193
  intervention 71, 143–4, 146–50
  society of states 20, 66, 71–3, 193, 196
  war 65, 72–3, 163–8
  world 59, 65, 72–3, 136, 178–87, 195–7
Realism 23–37, 44, 135
  alliances 17, 35, 121–3, 126–33, 134–5

commerce 26, 34–5, 129, 180–3
conflict 24, 102–4
diplomacy 35, 36, 131
international law 35–6
international organizations 35, 131
intervention 136–41
society of states 24, 27, 30
war 26, 28, 31, 123, 174–7
world 24, 182
reason 8, 38, 41, 46, 60, 76, 78, 82, 144,
  157, 161, 163, 165, 168, 191–7
religion 39, 51, 61, 66, 87, 153–4
  see also faith; God; gods; virtue, faith
Renan, Ernest 79
rights
  civil, economic, political 19, 47, 63,
    146, 197
  human, natural 19, 25, 47, 60, 83, 109,
    136, 138, 142, 144, 147, 149
Roman Empire 19, 25, 52, 66, 91, 112,
  162, 163, 175
Roosevelt, Franklin 123
Rousseau, Jean-Jacques 1, 29, 61, 81,
  112, 168

Sadat, Anwar 127
Salisbury, Lord 1, 36, 44
Sassoon, Siegfried 157
Savonarola, Girolamo 46
Schiller, Friedrich 120
Schwarzenberg, Prince 141
security 24, 26, 27, 31, 36, 46, 60, 149,
  180–1, 183, 189
  security association 71–3, 124–6, 133–
    4, 135–6
Seers, Dudley 81
Senior, Nassau 81
Shinn, Roger 43
Shonfield, Andrew 69
Sidgwick, Henry 185
Sismondi, J. C. L. Simonde de 189, 198
Smith, Adam 63, 189, 197
socialism 63, 64, 78, 87, 94, 178
society
  civil 59–60, 78, 178, 180, 194
  collectivism 13, 39, 178, 188, 190
  natural 59, 65, 66, 67, 71, 117
  social contract 25, 45, 60, 66, 71, 72,
    78, 144, 147, 166
  totalitarianism 13, 26, 76
  see also state, society of states
sociology 27, 82
Socrates 8, 110

solidarity and subsidiarity 12, 13
Sophocles 7
Spinoza, Benedict 25
Stalin, Joseph 26, 34, 86, 94, 135
state 12, 24, 45, 60, 81, 86, 89, 116
  constitution 12, 25, 46, 59, 61, 62, 69,
    80
  federation 18, 72, 112
  foundation 25, 26, 65, 86, 143, 144
  imperial 12, 27, 29, 52, 55, 65–6, 110,
    127–32, 158, 162
  imperialism 29, 55, 80, 88, 94–5
  internationally 14, 24, 27, 29, 34, 50,
    52, 88, 90, 107, 114, 124, 136, 151,
    182, 193
  international organizations 16–19, 35,
    50, 91, 94, 124–6, 131, 185, 186, 193;
    see also particular organizations
  nationally 12, 24, 26, 46, 61, 78, 86,
    136, 148, 181, 182, 183
  secession 143, 144, 147, 150
  society of states 12, 15, 24, 27, 30, 49,
    52, 66, 71–3, 90, 96, 186, 193, 196
  sphere of influence 34, 138, 139
  states-system 28–35, 44, 90–1, 94, 182,
    187
  toleration 14, 46, 47, 55, 61
  welfare state 13, 26, 39, 64, 181, 183–
    4, 185
  see also Church; freedom; group person;
    intervention; order; politics; powers;
    society
Stein, Freiherr vom 79
Stoics 2
strategy 16, 28, 169, 176
  see also armaments; force; military; war
Suárez, Francisco 11, 163
Sukarno 88

Tacitus 52
Talleyrand, Prince 36, 136
Taparelli d'Azeglio, Luigi 20
Tawney, R. H. 157
terrorism 173–5
theory 26–7, 46, 56, 62, 66, 74, 76–7, 81,
  85–96, 107, 108, 124, 141, 154, 189,
  190, 192, 198
Thomas Aquinas 7, 9, 11, 22, 40, 46
Thoreau, Henry 101
Thucydides 27, 32
Tocqueville, Alexis de 26, 81
tradition 80–3, 97, 108, 111, 119, 155,
  188, 193, 194, 198

Trier, Jost 156
Truman, Harry 176
Truman Doctrine 149
'two camps' 49–55, 95, 104, 154, 172

United Nations 18, 19, 35, 53, 72, 95, 124
utilitarianism 8, 58, 73

Valentine, Caesar Borgia, Duke 22
Vattel, Emmerich de 1, 67, 147
Vico, Giambattista 75
Victoria, Queen 66
Vienna, Congress of 31
Vienna Convention (1961) 15
Virgil 162
virtue
  courage 9, 37, 77, 170, 201
  faith 41, 44, 46, 55
  generosity 26, 48, 201
  hope 37, 46, 120
  humanity 11, 59, 64, 71, 166, 167
  joy 40, 41, 49, 55, 73, 155, 195
  justice 9, 41, 106, 107, 110, 201
  love 23, 40, 154
  magnificence 32, 77, 83
  mercy 40, 172, 173
  moderation 16
  obedience 40, 41, 45–8, 55
  prudence 8, 20, 26, 37, 46, 47, 53, 115, 116, 185, 201

self-mastery 9, 201
  see also honour
Vitoria, Francisco de 1, 11, 70, 144, 146
Voltaire (François-Marie Arouet) 65

Walsh, W. H. 82
war 15, 18, 31, 51, 71–3, 90, 110, 117, 118, 123, 157–77
  civil 27, 147, 154
  ius ad bellum 118, 161–4, 173
  ius in bello 164–70, 172
  neutrality 123, 125
  pacifism 42, 43, 171
  warfare 28, 164–76
  see also armaments; military; strategy
Warsaw Pact 127, 129, 133
Washington, George 64
Weber, Max 44
Wight, Martin 1, 33, 44, 136
Williams, Bernard 82
Wilson, Woodrow 1, 123, 129, 147
'Winter Queen' (Elizabeth Stuart) 147
world 2, 9–12, 20, 24, 49, 59, 65, 72–3, 91, 95–6, 111, 119, 120, 154, 177, 198
World Bank 18

Zechariah 171